AMERICAN HISTORY IN FOCUS SERIES

Under the Editorship of
William H. Goetzmann

THE AGE OF INSECURITY: AMERICA, 1920-1945

Interpretive Articles and Documentary Sources

Edited by

ROBERT A. DIVINE

University of Texas

▲ ADDISON-WESLEY PUBLISHING COMPANY

Reading, Massachusetts / Menlo Park, California / London / Don Mills, Ontario

Cover photograph courtesy of Wide World Photos.

PREFACE:
THE AMERICAN HISTORY IN FOCUS SERIES

History is the recorded deeds, ideas, and emotions of men. Living history is the re-recording of these deeds, ideas, and emotions by interpreters in each new generation. *The American History in Focus Series* seeks to provide the student with what might be called "the varieties of living historical experience," from a mid-twentieth century point of view. Each of the major historical epochs in American history is brought into focus by means of modern interpretive articles written by major scholars in the field, scholars who may be said to be on "the growing tip" of historical knowledge. Their interests span a vast range of historical methods and commitments. Collectively, they represent the multiple points of view of political, social, economic, diplomatic, military, and intellectual historians —historians who are nonetheless very much products of our own times and affected by current interests. These selections are concerned in almost every instance with answering that simple but all-important question— "so what?"—as it relates to our historical heritage. Of what relevance has past American historical experience been to the total course of human development, to the emergence of American values, achievements, problems, and predicaments? How did I, a citizen of the United States, get to be where and what I am today with all the privileges, burdens, and responsibilities that are entailed? What experiences of quality and nobility of conduct can be noted in the past against which we can measure our own aspirations and behavior—for we can the better recognize quality in our own lives for having seen it somewhere before in the recent or distant past?! By portraying realistically the complexities, relativisms, and ambiguities in the interpretations of time past, the editors and authors represented in these volumes provide new perspectives for determining our cultural identity.

Each of the volumes concentrates on a major period in American history, from colonial times to the present. Each is structured around focal, interpretive articles of modern historians with several varieties of history represented. These focal articles are supplemented by important and revealing historical documents of the particular era with which the historian is concerned. These are samples of the kinds of materials out of which he has constructed his interpretation. They are intended to serve two purposes: first, to give today's student a "feel" for the language and perspectives of the people of earlier generations; second, to provide materials with which to *test* the generalizations of the modern interpreters—to provide a laboratory situation whereby the student may critically examine some of the interpreter's answers and hopefully even some of his questions. For serious historical study requires constant criticism of historical generalizations, and it is too little recognized that such criticism might properly begin with the question, "did the historian ask the right questions of the period?"

Given the above, it should be obvious that these are experimental books especially designed as tools for learning. They are neither exercises in belletristic virtuosity, nor are they "canned" problems where the rules are clear and for the clever, the answers pat. Rather they are intended to be sophisticated, broad-based springboards to future discussion. As an added dimension we have experimented with the addition of pictorial materials which are not intended as idle embellishment but should rather serve as integral parts of the text—as further documents of the time. These, too, when examined with care, afford points of focus.

In attempting to draw a distinction between the nature of science and the nature of history, an historian of science, Derek de Solla Price, makes a striking analogy. He sees science as a "many-brained" machine into whose circuits all of the latest "growing tip" discoveries, however limited, can be wired so that advances in knowledge can result without the necessity for retracing in detail the historical steps involved in previous discoveries. History, on the other hand, is a "single-brained" enterprise in which each historian has to go back over all the sources and interpretations of the past before making his own generalization.* The *American History in Focus Series* attempts to draw upon the advantages of both. For the individual student it is clearly a "single-brained" experience. But in assembling between two covers modern interpretations, along with documents from the past, both written and pictorial, we have attempted to provide the advantages of a "many-brained" approach as well, so as to encourage the student to examine the nature of historical enquiry as a process of thought, and to address himself to the problem of cultural identity in a changing world.

William H. Goetzmann
General Editor

---

*Derek D. Price, "Two Cultures and One Historian of Science," *Teachers College Record*, **64**, 7, April 1963, pp. 528-531.

CONTENTS

III WORLD WAR II: SEARCH FOR A BETTER WORLD

GENERAL INTRODUCTION

The year 1920 was a year of demobilization. The army of more than two million men that had arrived in France in time to ensure Germany's defeat on the western front was disbanding; the young men were going back to the fields and factories they had left in such haste only three years before. Many still held the image of an older America, an America of tranquil tree-shaded streets, of large, rambling frame houses with broad front porches where one could swing lazily while life went on in an orderly and relaxed fashion. It was the America of ice-cream socials and church picnics, of family reunions and circus parades, that the returning soldiers remembered. Yet many knew that the old rural America, where life centered in the town, was passing, a victim of the industrialization which had transformed the American economy in the half-century before the First World War. A new urban civilization was emerging to take its place.

Twenty-five years later, another and even greater war ended. The society this generation of veterans returned to reflected the revolution that had taken place in American life. The cities of 1920 had grown into huge metropolitan complexes, surrounded by suburbs stretching for mile after mile along highways that converged on the urban core. Movies and radio had replaced the simpler entertainments of small-town America. The circus was dying, and the old houses had fallen into decay as families moved into tract houses with their compact rooms and drab, monotonous exteriors. Aesthetically the urban landscape seemed a great step backward, but there were significant rewards in the cultural realm. American literature had come of age, artists were finding unorthodox forms to explore, and music flourished in the new symphony orchestras and opera companies that were founded in city after city. An urban culture had developed which provided a far richer and more exhilarating way of life than the smug, closed society of the older America had ever offered.

The twenty-five years between 1920 and 1945 witnessed a profound series of dislocations. In the 1920's, so often viewed by Americans as a gay age of reckless abandon, the tensions between the new urban civilization and the passing rural culture produced the excesses of prohibition, racism, and intolerance. A glittering economic boom, despite its soft spots, altered the traditional patterns, transforming a nation of producers into a nation of buyers, as advertising and sales promotion experts desperately tried to sell the enormous output of new consumer-oriented industries to the public. Then in 1929 a massive depression overtook the nation, and slowly

1

American confidence gave way as industrial production declined and unemployment mounted. The advent of Franklin Roosevelt to the presidency in 1933 revived the sagging American spirits, and though the New Deal never achieved all its goals, it did restore faith in the future of America. While Americans underwent this series of shocks and adjustments at home, they tended to ignore the world. Businessmen and diplomats were active overseas in the 1920's, but with the depression the nation turned inward and only belatedly realized the threat to its security posed by the totalitarian regimes in Germany, Italy and Japan. The outbreak of the war in Europe in 1939 rekindled American interest in the world, and after the Japanese attack on Pearl Harbor the people accepted with characteristic zeal the responsibility of saving themselves and their allies from the perils of facism. In less than four years an unprepared America raised an army of nearly ten million men, created a navy and an air force larger than any other in the world, and finally harnessed the power of the atom to create an awesome weapon and usher in a new age of mass destruction. Yet despite these great successes, growing strains with the Soviet Union had become so ominous by 1945 that many Americans began to realize that the war would not bring the lasting peace they had so naïvely expected.

The articles and documents that follow chronicle these major transformations in American life. Each article provides an analysis of significant trends by a leading historian. The documents, chosen for their clarity, provide an insight into the character of the times. There has been no effort to be all-inclusive; instead, the emphasis is on a limited number of themes which in the editor's opinion reflect the dominant trends of the period. In the twenties, the focus is on social and economic change; in the thirties, on the New Deal and the political leadership of Franklin D. Roosevelt; in World War II, on the diplomacy of the Big Three. By concentrating on these themes, it is hoped that the reader will gain an understanding to which he can relate other aspects of this exciting and eventful twenty-five years of the American experience.

Robert A. Divine

1 / THE 1920'S: ERA OF TRANSITION

INTRODUCTION

The 1920's have long fascinated the American people. The period was barely over when Frederick Lewis Allen published his popular book, *Only Yesterday*, which captured many of the distinctive features of the decade. Allen stressed the giddy, wild, and exciting theme of the Jazz Age, and less perceptive imitators made the twenties a stereotype of a gay, carefree, and immoral society. Hollywood mined this nostalgic theme in movies dealing with crime, sex, and youth in rebellion, and later television exploited it with such series as "The Untouchables." In contrast to this popular view of the twenties, historians have tried to stress the profoundly tragic aspect of life in this decade. They have pointed to the panic of the Red Scare in 1919–1920, when thousands of suspected radicals were deported without due process of law; to the racism that flourished in the Ku Klux Klan and which was implicit in the restrictions imposed on immigration; and to the growth of organized crime, the gang-killings, and the disrespect for law engendered by prohibition.

This was a time when one way of life was yielding to another. The rural, small-town-oriented America composed of white, Protestant Anglo-Saxons was losing out to an urban, industrial, heterogeneous society in which Jews and Catholics, Italians and Poles, Negroes and Orientals were penetrating the mainstream of American life. This process of social change led to severe tensions which accounted for both the reckless abandon and the cruel intolerance of the age. The older middle-class America resented the change, and it responded in the cities by attempting to escape through exaggerated patterns of behavior—bathtub gin and speakeasies, short skirts and bobbed hair, even, in the case of intellectuals, physical exile in Europe. In the small towns and on the farms, the resentment took the form of counterattack. Men joined the Klan to strike out against the alien in their midst; Congressmen from the rural South and West voted as a bloc to enact immigration restriction; Protestant temperance crusaders forced prohibition on the reluctant American city. Yet none of these tactics would prevail. The Klan burned itself out before the decade was over, the quota system could not stop the children of earlier immigrants from gaining power in American politics and gradually attaining affluence, and the campaign against alcohol was bound to lead to its own demise. The new urban society was the wave of the future, and though historians still stress the conflicts of the twenties, the enduring change in American society remains the most important aspect of the decade.

Nor should the earlier emphasis on the destructive aspects of the 1920's obscure the significant developments in American political, economic, and cultural life. Throughout the decade, a silent revolution was taking place in voting behavior. In 1920, the Republicans were the majority party, dominating the countryside and winning a decisive edge in the nation's twelve largest cities. The Democrats were torn by sectional tensions, but by 1928 they were emerging as the new majority party. Even though Al Smith was overwhelmed by Herbert Hoover, he won a majority in the cities and thus opened up a new source of political strength that Franklin Roosevelt would exploit successfully in the 1930's. In the economic sphere even more fundamental shifts were taking place. The rise of new industries devoted to the production of such consumer goods as automobiles and electrical appliances led to a roaring prosperity and a better standard of living for millions of Americans. The boom proved to be short-lived; the sudden nature of the economic changes contributed to the severity of the depression that followed. But it is now clear that the economic developments of the twenties were not as pernicious as a depression generation once thought, and many of the most important features of the modern American economy, notably installment-buying, extensive advertising, and mass production, first came into their own in the twenties. Equally important trends took place in American culture. This ten-year period produced a stunning literary outpouring as Ernest Hemingway, Eugene O'Neill and Ezra Pound made American letters world-famous. American artists still followed European trends, but there was a new appreciation of painting and sculpture which led to the founding of many museums and the collecting on a private basis by wealthy patrons. America was no longer the cultural wasteland it had been in the nineteenth century; a new, sophisticated civilization was emerging in the 1920's.

INTERPRETATION

In the article that follows, Henry F. May, a social and intellectual historian at the University of California at Berkeley who has written books on both religious and cultural history, examines the changing views of the 1920's that historians and other writers have held. By showing us how time has changed our angle of vision, he is able to bring out the complexity of the decade and to suggest a way to see it whole.

HENRY F. MAY, *Shifting Perspectives on the 1920's*

To comment on the 1920's today is to put oneself in the position of a Civil War historian writing in the 1890's. The period is over and major changes have taken place. The younger historian himself belongs to a generation which barely remembers the great days. From the point of view of the veterans, still full of heroic memories, such a historian obviously has no right to talk—he was not there. Yet historians are led by their training to hope that one kind of truth—not the only kind and perhaps not always the most important kind—emerges from the calm study of the records.

Calm study of this decade is not easy. Like the Civil War itself, the cultural battles of the twenties have been fought again and again. Successive writers have found it necessary either to condemn or to praise the decade, though what they have seen in it to condemn or praise has differed. Perhaps this fact offers us our best starting point. If we can trace the shifting and changing picture of the decade through the last thirty years, and still better, if we can understand the emotions that have attached themselves to one version or another, we may be closer to knowing what the decade really meant. In the process, we can hardly help learning something of the intellectual history of the intervening period.

It is immediately apparent, as one turns through the literature about the twenties, that most of the striking contributions have not come from men we usually think of as historians, but rather from journalists, literary critics, and social scientists. This is perhaps not surprising, since most of

Henry F. May, "Shifting Perspectives on the 1920's," *Mississippi Valley Historical Review,* XLIII (December 1956), 405-427. Reprinted without footnotes by permission of the Organization of American Historians.

the excitement has centered in areas outside the historian's traditional domain. Historians today, of course, claim a territory stretching far beyond past politics; but this is a recent expansion, and all of us enter such fields as literature and science only with caution. Caution is necessary, but it must not prevent exploration. If the best insights into a period come from economists, or anthropologists, or literary critics, we must try to understand and even to assess them, hoping that our inevitable mistakes will be made in a good cause.

At least three pictures of the twenties had formed before the decade was over. For different reasons, spokesmen of business, social science, and literary revolt all wanted to get clear away from the past, to discard history. For this reason, all three groups were constantly discussing their own historical role. Perhaps the dominant current version was that proclaimed by the businessmen, the picture of the period usually conveyed by the phrase New Era itself. Out of the postwar upheaval was emerging, in this view, a new civilization. Its origin was technology, its efficient causes high wages and diffusion of ownership, its leadership enlightened private management. This picture of the period was far more than a matter of political speeches and *Saturday Evening Post* editorials. It was buttressed by academic argument and attested by foreign observers. To its believers, we must remember, it was not a picture of conservatism but of innovation, even, as Thomas Nixon Carver strikingly asserted, of revolution.

It is not surprising that this interpretation of the period gained the allegiance of many of its first historians. Preston W. Slosson, surveying his own time for the *History of American Life* series, came to a typical New Era conclusion on the basis of a typical New Era criterion: "Often in history the acid test of wealth has been applied to a favored class; alone in all nations and all ages the United States of the 1920's was beginning to apply that test to a whole people." James C. Malin found, with no apparent anguish, that political democracy was being replaced by self-government in industry. No serious dissent was expressed in Charles A. Beard's great synthesis, published in 1927. Beard deplored the politics and other obsolete folkways surviving in the postwar era. But he found the center of current development, and the climax of his whole vast story, in the achievements of the machine age. Continuous invention was the hope of the future. Standardization had made possible not only better living for all but a more generous support for the life of the mind. Those who feared the machine were lumped together by Beard as "artists of a classical bent and . . . spectators of a soulful temper." Lesser and more conventional historians usually struck the same note; and the textbooks of the period, if they ventured beyond Versailles, emerged into a few pages of peace and prosperity.

Sociologists of the period, full of the élan of their new subject, exultant over the apparent defeat of religious obscurantism, were as optimistic as the businessmen and the historians, though for different reasons. Their New Era lay in the future rather than the present; its motivating force was not technology alone but the guiding social intelligence. This picture of the decade as a transitional age emerges most clearly from the sociological periodicals of the early twenties, where one finds at least four important assumptions. First, the scientific study of society is just coming into its own. Second, social scientists are now able to abandon sentiment, impressionism, and introspection and seek accurate information, especially quantitative information. Third, this new knowledge should be, and increasingly will be, the guide for practical statesmanship, replacing custom and tradition. Fourth, Utopia is consequently just around the corner. The present may look chaotic, but the new élite will be able to lead us fairly quickly out of the fog of dissolving tradition and toward the end of controversy and the reign of universal efficiency.

To condense is always unfair, and it would be incorrect to assume that all social scientists in the twenties saw their role or their period this simply. Yet it is easy enough to find all these beliefs stated very positively in textbooks and even learned articles, with both the behaviorist dogmatism and the authoritarian implications full-blown. Part of the confidence of these prophets rested on real and important achievement by social scientists in the period, but those who had actually contributed the most new knowledge were sometimes less dogmatic than their colleagues. In *Middletown*, for instance, the social science interpretation of the twenties is buried in a mass of scrupulously collected facts, but it is there. At certain points in describing the decline of labor unionism or the standardization of leisure the authors seem to be deploring changes that have taken place since 1890. Yet in their conclusion they trace the tensions of Middletown to the lag of habits and institutions behind technological progress. Individual child-training, religion, and the use of patriotic symbols represent the past, while the future is represented by whatever is thoroughly secular and collective, particularly in the community's work life. The town has tended to meet its crises by invoking tradition in defense of established institutions. Their whole investigation, the Lynds conclude, suggests instead "the possible utility of a deeper-cutting procedure that would involve a reexamination of the institutions themselves."

The typical economic thought of the twenties, while it avoided Utopian extremes, shared with the other social sciences an unlimited confidence in the present possibilities of fact-finding and saw in the collection and use of statistics much of the promise and meaning of the era. In his brilliant **conclu**ding summary of *Recent Economic Trends,* Professor

Wesley C. Mitchell, for instance, found the main explanation for the progress of 1922–1928 in the new application of intelligence to business, government, and trade-union administration.

The third contemporary interpretation of the period, that offered by its literary intellectuals, differed sharply from the other two. Completely repudiating the optimism of the businessmen, it agreed with the social scientists only in its occasional praise of the liberated intelligence. For the most part, as we are all continually reminded, the writers and artists of the twenties saw their age as one of decline.

The most publicized group of pessimists was that typified by Harold Stearns and his colleagues of 1922, who, with their many successors, left an enduring picture of a barren, neurotic, Babbitt-ridden society. These critics have drawn a lot of patriotic fire, and indeed some of them are sitting ducks. They were often, though not always, facile, unoriginal, and ignorant. They seldom made clear the standards by which they found American society so lacking. Yet their lament is never altogether absurd or capricious. If one studies the civilization they saw around them through its press, one hardly finds it a model of ripeness or serenity. The fact remains, for historians to deal with, that American civilization in the twenties presented to many of its most sensitive and some of its gifted members only an ugly and hostile face.

A more thoughtful and sadder group of writers than most of the young Babbitt-beaters traced their own real malaise not to the inadequacies of America but to the breakdown of the entire Western civilization. The New Humanists had long been deploring the decline of literary and moral discipline. At the opposite extreme in taste the up-to-date followers of Spengler agreed that decay impended. Joseph Wood Krutch in 1929 described the failure first of religion and then of the religion of science to give life meaning: "Both our practical morality and our emotional lives are adjusted to a world which no longer exists. . . . There impends for the human spirit either extinction or a readjustment more stupendous than any made before."

Many accepted this statement of the alternatives, and chose according to their natures. Walter Lippmann, who had played some part in the confident prewar attack on tradition and custom, chose the duty of reconstruction and published, in 1929, his earnest attempt to find a naturalist basis for traditional moral standards. On the other hand, T. S. Eliot painted a savage and devastating picture of present civilization and left it to live in the world which Krutch thought no longer existent. As Eliot assumed the stature of a contemporary classic, his description of the Waste Land, the world of Sweeney and Prufrock, and also his path away from it, seriously influenced later conceptions of the period.

With the depression, the twenties shot into the past with extraordinary suddenness. The conflicting pictures of the decade, rosy and deep black, changed sharply, though none disappeared. Of them all, it was the New Era point of view, the interpretation of the decade as the birth of a new and humane capitalism, that understandably suffered most. Ironically, the most plausible and heavily documented version of this description, and one of the most influential later, appeared only in 1932 when Adolf A. Berle, Jr., and Gardiner C. Means described the separation of management from ownership. At the time, however, the economic order of the twenties was collapsing, and its harassed defenders retreated temporarily into the Republican last ditch.

The other optimistic vision of the decade, that of the social scientists, depended less directly on prosperity and in the thirties survived somewhat better, though it became difficult to see the preceding period as the triumphant application of social intelligence. It is a startling example of the prestige of the social science point of view in 1929 that a president should commission a group of social scientists to make a complete and semi-official portrait of a whole civilization. The fact that *Recent Social Trends* was not completed and published until 1932 probably accounts in part for its excellence; it is the most informative document of the twenties which we have and also a monument of the chastened social science of the thirties. The committee that wrote this survey still believed, as its chairman, Wesley Mitchell, had earlier, that much of the meaning of the twenties lay in the harnessing of social intelligence to collective tasks. Consciously and subtly, the various authors documented the contradiction between the period's individualistic slogans and its actual movement toward social and even governmental control. Yet they were conscious throughout that all this had ended in depression.

Like the authors of *Middletown,* the committee found its synthetic principle in the doctrine that change proceeds at different rates in different areas. Again like the Lynds, it assumed that society's principal objective should be "the attainment of a situation in which economic, governmental, moral and cultural arrangements should not lag too far behind the advance of basic changes," and basic here means primarily technological. Occasionally *Recent Social Trends* displays, as for instance in its chapters on the child and on education, a surviving trace of the easy authoritarianism of the preceding decade's social theorists, and occasional chapters refer in the early optimistic manner to the hope of solving all social problems through the new psychological knowledge. But in most of this great work, and particularly in its brilliant introduction, the authors left behind the social-science utopianism of the early twenties. It would take an increasingly powerful effort of social intelligence to bring us into equilibrium. Moreover, this effort must be a subtle one; the committee took pains to state that it was "not unmindful of the fact that there are important elements in human life not easily stated in terms of efficiency, mechanization, institutions, rates of change or adaptations to change." Therefore, what was called for was not a ruthless rejection of tradition but a reexamination leading to a restatement in terms of modern life. *Recent Social Trends* is in places a work of art as well as of social science, and it is one of the few books about the twenties that point the way toward a comprehensive understanding of the period.

The view of the previous decade presented in the thirties by most historians was far less subtle and complete. Instead of either a New Era, a liberation, or a slow scientific adaptation, the twenties became a deplorable interlude of reaction. This view, stated sometimes with qualifications and sometimes very baldly, has continued to dominate academic historical writing from the thirties almost until the present.

Most of the historians who were publishing in the thirties had received their training in the Progressive Era. Many had been deeply influenced by Frederick Jackson Turner, and had tended to look for their synthesis not to the decline of Europe but to the expansion of America. Though the Turner doctrine can be turned to pessimistic uses, Turner himself in the twenties prophesied that social intelligence would find a substitute for the disappearing force of free land. As this suggests, the outlook of John Dewey pervaded much of historical writing as it did the work of social scientists. Yet historians still tended to give most of their attention to politics. For these reasons, and because they shared the opinion of their readers, historians usually found the meaning of American history in the nineteenth-century growth of political and social democracy and the twentieth-century effort to adapt it to new conditions.

As we have seen, many of the historians actually writing in the twenties had not found their own period an interruption of this beneficent adaptation. The interruption had come in 1929 and then, after an interval of confusion and paralysis, Franklin D. Roosevelt had appealed for support partly in terms of the progressive view of history. Roosevelt himself justified his program by pointing to the end of free land and claimed the progressive succession from Theodore Roosevelt and Woodrow Wilson, his cousin and his former chief. Few historians were disposed to deny his claim, and accepting it made the twenties an unfortunate interregnum, sometimes covered by a chapter called "The Age of the Golden Calf," or "Political Decadence," or even "A Mad Decade."

This does not mean that an emphasis on the political conservatism of the decade, or a hostile criticism of the Harding-Coolidge policies, is in itself a distortion. Yet stubborn standpattism was only one ingredient in a varied picture. It is not history to make the twenties, as some of the briefer historical treatments do, merely a contrasting background for the New Deal. Sometimes even prosperity—an important fact despite the exceptions—is belittled almost out of existence, the prophets of abundance are denied credit for good intentions, the approach of the depression becomes something that nearly anybody could have foreseen, and the decade's many advances in science, social science, medicine, and even government are left out.

While they deplored the businessmen and politicians of the twenties, the progressive historians of the thirties and later tended also to belittle the period's literary achievement. This negative judgment was sustained by a powerful writer, Vernon L. Parrington, himself a thorough and fervent exponent of the progressive interpretation of American history. In Parrington's last, fragmentary volume, published in 1930, he read the younger authors of the twenties out of the American tradition as "a group of youthful poseurs at the mercy of undigested reactions to Nietzsche, Butler, Dadaism, Vorticism, Socialism; overbalanced by changes in American critical and creative standards, and in love with copious vocabularies and callow emotions." "With the cynicism that came with postwar days," said Professor Parrington, "the democratic liberalism of 1917 was thrown away like an empty whiskey-flask."

Though Parrington did not live to explain this rejection or treat it at length, he obviously believed that the liberal whisky was still there and still potent, and so, in the thirties and often since, have many of his readers. Some historians, understandably impressed by Parrington's great architectural achievement, willingly and specifically took over his literary judgments; others doubtless arrived at similar opinions independently. For whatever reason, by the thirties the most widespread historical picture of the twenties was that of a sudden and temporary repudiation of the progressive tradition by reactionary politicians and also by frivolous or decadent littérateurs.

Some of the historians writing in the thirties, and far more of the literary critics, found their historical principle not in American progressivism but in Marxism. John Chamberlain demonstrated to his own temporary satisfaction the futility of the preceding Progressive Era, and Lewis Corey and others depicted the resultant triumph of monopoly capitalism, characterized by a false prosperity and leading inevitably to the depression and (before 1935) the disguised fascism of the New Deal. At their worst, and in most of their specifically historical writing, the Marxist writers seem now unbelievably crude and schematic. But the Marxist version of the twenties came not only from the pamphleteers but also from gifted literary artists. For many of the generation that grew up in the thirties the concept of the previous decade was strongly influenced by the work of John Dos Passos. His brilliant sketches of Woodrow Wilson, Henry Ford, Thorstein Veblen, and other giants, the postwar violence, the defeat of hopes, and the gradual inevitable corruption of the "big money" form a picture that is hard to forget—that Dos Passos himself in sackcloth and ashes is entirely unable to wipe out. Among the many critics and literary historians who were then Marxists, most of them dull and fashion-ridden, were a few writers of insight. It is still suggestive to see the literary rebellion of the twenties, through the 1935 eyes of Granville Hicks, as a reflection of the insecurity of the middle class. Most of the rebellious writers *had* come from this class, and even from a particular segment of it that had lost prestige, and many of them had been self-conscious and worried about this origin.

Sometimes, despite their basic differences, the Marxist writers agreed in part in the thirties with the progressive historians. Often, however, the literary Marxists made a different combination. Starting in the twenties as rebels in the name of art, they had found their esthetic distaste for capitalism confirmed by prophecies of its inevitable doom. The resultant mixture of individualist rebellion and socialist revolution was unstable and short-lived, but in the thirties powerful. Edmund Wilson describes the representative mood, and the resultant attitude toward the twenties: "To the writers and artists of my generation who had grown up in the shadow of the Big Business era and had always resented its barbarism, its crowding-out of everything they cared about, these depression years were not depressing but stimulating. One couldn't help being exhilarated at the sudden unexpected collapse of that stupid gigantic fraud."

One other and opposite group of writers in the thirties contributed to the previous decade's bad press. This was the varied group stemming from T. S. Eliot's neo-classical essays and I. A. Richards' effort at a scientific criticism that came to be known as "the New Critics." This school of writers could almost be defined as a counter revolution against the individualist rebellion of the twenties, in which some of them, not surprisingly, had themselves played a part. Some of the New Critics called for a revival of the Catholic, or Anglo-Catholic, or humanist, or southern tradition; others hoped to find a new credo in literature itself. They agreed only in valuing such qualities as complexity, tension, and intellectual strictness. In the thirties, despite the noise made by opposite groups, it was the New Critics who were moving quietly toward a position of dominance in criticism and in the college teaching of literature; a position they clearly hold today.

Like their enemies, the Marxists and progressives, the New Critics found little to praise in the twenties. To begin with, they stoutly rejected any tendency to measure the progress of civilization in terms of technology or standard of living. Thus they saw both the business civilization of the New Era and the opposing humanitarian progressivism as two variants of the same shallow materialism. To them the social science Utopias forecast in the twenties were merely a repulsive climax to current tendencies. Allen Tate, for instance, associated social science not only with innocent barbarism but with the current triumph of the total state: "What we thought was to be a conditioning process in favor of a state planned by Teachers College of Columbia University will be a conditioning equally useful for Plato's tyrant state. . . . The point of view that I am sketching here looks upon the rise of the social sciences and their influence in education, from Comtism to Deweyism, as a powerful aid to the coming of the slave society." Looking back at the previous period, Tate remembered sadly "How many young innocent men—myself among them—thought, in 1924, that laboratory jargon meant laboratory demonstration."

Most of the New Critics rejected the rebellious literature of the twenties as completely as they did the business civilizations of the era. Exceptions had to be made, of course, for the more careful and rigorous poets—Marianne Moore, Eliot, sometimes Ezra Pound. The abler of the New Critics realized, as some moralists did not, that the writers of the twenties expressed, rather than caused, the disintegration of tradition which they deplored. Some of them were able to admire men like Ernest Hemingway and Hart Crane who bravely tried to give literary form to moral and intellectual disorder. But the general direction of the literature of the decade was, they agreed, disintegration.

Progressives, Marxists, and neoclassicists all found the twenties deplorable, yet in writers from all these camps, and in others who wrote in the thirties, a note of nostalgia often broke through the sermon. Frivolous, antisocial, and decadent as the literature of the twenties seemed, it had to be conceded the somewhat contradictory qualities of freshness and excitement. And nostalgia, in the thirties, extended beyond the previous decade's literature to its manners and customs. In 1931 Frederick L. Allen performed a remarkable feat of impressionist recall of the period just over, and in 1935 Mark Sullivan brought back vividly its clothes and songs and sensations. Already in the work of these two excellent reporters, and later in the versions of a number of minor and more sentimental merchants of nostalgia, the twenties appeared strange, fantastic, and appealing. They appealed with particular strength to those who did not remember them; it was the peculiar feat of these reporters to fill the new generation with nostalgia for scenes they had not seen. For the college student of the next decade, if the twenties was one half the betrayal of progress, the other half was the jazz age. Irresponsibility, to the solemn and uneasy thirties, was both deplorable and attractive.

This paradoxical attitude toward the twenties continued and the paradox sharpened in the next period. In the dramatic and tragic days of World War II, few found much to admire in the age of Ford and Coolidge. James Burnham, combining Berle and Means's data on the separation of owner-ship and control with an apocalyptic vision of the rise of the total state, made the New Era into the beginning of the "Managerial Revolution." To the F. D. R. liberals, who already blamed the twenties for abandoning progressivism, the period's major crime was now its rejection of the Wilsonian international program. Teachers worried whether the earlier postwar disillusion, which they had helped to propagate, would make it impossible to revive a fighting spirit—a worry which proved unnecessary and perhaps a little conceited. Editorial writers wondered whether the country would again fail in its responsibilities after the war. Above all, those who responded most generously to the call for the defense of West-ern culture feared that the literary rebels of the twenties had done great, even disastrous, damage to the nation's morale.

Even before the war broke out, Walter Lippmann was concerned about the lack of fighting convictions among civilized men and blamed, in part, the rejection of tradition in which he had long ago taken part. Archibald MacLeish blamed both the artists and the scholars of the previous period for their different kinds of detachment. Van Wyck Brooks, looking back at the writers who had answered his own summons for a new literature, found that they differed from all previous writers in one striking way: they had ceased to be "voices of the people." "How could a world," he wondered, "that was sapped by these negative feelings resist the trium-phant advance of evil."

This high estimate of the power and responsibility of literature seemed to be shared by Bernard DeVoto, though he took writers to task for making literature the measure of life. Writers of the "Age of Ignominy" had con-demned their period partly out of sheer ignorance. In his eagerness to demonstrate this DeVoto revived, earlier than many, some of the New Era interpretation of the twenties. "What truly was bankrupt was not American civilization but the literary way of thinking about it." Actually, "The nation that came out of the war into the 1920's was . . . the most cheerful and energetic society in the world." A true picture of it would have emphasized its achievements in education, medicine, humanitarian improvement, and the writing of local history.

MacLeish, Brooks, DeVoto, and others condemned the writers of the twenties for damaging the nation's fighting morale, and strangely enough,

Courtesy of Harms, Inc., New York City, and The Bettman Archive.

Charles and Mary Beard, writing in 1942 of the American Spirit, made the same charges from an isolationist point of view. For the Beards, American cynicism had come from Europe: "In the tempers and moods fostered by foreign criticisms and by American weakness displayed in reactions to the impacts, multitudes of young men and women were brought to such a plight that they derided the whole American scene."

All these works, including in part that of the Beards (which was not one of the major productions of these great historians), were wartime pamphlets rather than history. None of them offered a halfway satisfactory explanation of the alienation they discussed, which was certainly a more important phenomenon than the inadequacy of a few individuals. Yet one thing the wartime writers said was true and worth saying, that in the twenties a deep chasm had opened between the views of life of most writers and their fellow citizens. Perhaps the importance of this fact could not be emotionally grasped until the years when DeVoto heard Ezra Pound on the Italian radio.

Yet, even in wartime, and for some perhaps especially in wartime, the freedom and creativity and even the irresponsibility of the previous generation of writers had a paradoxical attraction. Alfred Kazin's admirable and by no means uncritical chapters on the period, which appeared in 1942, were called "The Great Liberation (1918–1929)." And the paradox seemed to reach its most acute form in DeVoto himself. In the same short volume the literature of the twenties was "debilitated, capricious, querulous, and irrelevant" and yet the decade was "one of the great periods of American literature, and probably the most colorful, vigorous, and exciting period." It was a literature that was "not . . . functional in American life," but "idle, dilettante, flippant, and intellectually sterile," and yet one which had "achieved something like a charter of liberties for American writers."

In the nineteen-fifties, as in other periods, it is dangerous to equate the latest insights with truth. Yet it is hard not to conclude that now, in the second postwar period, some writers are converging from various directions toward a better understanding of the twenties. For one thing, the decade is longer past and it is no longer acutely necessary to break with its viewpoint. Fairly recently the twenties have come to be a fair field for the dissertation and the monograph, which bring at least a different kind of knowledge. One survivor of the period says that instead of being revived, it is being excavated like a ruin, and another complains that he and his friends are already being preserved in complete bibliographies while yet, as far as they can tell, alive.

Disapproval and nostalgia, of course, remain. Editorials worry about the effect on Europe of the vogue there of the literature of the twenties.

Professor Howard Mumford Jones has continued something like DeVoto's charges in more analytic tones, accusing the postwar writers both of brilliance and of detachment amounting to solipsism. The choice of Scott Fitzgerald for revival and in some quarters canonization indicates the perverse attraction which self-destruction seems to hold for our period. Budd Schulberg's novel specifically contrasts a romantic and defeated alcoholic writer of the twenties with a crass, earnest young radical of the thirties to the latter's obvious disadvantage.

In general, however, literary opinion seems to have gone beyond both nostalgia and reproof into a more mature and solidly based appreciation of the achievements of this era now so safely in the past. To many, the apparent sterility of the present literary scene furnishes a depressing contrast. Whatever else they rejected, writers of the twenties took their writing seriously, and, as Cowley has pointed out, publishers made it possible for them to do so. Professor Frederick J. Hoffman in the most thorough of many recent accounts finds the period's literature full of daring, variety, and technical brilliance. This estimate by now represents more than a cult; it is an accepted consensus.

One achievement of the twenties which has received only a little specific comment is nevertheless widely recognized today. The period of alienation and exile gave rise, curiously enough, to a thorough, rich, and continuing inquiry into the whole American past. The sources of this inward turn are as complicated as the decade itself. Many of the major historians who wrote then, including Parrington, Beard, Carl Becker, and Arthur M. Schlesinger, Sr., belong to the group that always found its major synthesis in the course of democratic progress. But others turned to the past with Van Wyck Brooks, partly in a spirit of cultural nationalism, to destroy the English and Anglophile genteel tradition and replace it with something native. Still others went first through a phase of violent rejection of American culture and then, finding Europe essentially unavailable as a substitute, returned to look desperately for roots at home. By the forties and fifties it was possible to see the lines converging in a cultural history which, at its best, could be critical, conscious of irony and failure, and yet, in a meaningful and necessary way, patriotic.

With the literature and historical research of the twenties, its economic achievement, once overvalued and then rated too low, has again turned the corner into a rising market. In the years of the Marshall Plan, when American capitalism was called on to shoulder an immense burden, it was hard to think of it as a failure and a mistake. And in the still rising prosperity of the Eisenhower period, far more widespread and soundly based than that under Coolidge but inevitably reminiscent, a reassessment of the earlier period was natural enough.

Part of the reassessment arose from the increasing complexity of economics and the development of a new economic history. Beginning about 1940, a number of economists and historians had demanded that American economic history separate itself from the political framework and give more attention to such matters as real wages and volume of production, and somewhat less to labor organization and the political struggles between farmers and merchants. Even earlier, the business historians had been asking for a more analytic and less emotional approach to the history of management. By the forties, it was impossible for an informed historian to duplicate the sweeping judgments about the boom and crash that had been easy ten years earlier. In 1947 George Soule, in his detailed economic history of the twenties, concluded perhaps rather to his own surprise that the rich grew richer without the poor growing poorer, that new amenities became available on a scale impossible to ignore, and that no measures then available would certainly have prevented the crash. Most of the more recent economic history textbooks seem either to suggest a similar assessment or to avoid passing judgment altogether. Even the economic foreign policy of the twenties, long a favorite target of liberal historians, has been presented by Herbert Feis as a well-intentioned though ineffective forerunner of Point Four. In 1955 John K. Galbraith, even in a book on the "Great Crash," took historians mildly to task for underrating what was good in the Coolidge era, and unfairly blaming Coolidge himself for a failure of prophecy.

Such opposite kinds of writers as Peter Drucker, Frederick L. Allen, and the editors of *Fortune* have argued, without special reference to the twenties, that American capitalism since about the turn of the century has been evolving into a new kind of democratic and humane economic order. Most recently David M. Potter concludes that we have always been the "People of Plenty" and that this fact, more than the frontier or political freedom, has shaped our mores. Professor Potter, more sophisticated than earlier prophets of abundance, has learned from the social scientists that a country has to pay for production in competitive strain, and perhaps later for security in loss of mobility. Yet his perspective, like that deriving from our whole political and economic climate, shifts the meaning of the earlier prosperity era. If productivity holds much of the meaning of American history, it is the depression and not the twenties that marks the interruption in a steady development. The New Era represents at worst a promising try at a new economy, a chapter in a book with a happy ending.

There is much in this reassessment that is invigorating, especially in a period when the leftist clichés are the tiredest of all. Yet several cautions are in order. Historians must remember, first, that the early 1880's and the 1920's and the 1950's are different and separated periods of prosperity, no matter how similar; second, that the depressions, even if in the long run temporary interruptions, did not look that way to their victims; and third, that even complete economic success does not, either now or for the twenties, refute all criticisms of American culture.

There is little danger that we will altogether forget this last caution. While some contemporary writers present a view of our recent history that emphasizes economic success, to another group such success is not so much false as irrelevant. The anti-optimists today are not rebels but traditionalists, a group that can be lumped together as antimaterialist conservatives. Some of these derive from and continue the new criticism, others reflect the revival of theology, and still others rely partly on new scientific theory. All have been led or forced, during the recent era of world catastrophe, to place their trust not in secular progress but primarily in moral and religious tradition, and from this standpoint the twenties are difficult to rehabilitate.

Joseph Wood Krutch has devoted a volume to repudiating the mechanistic determinism he voiced so powerfully in 1930, and Walter Lippmann has even more specifically repudiated his early relativism. In 1955 Lippmann concluded that the whole debacle in international politics, starting in 1917 and continuing through and after Versailles, resulted primarily from "the growing incapacity of the large majority of the democratic peoples to believe in intangible realities," specifically in a transcendent, universally valid, natural law.

Many powerful contemporary writers agree with Lippmann not only in his diagnosis of the trouble but in his fixing the responsibility for breakdown in the 1920's. Some of these, however, find in the decade enough just men to save it from complete condemnation. Russell Kirk, for instance, resurrects the New Humanists and marvels that "these years of vulgarity and presumption" produced the coming of an age of American conservatism in a group of thinkers who struggled against "the vertiginous social current of the Harding and Coolidge and Hoover years." (It marks perhaps the high point in this reassessment to make Coolidge, rather than Freud or Einstein, a symbol of vertigo.) A more subtle conservative and antimaterialist finds in the literary rebels the saving remnant. In his curious, dogmatic, but occasionally suggestive *Yankees and God,* Chard Powers Smith suggests that the young iconoclasts of the twenties were really the last, or next-to-the-last, wave of Puritanism, despite their use of the term Puritan as the ultimate of abuse. This apparently bizarre thesis is really neither absurd nor entirely original. Perry Miller in 1950 gave the rebels of the twenties a similarly respectable pedigree when he compared them to the transcendentalists. Both of these movements spoke for the spirit against the rule of things, and both, said Professor Miller, belonged in a series of "revolts by the youth of America against American philistinism." One can go a very little further and agree with Mr. Smith that both are basically Protestant; it is not hard to recognize in the young intellectuals of the twenties together with their iconoclasm a tortured uneasiness, a conscious responsibility for the faults of the era that are suggestive of a long heritage.

In the 1950's, then, the familiar division continued. Spokesmen of the New Era rehabilitated the twenties by using one set of standards while antimaterialists blamed or praised them according to another. At the same time, however, a number of scholars of varying views were reaching toward an understanding of such paradoxes by treating the twenties as a period of profound social change. Most of these students derived their insights to some extent from the sociologists, and it is interesting that some of the gloomiest insights stem today from this once exuberant science. David Riesman's strikingly influential vision of the shift from inner-direction to other-direction is not strictly dated by its creator, but it often seems to be a description of the end of the genteel tradition and the birth of the New Era, the defeat of Wilsonian moralism and the victory of the Babbitts. In different terms and with a more clearly stated value judgment, C. Wright Mills has documented the rise of a regimented, rootless, and docile new middle class to the arbitral position in American society. The increase of the white-collar salariat and its implications extended before and after the twenties but went especially fast in that period, as the authors of *Recent Social Trends,* among others, pointed out. Samuel Lubell and others have seen another social change in the twenties, the beginning of the coming-of-age of the new immigration. Drawing together Lubell's interpretation and Mills, Richard Hofstadter emphasizes the "Status Revolution" as a main event of the period about the turn of the century. The Protestant upper middle class, long a semi-aristocracy with a monopoly on advanced education, had declined, and so had the independent farmers. In their places other groups had grown and gained some power—the new middle class, the ethnic minorities, and labor. All these processes of change had, by the twenties, proceeded a long way, and all were continuing and accelerating, with the partial exception of the rise of labor. Surely this social upheaval, impossible to see clearly until our own time, has considerable meaning for the intellectual history of the twenties as for its politics, for the collapse, that is, of a long-frayed moral and literary tradition.

The nearest we can come to summarizing or explaining the shifting opinions of the twenties may well be to see the period in some such terms as these, and to see it as a disintegration. There is certainly nothing original about such a conclusion, but perhaps we are now in a position to give disintegration a fuller and more various meaning. The twenties were a period in which common values and common beliefs were replaced by separate and conflicting loyalties. One or another of the standards arising from the age itself has been used by each of its historians ever since. This is what has made their judgments so conflicting, so emotional, so severally valid and collectively confusing. It is equally true and equally partial to talk about the rising standard of living and the falling standard of political morality, the freshness and individuality of literature and the menace of conformity, the exuberance of manufacturers or social scientists and the despair of traditional philosophers. Somehow, we must learn to write history that includes all these, and the first step is to understand the decade when the fragmentation first became deep and obvious.

At least two recent writers are useful to those who want to look at the twenties from this point of view. One is Lionel Trilling, who deplores and analyzes the split between liberalism and the imagination, between the values we take for granted as socially desirable and those that have now the power to move us in art, between collective welfare and individual dignity. What is lacking, says Trilling, and what has been lacking specifically since the twenties, is a view of the world, in his word a faith though not necessarily a religion, that will give meaning both to society and to art, to progress and to tragedy. Professor Henry Nash Smith in a recent address has sketched, somewhat similarly, two diametrically opposite points of view which, he says, have divided our culture since 1910. One he calls the realistic-progressive view and the other the counter-enlightenment; one takes for its standards measurable welfare and humanitarian progress and equality; the other values only the individual imagination, nourished on tradition, holding out desperately against a mechanized culture, and accepting if necessary alienation and despair as the price of its survival.

The conflict of values that culminated, for it certainly did not begin, in the twenties was more than two-sided, and neither of these two critics has completely explored it. But they have indicated the right starting point. The way to understand our recent cultural history is to understand why and how its exponents fail to agree.

How can historians proceed further along this path? First, it hardly needs saying that to understand the twenties better we must make use of techniques drawn from various fields. The most important developments in the decade did not take place in the realms of politics, or economics, or literature, or science alone, but in all these areas and the relation, or lack of relation, among them. If one uses one kind of sources one will inevitably emerge with one point of view, which will be inadequate to understand the others.

Second, it seems clear that one cannot say much about the twenties as a disintegration or revolution without giving more attention to the old regime, the presumed prewar agreement. There seems to have been a greater degree of unity in American culture before 1917 or perhaps 1910, but a description of it is not easy and a casual reference to the genteel tradition or the cultural inheritance will not suffice. Immediately prewar America must be newly explored. We must look not so much at its articulate political or philosophical beliefs and more at its inarticulate assumptions—assumptions in such areas as morality, politics, class and race relations, popular art and literature, and family life. In short, we must concentrate on what Tocqueville would have called its manners. We are now, perhaps, in a position at least to undertake this recapture in an impartial mood. In 1956 we do not need to lament or rejoice at the destruction of the America of 1914; it is nearly as far off as Greece or Rome, and as inevitably a part of us.

Third, we must try to look at the succeeding disintegration, the revolution of the twenties, with a similar absence of passion. The literary scoffers who have been so thoroughly scolded were not, after all, the only rebels. The prophets of mechanization and welfare, the Fords and Edisons who scorned history and tradition, were equally revolutionary. Most revolutionary of all, perhaps, were the prophets of psychology and social science, with their brand new societies full of brand new human beings.

Finally, if we can really look back on this revolutionary decade from a perspective which has the advantage of thirty years of continuing revolution, we may be able to see which of the separate movements of the twenties has lasted best, and whether any of them are beginning to come together. Are there really in this decade of novelty beginnings as well as ends? Is it possible by now really to glimpse what so many have announced: the beginnings of a new period of American history and even of a new civilization?

THE INTOLERANCE OF THE TWENTIES

One of the ugliest but most pervasive forces underlying American life in the 1920's was racism. In 1916 a New York lawyer and amateur anthropologist named Madison Grant wrote a book entitled The Passing of the Great Race. Grant exploited racist ideas already popular in Europe to argue that the United States was founded and had flourished because of the efforts of the Nordic peoples of Northwestern Europe. In the latter part of the nineteenth century, immigrants from southern and eastern Europe began entering the nation in very large numbers, and Grant feared that their continued influx, combined with a high birth rate, would enable them to overwhelm the original Nordic population.

Many old-stock Americans shared Grant's fears. During the war immigration had nearly ceased, but with the return of peace it was believed that the devastation of Europe would trigger a massive flow of human beings across the Atlantic to the United States. In 1920, the editor of the Saturday Evening Post sent Kenneth Roberts, a New England writer of historical novels, on a European tour to alert the American people to the danger. Roberts wrote a series of articles which appeared in the Post and which were then published in 1922 under the title, Why Europe Leaves Home. In the following selections, Roberts expresses the racist antipathy to immigrants that was characteristic of middle-class Americans of his time.

KENNETH ROBERTS, Why Europe Leaves Home

During the thirty-five years before the war, the bulk of the immigrants who surged so freely into the United States came from three countries—Austria-Hungary, Italy and Russia. They were running neck and neck when the war broke; and on an average about a quarter of a million immigrants were entering America from each of the three countries. Austria-Hungary, however, showed unmistakable signs of nosing out the other two. In the ten years before the war broke out, 2,347,636 immigrants had entered the

From Why Europe Leaves Home, by Kenneth L. Roberts, pp. 2-6, 47-49, 113-114, copyright, 1922, by the Bobbs-Merrill Company, Inc., R. 1949, by Kenneth L. Roberts; reprinted by permission of the publishers.

United States from Austria-Hungary as against 2,196,884 from Italy and 1,991,284 from Russia. In the big immigration year of 1907, Austria-Hungary alone sent to America the staggering total of 338,452 emigrants. This was the greatest number of people that ever moved from one country to another country in one year's time in the history of the world. Part of them went because the agents of steamship lines painted glowing pictures of the ease with which money could be made in America; part of them went because agents of big manufacturing concerns circulated through the crowded districts and offered jobs in American mills at wages which seemed fabulous to the poor peasant; and by far the largest part went because relatives and friends and acquaintances who had already gone to America wrote back to their home towns telling of easy money and bright lights and fine clothes, and filling the minds of the stay-at-homes with a red-hot, sizzling desire to be up and doing in order to participate in the delights of America—especially in the easy-money part.

Today Austria-Hungary no longer exists. It has become Czecho-Slovakia, Hungary, Austria, a part of Poland, a part of Rumania, a part of Italy and a part of Jugo-Slavia. The inhabitants of these new divisions of an old empire have as little in common as they had before the war; but the few things which they have in common have grown greatly during the last few years. They hate one another even more passionately than they hated one another in 1914; they are even more dissatisfied with their governments, for the most part, than they used to be; and their longing to go to America is so violent and poignant and all-pervasive that they would willingly permit themselves to be kicked all the way from Warsaw to Paris or from Belgrade to Danzig—both of which trips would require a vast amount of kicking, to say nothing of a frightful amount of wear and tear on the garments of the kickee—if the final kick deposited them aboard a ship bound for America. They would do anything to get to America. They would lie with a fluency that would cause the bones of Baron Münchhausen to rattle feverishly in his grave; they would steal anything which could be stolen by human hands; probably they would willingly commit murder; for human life is not highly valued in Europe at the present time, what with several years of war, and the menace of Bolshevism, and the low rate of exchange, and one thing and another.

Before the war there was a great pother over the vast quantities of immigrants which were pouring into the United States each year. The United States Immigration Commission proved conclusively that the bulk of the more recent immigrants from Central and Southeastern Europe hived up in settlements of their own, where they retained the customs and the languages and the ideals of the countries from which they came, and failed utterly to become Americans. They had their own publications and occasionally their own laws. They were too frequently the sources of unrest and dissatisfaction, as well as of sedition and of innumerable varieties of revolutionary and anarchistic doctrines. In the cant phrase of the day the majority of the more recent immigrants didn't assimilate. An ostrich could assimilate a croquet ball or a cobblestone with about the same ease that America assimilated her newcomers from Central and Southeastern Europe. Most of them seemed to have been inoculated against assimilation before leaving home. Their standard of living in their home countries was as low as any standard of living could possibly be. If it had been any lower, it would have ceased to be a standard, and would have become a hole or socket.

The immigrants brought many of these standards with them, and clung to them determinedly in America. No matter how meager their wages might be, they lived on them handily and saved money, which they sent back home. That was what most of them came to America for—to save money and send it back home. Now there is nothing wrong with the saving of money by an immigrant; and when he has saved it, he is entitled to do what he pleases with it; for he has paid for the money with hard work. But it is a different matter when great numbers of men, accustomed all their lives to living on starvation rations, come to America and take jobs at low wages and then, in their determination to save money, crowd into wretched quarters and live in squalor and filth and darkness on a fraction of the money which an American workman must spend in order to live decently. Such a proceeding lowers the standard of living in America. The 1920 platform of the Republican party voiced the opinion of most political economists when it declared that, "The standard of living and the standard of citizenship of a nation are its most precious possessions, and the preservation and elevation of those standards is the first duty of our Government," and added that, "The immigration policy of the United States should be such as to insure that the number of foreigners in the country at any one time shall not exceed that which can be assimilated with reasonable rapidity, and to favor immigrants whose standards are similar to ours." No prophet who ever lived, and no student of immigration, no matter how weighty his brain, is capable of figuring out the number of foreigners who can be assimilated by the United States in a given period of time. If they are allowed to live in the slums and Ghettos and foreign settlements in which they are now living, they can not be assimilated. There isn't a chance of it. There isn't even a shadow of a chance of it. Such chance as there is, would, in fact, have to stand twice on one spot in order to cast a shadow. The people from these foreign settlements work all day by the side of other aliens. When they leave their work, they go back to crowded homes in which the only atmosphere is one of dirt and Europe. They come in contact with practically nothing which can be regarded as an Americanizing influence. So long as foreigners are permitted to enter this country and segregate themselves, just so long will they resist the rudiments of assimilation. Numbers have nothing to do with it. In approaching the subject from that angle, therefore, the Republican platform was disseminating a large amount of hot air. The idea behind the hazy words, however, was good. The idea proclaimed that the United States, in the past, had bitten off more than it could chew as regards immigrants, and that in the future smaller bites must be taken. . . .

There are many facts connected with the matter of immigration that are difficult to face. One of the most difficult is the matter of race. It is the constant cry of sentimentalists and individuals whose interest in immigration arises from nonpatriotic reasons that America consists of layer upon layer of immigrants, and that to stop immigration is to stop the growth and impair the greatness of America. Such people refuse to realize or to recognize that practically all immigration to America prior to 1880 was composed of people of the Nordic race—the tall, blond, adventurous people from the northern countries of Europe: from Sweden and Norway and Denmark and England and Scotland; from certain sections of Germany and Belgium and Ireland and France and Holland. The Nordic people possess certain characteristics: they have long skulls and blond hair— hair, that is, which is lighter than black; they possess to a marked degree the ability to govern themselves and to govern others; and from their ranks have been recruited the world's voluntary explorers, pioneers, sailors and adventurers. The early colonists of every undeveloped country in modern times have invariably been Nordics. America, then, was a nation of Nordics.

Since 1880 the bulk of immigration to the United States has been composed of people from the other two main races of Europe, known to biologists and ethnologists as the Alpine race and the Mediterranean race. The Alpines are the stocky, slow, dark, round-skulled folk who inhabit most of Central Europe and whose chief representatives are the large part —not all, but the large part—of the different Slav countries, the Czechs, the Poles, the Slovaks, the Russians, the Ruthenians and so on. The Mediterraneans are the small, swarthy, black-haired, long-skulled people which form the bulk of the population in Southern Italy, Greece, Spain and the north coast of Africa. These two races, plus the Hebrew, which is an Oriental instead of a European race, were pouring into America at the rate of a million a year during the ten years before the war; and given sufficient ships and an absence of immigration restrictions, they will pour into America at the rate of two million a year and more for years to come. These people who have been pouring in since 1880—and only since 1880— have displayed one marked characteristic throughout the centuries. Never have they been successful at governing themselves or at governing any one else. They have rushed to the spot where a stronger and hardier people have established successful enterprises; and by their low standards of living and their willingness to subordinate everything to immediate gain, they have forced out the people who preceded them. One of the oldest stories in history is the repeated influx of Alpine and Mediterranean peoples into Nordic people, and the resultant and almost invariable breeding out of the Nordics by the Alpines and Mediterraneans. To these people, who for centuries have demonstrated their incapacity to govern themselves, America is blindly and fatuously offering the keys of her cities and her reins of government, and that is why Americans all over Europe, after watching and studying the type of immigrant that is rushing to America, are writing and cabling to their people in America and to the Department of State that immigration is a matter of life and death to the American people; death if it continues unrestricted, and life if it is stopped. There will be many to smile at this statement as being an exaggeration. It is no exaggeration, but a matter of cold fact; and it will be upheld by every American who has seen European emigration and its sources—with the exception of those whose racial or business affiliations have impaired their eyesight. . . .

It is not particularly pleasant to continue to harp on the necessity of keeping the United States a nation of Nordics; for there are always a large number of sentimentally inclined readers, whose belief in the whimsical fairy tale of the melting pot is stronger than their common sense, who write hectic and vitriolic replies to any remarks on the respective merits of a continued Nordic strain of people and a mixed strain. So far as I have been able to gather from the letters that frequently reach me on this subject, no mention should be made of racial differences because all people are equal in the eyes of St. Peter. This is probably true; and everybody will unquestionably be delighted if it is. Here on earth, however, there are certain biological laws which govern the crossing of different breeds, whether the breeds be dogs or horses or men. If an otter hound is crossed with a Welsh terrier, the result is a mongrel. But if other otter hounds are crossed with other Welsh terriers, and the results of these crossings are mated in turn, the result is an Airedale, which is a very excellent dog. Excellent results can usually be obtained from crossbreeding followed by inbreeding. But the only results that can ever be obtained from promiscuous and continued crossbreeding is mongrelization; and a mongrel —in spite of the excellence of the stock from which he may have sprung— is a total loss. The same thing is true of humans. A mongrelized race of people is incapable of producing great artists or authors or statesmen or poets or architects or sculptors, or explorers or warriors. A mongrelized race sinks to the dead level of mediocrity. Its government becomes corrupt, its art and its literature become degenerate and silly, its judiciary becomes venal, its public and its private morals become depraved. Nothing is left to it but the sharpness, the trickiness and the cunning of its unscrupulous traders and an exalted opinion of its own importance, based on the records of the pure but vanished race which it supplanted. These facts should be of considerable interest to a great many citizens of the United States; for so many millions of non-Nordic aliens have poured into this country since 1880 that in several of America's largest cities the foreign-born and the children of foreign-born far outnumber the native Americans. The inevitable result of such a state of affairs, unless it is checked at once and forever, is mongrelization; and many of America's large cities are already displaying all the earmarks of mongrelization. There are still many millions of good Americans who hold, in the innocence of their mistaken belief in the equality of mankind, that the person who believes in race purity is a snob; but before many years have gone by, he will be a benighted American who doesn't know that race purity is the prime essential for the well-being of his children and the continued existence of the things that made his country great.

THE DIVIDED DEMOCRATS

The racism preached by Roberts and Grant led to the adoption of stringent immigration restriction legislation, at first on a temporary basis in 1921, and then permanently in April, 1924 with the passage of the National Origins Quota Act which limited immigration from Europe to 150,000. Of this quota 80 % was allotted to the Nordic countries, thereby discriminating against immigrants from southern and eastern Europe.

Two months later, in June 1924, the Democratic National Convention was held in New York City, and racism was a major issue. Under Woodrow Wilson, the Democrats had barely managed to hold power for two terms, and in 1920 the Republicans had easily swept back into office with Warren Harding. When Harding died in the summer of 1923, serious scandals were just becoming public knowledge, but the new President, the flinty Vermonter Calvin Coolidge, was able to restore the reputation of his party. A group of dissident reformers nominated Robert La Follette on a Progressive Party Ticket in 1924, but he failed to attract widespread public support. The Democrats were in disarray when they gathered in New York. One wing of the party, representing the urban East and Middle West, championed Al Smith, the Catholic Governor of New York, while the rural Democrats of the South and Far West supported William Gibbs McAdoo of California. The conflict became so intense that a deadlock ensued, and finally on the 103rd ballot, the delegates chose John W. Davis, a conservative Wall Street lawyer, as a compromise candidate.

The bitterness of the division inside the party was most evident in the debate over the platform. The northern Democrats wanted to include a plank specifically denouncing the Ku Klux Klan as a racist organization whose ideas ran counter to the principles of the party. They particularly condemned the Klan's virulent anti-Catholicism. Southern and western Democrats countered with a milder plank that simply denounced secret societies without mentioning the Klan. On the fifth day of the convention, the platform committee reported out the milder plank, but a minority report led to a floor debate. The final speech was delivered by William Jennings Bryan, three times the Democratic candidate for President. His famous voice weakened by age, Bryan was frequently interrupted by the hostile New York audience. Nevertheless, he delivered an eloquent plea for unity which helped sway the delegates into upholding the platform committee by a vote of 542 and a fraction to 541 and a fraction.

WILLIAM JENNINGS BRYAN,
Speech to the Democratic National Convention

The Chairman: Mr. Cummings yields twenty-five minutes to that revered Democrat, the Hon. William J. Bryan from Florida. (Loud applause.)

A Voice: The head of the party, Mr. Bryan.

Mr. Bryan: Mr. Chairman, ladies and gentlemen, members of the convention: It is now twenty-eight years since Democratic conventions be-

The New York Times (June 29, 1924), p. 4.

came gracious enough to invite me and patient enough to listen to me, and I have not words in which to express my gratitude for the love and loyalty of millions of Democrats who have been my co-laborers for more than a quarter of a century. (Applause.)

I have spoken to you on many themes, never on themes more important than today; and since they take applause out of my time, and since I am speaking to your hearts and heads and not to your hands, keep still and let me speak to you. (Cries of "We'll do it.")

I have only a short time in which to lay before you the arguments that seem to be pertinent to this occasion, when we are about to decide not only the line of our campaign this fall, but in which we may affect larger things than parties.

Let's understand each other. Let's eliminate the things that are not in this issue and come down to the three words that these, our good friends, as honest, as patriotic and as anxious for the welfare of the party, take out of the language and exalt above any other three words that will be used in this campaign. Note, my friends, that they take our report, every word of it, and note also that we offered to take every word of their report, but three. We said: "Strike out three words and there will be no objection." But three words were more to them than the welfare of a party in a great campaign. (Applause.)

You have listened to the applause when we have had read to you the best Democratic platform that was ever written, the noblest principles that have ever been written into a platform. We have there pleas pathetic for people in distress, but none of our principles, none of our pleas stirred the hearts of these men like the words, "Ku Klux Klan." [Long and continued hisses, boos and jeers.)

(The Chairman raps for order.)

The Chairman: The delegates of the convention will preserve order. I shall have to call Mr. Bryan when the time has expired unless you permit him to proceed.

Mr. Bryan: I call you to witness, I call you to witness that these men never took the standards of their States and marched when we appealed on grand principles. It was only when they said the Ku Klux Klan, that's the only thing—(Hisses, boos, and jeers.)

The Chairman: The officers will preserve order.

A Voice: Clear the galleries of the hoodlums.

The Chairman: Or these proceedings will cease. Please let us have order here.

Mr. Bryan: Citizens of New York, you show your appreciation of the honor we did you in holding our convention here. (A confusion of cries from the floor with the Chairman rapping for order.)

Courtesy of Wide World Photos.

Ku Klux Klan parade in Tulsa, Oklahoma, 1923.

The Chairman: If the speaker is again interrupted by the galleries, they will be cleared. (Applause and some hisses.) I shall order this in the name of the delegates of this convention, for whom I speak. I warn the delegates that this speaker is to continue, and without interruption from them.

Mr. Bryan: Let me place before you the five reasons which I submit to your judgments and your consciences. First, this plank, these three words, are not necessary.

A Voice: Yes, they are.

Other Voices: Put him out! Put him out!

Mr. Bryan: There is not a State in the Union where anybody whose rights are denied cannot go and find redress (applause); not a State in the Union; and the Democratic Party in its platform, the part of it on which we all agree, in words as strong as can be written, with emphasis as great as can be employed, puts all the strength of party back of every right, and especially back of the right of religious liberty for which we stand (applause), as well as those who call us cowards because we do not take three words with which they seek to conjure.

It is not necessary, I repeat, first because the laws protect every one. Second, it is not necessary to protect any church. I, my friends, have such confidence in the Catholic Church, which was for over a thousand years my mother church as well as yours (applause).

A Voice: That is your faith.

Mr. Bryan: It was the Catholic Church that took religion from its founder and preserved it, the only custodian, for over a thousand years. And when they did it for the Catholic, they did it for me and for every Protestant.

The Catholic Church, with its legacy of martyred blood and with all the testimony of its missionaries who went into every line, does not need a great party to protect it from a million men. (Cheers and applause.) The Jews do not need this resolution. They have Moses. They have Elijah. They have Elisha, who was able to draw back the curtain and show upon the mountain tops an invisible host greater than a thousand Ku Klux Klans. (Cheers and applause.) And both the Catholic Church, as well as the Jewish faith, has its great characters today who plead for respect for them, and whose pleading is not in vain. It is not necessary, and, my friends, the Ku Klux Klan does not deserve the advertisement that you give them. (Cheers and applause.)

The minority, the fourteen members of our committee, who could not join with me in a report that would leave out these three magic and mystic words, have raised the Ku Klux Klan to a higher altitude than the Ku Klux themselves ever raised their fiery cross. (Cheers and applause.) Mr. Colby tells you that this is a transient organization; that it will soon die. If that be true, then really, my friends, the motto of the minority ought to be, "Hurry up if you would see George, he is nearly gone." (Laughter.)

My friends, one objection that I have to making this issue the paramount issue of this campaign is that I am not willing to lift up the dying embers and start a prairie fire and carry this Klan into every Congressional district of the United States. (Cheers and applause.)

My third objection is that we have no moral right to let them divert us from as great a mission as our party ever had. (Applause.)

They say we are cowards. My friends, it requires more courage to fight the Republican Party than it does to fight a Ku Klux Klan. Here we have farmers driven into bankruptcy, a million driven from the farms in a single year. We find monopoly spreading. We find nearly every great line of industry in the control of gigantic combinations of capital.

And while we have distress in this country that cries aloud for relief and while we have a war-worn world across the Atlantic that needs our help and needs our guidance, these minority men say that we lack courage if we do a big work instead of starting out on a little hunt for something which is nearly dead and which will soon pass away. (Applause.)

You may call me a coward if you will, but there is nothing in my life to justify the charge that I am a coward. (Applause.) But, my friends, I would rather have the anathemas of these misguided Democrats than have to answer on Judgment Day for a duty disregarded and a trust deserted. Anybody can fight the Ku Klux Klan, but only the Democratic Party can stand between the common people and their oppressors in this land. (Applause.)

Then, I am not willing to bring discord into my party. The Democratic Party is united on all the economic issues. We have never been so united since I have known politics, and nobody has had more reason than I to regret discord. (Laughter and applause.) Now, when we are all united and all stand with a dauntless courage and enthusiasm never excelled, these people tell us that we must turn aside from these things and divide our party with a religious issue and cease to be a great political party. Why, they tell us that if we do not do so and so, the Democratic Party is going to lose a large number.

My friends, if the Democratic Party will lose a considerable number because it insists on being what it has been, how many will it lose if it tries to be what it has never been? The Democratic Party has never been a religious organization. The Democratic Party has never taken the side of one Church against the other. The Democratic Party must remain true. It cannot surrender its right to exist and the mission that was given to it in the days of Jefferson, that it remained true to in the days of Jackson and to which it was still loyal in the days of Woodrow Wilson.

But, my friends, I have left for the last what I regard as the greatest argument. If the Democratic Party is diverted from its duty some other party will take up its task. (Cries of "No!" "Boo!")

But no party that takes up a noble task will find its leaders in the gallery today. (Laughter and prolonged applause.)

I repeat, that if our party is turned aside from its transcendent duty as champion of the rights of the masses, another party can take our place. Even if our party were destroyed, another party would grow up to do its work.

And now I want to tell you my last and strongest objection, and let the galleries scoff if they dare: I say I am not willing to divide the Christian Church when we ought to stand together to fight the battles of religion in this land. (Cheers and applause.)

My friends, I am not responsible for your opinions. I am for mine. I have tried to defend the Democratic Party because of all I owe to it. It took me up when I was ten years younger than any other man had been when he was nominated by a great party, and it found me in a Western State, farther West than it had ever gone before, and it gave me a million more votes than it had ever given any Democrat before (applause), and it nominated me twice afterward, and I never had to use any money, and I had no organization. (Applause.)

The Democratic Party has done more for me than for any other living man, and, my friends, I am grateful. I cannot express my gratitude. I can paraphrase the words that are familiar when I express my sentiments:

"Partisans, spare that party, touch not a single bough;
In youth it sheltered me and I will protect it now."

(Loud cheers and applause.)

But, my friends, much as I owe to my party, I owe more to the Christian religion. If my party has given me the foundations of my political faith, my Bible has given me the foundations of a faith that has enabled me to stand for the right without stopping to count how many stood to take their share with me. (Applause and cheers.)

My father taught me that I could afford to be in a minority, but I could not afford to be wrong on any subject. He believed in the Bible and in God, and he believed that God stood back of every righteous cause with an arm strong enough to bring victory to his side; and that has been my faith. And, my friends, I believe religion is of more importance than politics, and I believe the world needs now not so much to get into a fight between denominations as it does to get back to God and a sense of responsibility to God. (Applause.)

Burglars stole $65,000,000 in a year and pickpockets stole nearly as much, and bank robbers and bandits took large sums; but the swindlers took $2,000,000,000, ten times as much as all the people in the penitentiary took. Isn't it worthwhile, my friends, to unite the Christian Church in behalf of the Ten Commandments and the Sermon on the Mount, instead of dividing them in warring factions? (Applause.)

The world is coming out of the war, the bloodiest ever known. Thirty millions of human lives were lost; $300,000,000,000 of property was destroyed, and the debts of the world are more than six times as great as they were when the first gun was fired. My friends, how are you going to stop war? Oh, they say, commerce will do it; but commerce did not do it, and commerce reached its highest point just before the war began.

They said education will do it; but education did not do it. Education reached its highest point just before the war began. Some say science will do it, but science did not do it, for science had reached the highest point just before the war began. Yes, my friends, science instead of preventing war, mixed the poisonous gas and made the liquid fire. It was science that made war so hellish that civilization was about to commit suicide.

Science cannot do it. There is only one thing that can bring peace to the world, and that is the Prince of Peace. (Applause.) That is, my friends, the One who, when He came upon the earth, the angels sang, "On earth peace, goodwill toward man."

My friends, Jew and Gentile, Catholic and Protestant, stand for God, on whom all religion rests, and Protestant and Catholic stand for the Prince of Peace. Is it possible that now, when Jesus is more needed, I say the hope of the world—is it possible that at this time, in this great land, we are to have a religious discussion and a religious warfare?

Are you going, my friends, to start a blaze that may cost you innumerable lives, sacrificed on the altar of religious liberty? I cannot believe it; I call you back in the name of our party, I call you back in the name of our God, I call you back in the name of the Son of God and Saviour of the world. Christians, stop fighting, and let us get together and save the world from the materialism that robs life of its spiritual values. (Applause.)

It was Christ on the Cross who said, "Father, forgive them, for they know not what they do." And my friends, we can exterminate Ku Kluxism better by recognizing their honesty and teaching them that they are wrong. (Boos and hisses, followed by applause.)

THE RURAL SOUTH PROTESTS

The *fatal division within the Democratic party enabled Coolidge to win easily in 1924. Four years later he chose not to run again, and the Republicans nominated Herbert Hoover, Secretary of Commerce since 1920. Though opposition to Smith remained strong in the South and West, the Democrats nominated him without a fight in their convention in Houston. In the accompanying platform, the party tried to retain the loyalty of the "dry" forces who supported prohibition by adopting a plank promising to enforce the laws against drinking more strictly. Yet before the convention adjourned, Governor Smith, who was known to be a "wet," came out for "fundamental changes" in the prohibition code.*

Bishop James Cannon, Jr., Methodist clergyman, leader of the Anti-Saloon League, and personification of the rural values of the South, decided to challenge Smith. Though Cannon took his stand on the prohibition issue, he continually referred to Smith's religion in an effort to persuade fellow southerners to break with tradition and vote for the Republican candidate. Cannon began his successful effort to discredit Smith in the South with the following attack in the liberal weekly, The Nation, only a week after the Democratic convention.

JAMES CANNON, JR., *Al Smith—Catholic, Tammany, Wet*

If it were necessary to explain this in a single sentence, I should say: Governor Smith is personally, ecclesiastically, aggressively, irreconcilably Wet, and is ineradicably Tammany-branded, with all the inferences and implications and objectionable consequences which naturally follow from such views and associations. In the issue of *The Nation* of November 30, in an article discussing Governor Smith as a "Presidential possibility," Mr. Villard said:

> Do you believe in electing to the Presidency a man who drinks too much for his own good, and is politically a rampant Wet? . . . Does "Al" drink and does he drink too much? Well, I am reliably informed that he drinks every

---

James Cannon, Jr., "Al Smith—Catholic, Tammany, Wet," *The Nation,* CXXVII (July 4, 1928), pp. 9-10.

day, and the number of his cocktails and highballs is variously estimated at from four to eight. It is positively denied that he is ever intoxicated, much gossip to the contrary notwithstanding. He is a Wet, and he lives up to it, and for that consistency he is to be praised. . . . One may regret with all one's heart, as does the writer of these lines, that, being in an exalted position, he cannot set an example of abstinence to the millions whose State he governs, but at least one knows where he stands.

It is now over six months since that statement concerning Governor Smith's personal habits was printed and quoted, and there has been no official denial of its accuracy. It coincides with the private statements of other reliable persons. The facts certainly appear to warrant the asking of this question: Shall Dry America, a country with prohibition embedded in its Constitution, elect a "cocktail President"?

It is true that a man's personal attitude toward the prohibition amendment and toward the use of intoxicants is not the only important question to be asked concerning his fitness for the office of President of the United States. But one's personal opinion on the principle of prohibition cannot be considered apart from the broader question of loyalty to the Constitution, as long as the prohibition amendment is a part of that Constitution. Furthermore, while it is true that the prohibition amendment does not prohibit the use of intoxicating liquor for beverage purposes, it is also true that it is the natural, logical consequence of the prohibition law that within a comparatively short time all legal use of beverage intoxicants will be eliminated. There are doubtless some law-abiding citizens who still use no intoxicants except those which they possessed at the time that prohibition went into effect, but that number is small and steadily decreasing. Can any law-abiding American citizen want a man to be elected President who not only disbelieves in the principle of prohibition, but, although sworn to uphold the Constitution of the United States, yet will continue to indulge his appetite for strong drink in the Executive Mansion? What an interesting public document for future generations to inspect would be the application of the President of the United States for a permit from the Prohibition Department to move from his residence to the White House an itemized list of the bottles, casks, barrels, and other containers of intoxicating liquor, traffic in which is prohibited by the Constitution which the said applicant is sworn to uphold!

But not only is Governor Smith personally Wet today, but his entire record is Wet. He was a frequenter of saloons while they existed; he put his foot on the brass rail and blew the foam off the glass; in his social and political activities he recognized the saloon as an important factor. As a legislator he not only opposed every measure to restrict the privileges of saloons, but endeavored to remove existing restrictions. He fought the ratification of the Eighteenth Amendment and the passage of the Mullen-Gage State Law Enforcement Code, and after that code had been enacted by the New York State Legislature, he labored aggressively and persistently to obtain its repeal. He is now advocating modifications of the prohibition laws to permit each State to determine what shall be the legal alcoholic content of the beverages permitted.

When all his background is considered, it is not surprising that Governor Smith should have persistently and aggressively fought prohibition. Tammany-bred, a pupil, a follower, a protege of Croker, Foley, and Murphy, he is today the outstanding personality and most influential factor in Tammany Hall. It is true that Mr. George Olvaney, the titular head of Tammany Hall, declared on oath before the Senate Committee that Tammany was not a political organization at all, but simply a "patriotic society." But whatever it be called Tammany is, as was declared in *The Nation* for June 13, a "society held together by the cohesive power of public plunder." Governor Smith has for thirty-three years been a worker in or an official of that society. Nor has he condemned the Tammany graft and corruption which has recently come to light. Indeed, he has only recently been reinstated as a sachem.

Moreover, Governor Smith is ecclesiastically Wet. There was published in the secular press on January 2, 1928, a quotation which has not been denied from the *Osservatore Romano,* the official organ of the Vatican, stating that "the attempt to enforce prohibition in America has become so useless, not to say dangerous, that it would be better to abolish it, especially since unbridled passion is always more rampant as soon as there is an attempt to enforce complete abstinence." This attack upon the prohibition law of the United States by the Vatican organ is in full agreement with the open criticism of the law by the Cardinal Archbishop of New York and Boston and other Roman Catholic dignitaries.

I concede the right of the Pope, cardinals, archbishops, and other Roman Catholics to declare their attitude as freely as Methodist, Baptist, Presbyterian, or other Protestant bodies or ministers or laymen upon this question. Nor would I even intimate that these Roman Catholic leaders are not sincere in their opposition to the prohibition law. But it is not surprising, indeed it is to be expected, that this position of high dignitaries of the Roman church will be reflected in the attitude of many loyal Catholics who are members of legislatures, or of Congress, or who hold other official positions. It is a fact that the attacks in Congress upon the prohibition law are made chiefly by men who are themselves Roman Catholics or who represent constituencies with large Roman Catholic populations. Certainly it is likely that Governor Alfred E. Smith is influenced by the views of the Pope and the cardinals on the subject of prohibition.

I repeat that because Governor Smith is personally, ecclesiastically, aggressively, irreconcilably Wet and is ineradicably Tammany-branded, the South's Dry Democrats will oppose him. It is unthinkable that the moral, religious leadership of the South could be a party to the nomination or election of such a man as Governor Smith, thus being guilty of an open betrayal of a great social, economic, and moral reform which was won after years of unselfish labor. If the Houston convention should nominate Governor Smith for President, multiplied thousands of lifelong Democrats will decide that Democracy will be better served by the defeat of the Wet Tammany sachem than by his election, and will act accordingly.

THE DISMAY OF THE MIDDLE CLASS

Racism and intolerance was only one form of reaction to social change in the 1920's. Many middle-class critics of the "new era" concentrated on the transformations taking place in the American economy. They lamented the emphasis on materalism and consumption of goods and they questioned whether the continued industrialization was leading to a better way of life for all Americans. In particular, they regretted the undermining of the older American values of thrift and industry. James Truslow Adams, historian of New England and popular essayist, presented the most telling indictment of the economic trends of the twenties in Our Business Civilization, which appeared in 1929. The following selection is excerpted from the second chapter.

JAMES TRUSLOW ADAMS, *The Cost of Prosperity*

Not long ago a despatch from Washington announced that "the highest standard of living ever attained in the history of the world was reached last year [1926] by the American people," and gave as basis for the state-

---

James T. Adams, *Our Business Civilization* (New York, Liveright, 1929), pp. 35-38. 50-52, 54-55, 58-59.

ment the government's figure for the income of our population, which income was set at ninety billion dollars. The "high standard" thus indicated is unhesitatingly accepted by almost everyone; but even if we do accept as a fact, though it is far from being a universal one, the ability of all persons to spend more and to buy more things than ever before, it may be worth while to consider what some of the by-products of the processes involved have been. Overwhelmed by the material advance made in the past five decades or so and by the vast amount of Pollyanna literature with which we are flooded by politicians and business executives with axes to grind, we are apt to lose sight of the law of compensation and to think of all change as unalloyed improvement.

Change may or may not be "progress," but whether it is or not it is bound to involve compensatory losses. Man may have advanced far from his ancestor which lived in the primeval slime, but that lowly progenitor could breathe either in air or water and if he lost a leg could grow another. Today man can make his voice heard three thousand miles away, but he dies if you hold his nose in a water basin and is a cripple for life when he loses a foot. What he gains in one direction he drops in another, unpopular as Nature or anyone else may be when they tell him so. One is not necessarily a pessimist, therefore, when one chooses to consider what losses may have been entailed by attaining to the present "highest standard of living."

Two points are notable in the popular belief as to that standard. One is that all classes in the community are supposed somehow to share in its beneficences, and the other is that the measuring rod used is material and economic. The leaders in the "marvellous advance" are automobiles, radios, vacuum cleaners, electric washing machines, telephones, etc. It is assumed that spiritual and intellectual progress will somehow come also from the mere accumulation of "things," and this assumption has become a sort of American religion with all the psychological implications of religious dogma. In business circles, mass production, on which our present prosperity is based, is not considered merely as a transient and possibly an unsound economic phase, but as the creator of "the highest standard of living ever attained," and, as such, as little to be doubted or questioned as God the Creator before Darwin. At any rate, mass production is so closely linked to the ninety billion dollars that the two may be considered as the heads and tails of the same coin, and the by-products of one those of the other.

It may be noted that, although ninety billion dollars is a staggering sum to contemplate, we receive something of a shock when we read farther that the average income of all persons "gainfully employed" was $2210 a year. When we turn to another statistical source and find that nearly ten thousand persons paid taxes on incomes of from $100,000 to $1,000,000 [a] year each, two hundred and twenty-eight on incomes over $1,000,000, and fourteen on incomes of over $5,000,000 each, we begin to wonder whether the masses are getting quite their share of the benefits of mass production. It is evident that however great the "national" wealth may be, there is something very queer about its distribution, and that the gulf between the average man and the rich man has widened with appalling rapidity.

We are not here concerned primarily with that point nor with the average person "gainfully employed," whose income is evidently not much above $2000, but we may glance a moment at the condition of the latter in order to get some standard of income measurement. In 1917 the street railway employees in Seattle submitted a minimum budget for living in a dispute with their company over wages. They figured that $1917.88 annually for a family of five would allow, among other things, $12 for the education of the children, $30 for reading matter of all kinds, and $120 each for insurance and old-age savings. The company was able to reduce this to $1505.60 by eliminating all reading matter, including newspapers, reducing education from $12 to $11, old-age savings from $120 to $100, and insurance from $120 to $30. Carfare was reduced to $35.70 annually, with the somewhat ironical result that the members of the families of the men engaged in running the street cars were allowed only enough to use a car themselves on an average of once every six days! As $5 a year per person was allowed for "recreation" and $4 for all "miscellaneous," we need not linger over the average man in our total population who is "gainfully employed" when considering for the moment the high standard of living. We are here concerned with the persons between those and the ultra wealthy—the persons who both suffer from and enjoy factors in that standard.

One of the outstanding features of life today is its frightful and steadily increasing cost. Apart from taxation, it is much higher in the United States than in any of the other ten countries in which I have spent longer or shorter periods in the past few years. This is in part due to the intentionally prohibitive tariff, in part to the terrific increase in wages, and in part to the increase in the kind and number of things we are supposed to have in order to be happy. . . .

What has been the effect on the professional and intellectual classes? Of couse where they have linked themselves to big business or made their work fit into mass production they have weathered the storm of the high standard very well. No one need worry about the general counsel of a motor-car company, the artists who draw the syndicated comic strips, or the movie stars. But there are whole classes who do not or cannot thus fit in. A nationally known trust company officer recently wrote that most of those who disliked the present situation and who were given to dire comment or prophecy were merely those who had had comfortable incomes before the present high standard hit us and who had been unable to adjust themselves to it, that is, make *large* incomes. But according to the present modes of dividing the national income, how *can* these classes adjust themselves except by abandoning their work and going into business?

Our glance at the minimum wage budget prepared by the street railway men has shown us what can be done on $1900 a year: $12 a year for education, $30 for all reading matter (one-third of which would be consumed by one daily paper), and $12.20 for tobacco and all recreation. The average pay of all clergymen throughout the United States is $735 a year. Even if this frequently includes a house, how are they to adjust themselves? To attain even to the minimum budget of the street railway worker they would nearly have to more than double their income, that is, to give approximately one-third of their time to the work of their ministry and two-thirds to making money solely. Even if they could do so, what would they get as their share of the "high standard"? We have seen that even the street railway company had to cut out all reading matter, even newspapers, from the homes of its men if they were to live on $1505. Yet under the high standard the country allows its clergy scarcely half that sum and complains that the church is failing in leadership.

Let us turn to another class, which is great numerically and should be great in influence, and which we shall consider more particularly in a later chapter. The average pay of teachers throughout the country districts of the Middle Atlantic States, including that manufactory of millionaires, Pennsylvania, is $870 a year; in the villages it is $1244. Let us bear in mind the bleak budget of $1900 of the street railway men and remember also that the conductor of a railway freight train gets about $3750 a year and the engineer about $4700. What are the opportunities and prospects for a man of scholarly tastes, attainments, and pursuits? The average pay of over eleven thousand members of college faculties is less than $3000 a year, and, although in rare institutions a comparatively few men may attain to $8000 or $10,000, a man is fortunate indeed who gets from $5000 to $7000. How are these men to adjust themselves? Most of them do do extra work to earn money as, in forty percent of the cases, do the wives also. In the days before the "high standard" a vacation was a vacation, a period in which the professor, fagged from nine months' drilling of immature minds, could rest and catch up on his professional reading, get fresh points of view and prepare for the next nine months' bout with inquiring or resisting youth. Now, we read, one-third of the faculty could take no vacation at all; 40 percent took less than two weeks, and 60 percent

less than four weeks; yet yesterday the men in the building trades in
New York laid down their demand for every Saturday off on full pay,
equivalent to six and a half weeks' vacation from purely physical work
requiring practically no mental preparation or recuperation. Is it any
wonder that a professor at Berkeley on $3000 a year goes into business
at $20,000 a year, that a professor from an Eastern university on about
$6,000 a year becomes president of a business company with $75,000 a year
drawing account, and that another turns from teaching history to writing
advertisements, to mention the three who occur first to me? . . .

Before we leave this phase of the question, let us glance at some of the
office workers under the new standard. What mass production methods
have done in the way of deadening routine for the factory workers is too
well known for repetition, in spite of much glossing over, but what is going
on in office work may be less generally understood. The new idea of the
relations between employer and employee in mass production is that
the employer buys "production," that is, "output," from the employee.
Thus we read in a book on office technic how improvement was made
in an up-to-date office. Motion pictures were taken of the clerks opening
the morning mail. As a result of a study of these pictures, the motions
of the clerks were "reduced from thirteen to six and the output increased
from 100 pieces an hour to 200 an hour. A further refinement in the manner
of arranging the opened and unopened letters on the table brought the rate
of 250 an hour. Output was still further increased by the use of a 'motion-
studied table' to 300 an hour."

Stenographers, of course, have been included in this speeding-up process.
We read that "in measuring production of this kind several systems are
in use. One is that of measuring production by the square inch, with a
transparent celluloid, but in most cases a cyclometer is used, which is
attached to the machine and records the number of strokes." Production
is counted by "points," each "point" being equal to a certain number of
strokes, and pay is given accordingly. 250 strokes are deducted for an
ordinary error and 1275 strokes for an error on an envelope. 10,000 strokes
are added for "a perfect desk," that is one on which every minute of the
week, every implement is so placed as to permit of the greatest speed.
Medals and vacation allowances are given for records, and contests are
held—though, as to these last, the expert admits that "as a general rule,
office contests are not to be recommended. Spurts of speed of any kind
are bound to have their reactions and the contest is *often succeeded by
a certain amount of lethargy after the goal has been won.* [Italics mine.]
But for clearing out an accumulation of work or to rouse the office force
they may be very effective." One rubs one's eyes and wonders whether he
is reading about America under the highest standard of living ever attained

or England at the beginning of the Industrial Revolution. Stenographers share in the high standard to the extent of from $1250 to $170 a year. . . .

There are evidences that a great change may be in prospect. Mass production requires a steady and enormous flow of sales. On the one hand, the jaded buyers are showing signs of restiveness and of becoming tired of wasting their lives in buying, buying, buying, and paying, paying, paying. They have to be whipped into it by more and more expensive salesmanship. On the other hand, office and sales forces are getting tired of being speeded up as they compare their share in the high standard with that of the men above them, and have to be whipped by the most improved technical methods into greater and greater activity. And all for what? That mass production shall not falter or fail. The overhead costs of distribution have become staggering. If the public begins to economize and does not buy, then we are told that mass production will fall down and in the crash to follow no one will have money with which to buy anything. Better than that, we are told, is to buy what we do not really want or cannot afford.

There is no rest from the effort to make money in ever larger and larger amounts. There is no prospect of comfortable retirement in old age. For many who never thought of it in the old days there is the ever-present spectre of illness or incapacity. As has been said, our prosperity can be maintained only by making people want more, and work more, all the time. Those, and they are many, who believe that our recent prosperity has been mainly caused by the phenomenal expansion of the automobile business tell us that it will soon be necessary to find some other article which will similarly take the public fancy and create billions of sales—and billions of expense to men already tired of doing nothing but meeting new expenses.

"The highest standard of living ever attained in the history of the world"?

THE PLIGHT OF THE WORKER

Social scientists criticized the changing social and economic order from a very different perspective. Sociology was just developing its new analytical tools in the 1920's, but its devotees had enormous confidence in their ability to diagnose American social ills and suggest the proper remedies.

Robert and Helen Lynd, as Henry F. May notes, were more cautious than many sociologists in imposing their views, but they shared the prevailing notion that social institutions had failed to keep pace with technological progress.

The Lynds conducted a systematic field investigation of Muncie, Indiana, which they selected as a typical small American city. Employing extensive personal interviews with a cross section of the population, they compared the city in the mid-1920's with patterns of life there in 1890. Though their primary aim was to present a careful portrait of contemporary American society, their own dismay at the difficulties the average factory worker faced in his daily routine comes through clearly. The following selections are taken from chapters entitled "The Long Arm of the Job" and "Why Do They Work So Hard?"

ROBERT and HELEN LYND, Middletown

As one prowls Middletown streets about six o'clock of a winter morning one notes two kinds of homes: the dark ones where people still sleep, and the ones with a light in the kitchen where the adults of the household may be seen moving about, starting the business of the day. For the seven out of every ten of those gainfully employed who constitute the working class, getting a living means being at work in the morning anywhere between six-fifteen and seven-thirty o'clock, chiefly seven. For the other three in each ten, the business class, being at work in the morning means seven-forty-five, eight or eight-thirty, or even nine o'clock, but chiefly eight-thirty. Of the sample of 112 working class housewives reporting on this point, forty-eight (two out of five) rise at or before five o'clock, seventy-nine (nearly three-fourths) by five-thirty, and 104 (over nine-tenths) are up at or before six. Among the group of forty business class housewives interviewed, none rises before six, only six at six, fourteen at any time before seven, and twenty-six rise at seven or later.

This gap between the rising hours of the two sections of the population touches the interlocked complex of Middletown life at many points. A prominent citizen speaking on the curtailing of family life by clubs, committees, and other organized activities urged the parents of the city to "Help solve the boy problem by making breakfast a time of leisurely family reunion."

He did not realize that such a solution could apply to only about one-third of the city's families, since in the other two-thirds the father gets up in the dark in winter, eats hastily in the kitchen in the gray dawn, and is at work from an hour to two and a quarter hours before his children have to be at school. Or take another local "problem"—the deadlock between north and south sides of the city in the spring of 1925 over daylight saving time; the working class majority overwhelmed the measure before the city officials on the plea that in summer their small dwellings cool off slowly, often remaining warm until after midnight, and that they can ill spare an hour of cool early-morning sleep before they must get up to work. The business men, on the other hand, urged the need of daylight time because of golf and because standard time put local business at a two-hour disadvantage in dealing with Eastern business. Each group thought the other unreasonable.

The rising hours of business and working class differed less thirty-five years ago, as early rising was then somewhat more characteristic of the entire city. Nowadays one does not find doctors keeping seven to nine o'clock morning office hours as in 1890. During the eighties retail stores opened at seven or seven-thirty and closed at eight or nine, a thirteen-hour day. About 1890 a six o'clock closing hour, except on Saturdays, was tried by a few merchants, and gradually the practice prevailed. Today stores open at eight or eight-thirty and close at five-thirty.

Ten hours a day, six days a week, was the standard rhythm of work for Middletown industrial workers in 1890. In 1914, 73 percent of them, according to the Federal Census, worked sixty hours a week or longer. By 1919 only 33 percent worked sixty hours or longer, although another 35 percent worked from fifty-five to sixty hours a week. The coming of the now almost universal Saturday half-holiday is the outstanding shift in industrial hours of work since 1890.

Year in and year out, about 300 working men work all night and sleep during the day. Periodically, however, a force of 3,000-4,000 men is either shifted from day work or recruited afresh by leading plants to work at night, thus establishing continuous day and night use of machinery. These periods of night work continue usually five to six months, after which the workers are discharged or shifted to day work. The repercussion upon home, leisure time, community life, and other activities of these periodic dislocations of the rhythms of living, when anywhere from several hundred to three or four thousand heads of families "go on night shift," should be borne in mind; the normal relations between husband and wife, children's customary noisy play around home, family leisure-time activities, lodge life, jury duty, civic interest, and other concerns are deranged as by the tipping over of one in a long line of dominoes. "I work nights, judge, and sleep during the day, and I haven't been able to keep in touch with George," pled a father to the judge of the juvenile court in behalf of his son. The fact that, with few exceptions, this dislocating factor affects only the working class has direct bearing upon the differential concern of the two groups for such things as the civic welfare of "Magic Middletown."

Not only does the accident of membership in one or the other of the two main groups in the city determine the number of hours worked and liability to night work, but it also determines to a considerable degree whether one is allowed to get a living uninterruptedly year after year or is subject to periodic partial or total debarments from these necessary activities. The most prosperous two-thirds of the business group, at a rough estimate, now as in 1890, are virtually never subject to interruptions of this kind so long as they do good work, while the other third is somewhat subject to cessation of work, though to a less extent than the working class. When "times were very bad" in 1924 the leading department store laid off small groups of clerks alternate weeks without pay. During 1923 the office force of a leading machine shop plant dropped at one time during the year to 79 percent of its peak number, while the wage earners declined to 32 percent of the peak.

Among the working class, however, the business device of the "shut-down" or "lay-off" is a recurrent phenomenon. If the number of working men employed in seven leading Middletown plants on June 30, 1920, be taken as 100, the number allowed to get a living was:

December 31, 1921	68
December 31, 1922	93
June 30, 1923	121
December 31, 1923	114
June 30, 1924	77
December 31, 1924	61
June 30, 1925	81

The month-by-month record of one of these plants, a leading machine shop, during 1923, again taking the number employed on June 30, 1920, as 100, was:

January	61	May	117	September	57
February	75	June	92	October	48
March	93	July	66	November	43
April	110	August	63	December	46

In one leading plant 1,000 is regarded as the "normal force." When interviewed in the summer of 1924, about 250 men were actually getting a living at this plant, though the bosses "think of about 550 [of the normal 1,000] as our men." The other 450 are floaters picked up when needed. In another large plant the number of men employed on December 31, 1923, was 802, and six months later, June 30, 1924, was 316, but only 205 of these men worked continuously throughout the entire six months with no lay-offs.

Of the sample of 165 working class families for whom data on steadiness of work was secured, 72 percent of the male heads of families lost no time at work in the twelve months of 1923 when "times were good," another 15 percent lost less than a month, and 13 percent lost a month or more; during the first nine months of 1924, throughout the last six of which "times were bad," only 38 percent of the 165 lost no time, another 19 percent lost less than a month, and 43 percent lost a month or more. Among the forty families of business men interviewed, only one of the men had been unemployed at any time during the two years, 1923–24—and that was not due to a lay-off. . . .

One emerges from the offices, stores, and factories of Middletown asking in some bewilderment why all the able-bodied men and many of the women devote their best energies for long hours day after day to this driving activity seemingly so foreign to many of the most powerful impulses of human beings. Is all this expenditure of energy necessary to secure food, clothing, shelter, and other things essential to existence? If not, precisely what over and beyond these subsistence necessaries is Middletown getting out of its work?

For very many of those who get the living for Middletown the amount of robust satisfaction they derive from the actual performance of their specific jobs seems, at best, to be slight. Among the business men the kudos accruing to the eminent in getting a living and to some of their minor associates yields a kind of incidental satisfaction; the successful manufacturer even tends today to supplant in local prestige and authority the judge, preacher, and "professor" of thirty-five to forty years ago. But for the working class both any satisfactions inherent in the actual daily doing of the job and the prestige and kudos of the able worker among his associates would appear to be declining.

The demands of the iron man for swiftness and endurance rather than training and skill have led to the gradual abandonment of the apprentice-master craftsman system; one of the chief characteristics of Middletown life in the nineties, this system is now virtually a thing of the past. The master mechanic was the aristocrat among workmen of 1890—"one of the noblest of God's creatures," as one of them put it. But even in the nineties machinery was beginning to undermine the monopolistic status of his skill; he was beginning to feel the ground shifting under his feet. The State Statistician recorded uneasy protests of men from all over the State. Today all that is left of the four-year apprentice system among 9,000 workers in the manufacturing and mechanical industries is three or four score apprentices scattered through the building and molding trades. "It's 'high speed steel' and specialization and Ford cars that's hit the machinists' union," according to a skilled Middletown worker. "You had to know how to use the old carbon steel to keep it from gettin' hot and spoilin' the edge. But this 'high speed steel' and this new 'stelite' don't absorb the heat and are harder than carbon steel. You can take a boy fresh from the farm and in three days he can manage a machine as well as I can, and I've been at it twenty-seven years."

With the passing of apprenticeship the line between skilled and un-skilled worker has become so blurred as to be in some shops almost nonexistent. The superintendent of a leading Middletown machine shop says, "Seventy-five percent of our force of 800 men can be taken from farm or high school and trained in a week's time." In the glass plant whose shift in processes is noted in Chapter VI, 84 percent of the tool-using personnel, exclusive of foremen, require one month or less of training, another 4 percent not more than six months, 6 percent a year, and the remaining 6 percent three years. Foundry workers have not lost to the iron man as heavily as machinists, but even here the trend is marked. In Middletown's leading foundry in the early nineties, 47 percent of the workers (including foremen) had three to six years' training. This trained group today is half as great (24 percent) and 60 percent of all the castings produced are made by a group of newcomers who cast with the help of machines and require only a fortnight or so of training.

"Do you think the man who runs a complicated machine takes pride in his work and gets a feeling of proprietorship in his machine?" a responsible executive in charge of personnel in a large machine shop was asked.

"No, I don't," was his ready reply. "There's a man who's ground diameters on gears here for fifteen years and done nothing else. It's a fairly highly skilled job and takes more than six months to learn. But it's so endlessly monotonous! That man is dead, just dead! And there's a lot of others like him, and I don't know what to do for them."

"What," asked the questioner, "do you think most of the men in the plant are working for?—to own a car, or a home, or just to keep their heads above water?"

"They're just working. They don't know what for. They're just in a rut and keep on in it, doing the same monotonous work every day, and wondering when a slump will come and they will be laid off."

"How much of the time are your thoughts on your job?" an alert young Middletown bench molder was asked.

"As long as there happens to be any new problem about the casting I'm making. I'm thinking about it, but as soon as ever I get the hang of the thing there isn't 25 percent of me paying attention to the job."

The shift from a system in which length of service, craftsmanship, and authority in the shop and social prestige among one's peers tended to go together to one which, in the main, demands little of a worker's personality save rapid, habitual reactions and an ability to submerge himself in the performance of a few routinized easily learned movements seems to have wiped out many of the satisfactions that formerly accompanied the job. Middletown's shops are full of men of whom it may be said that "there isn't 25 percent of them paying attention to the job." And as they leave the shop in the evening, "The work of a modern machine-tender leaves nothing tangible at the end of the day's work to which he can point with pride and say, 'I did that—it is the result of my own skill and my own effort.'" . . .

THE ORGY OF SPECULATION

The most glamorous feature of the economic revolution of the twenties took place in the stock market. Here the well-to-do and the wealthy who received the rewards of the new industrial system invested their money in hopes of achieving even greater financial gain. During the first half of the decade, the investment was sound; after a brief but intense postwar recession, the economy boomed as demand for the products of American factories kept pace with the ever-increasing industrial production. But in most industries, sales began to level off by 1927. At this point, the stock market lost touch with reality as investors continued to bid up stocks in a speculative frenzy that reached its zenith in the summer of 1929. Charles Merz, a popular writer and shrewd observer of the contemporary scene, describes the workings of the stock market as it approached its peak.

CHARLES MERZ, *Bull Market*

Under a round glass globe of the sort that used to cover the wax flowers on grandmother's parlor table, in the years before the nation discovered a broad and easy road to wealth, a small brass mechanism purrs and stutters. Click, click, click. Two little rollers pause just long enough to rub their hands in printer's ink, then beat a light tattoo on the strip of tape that runs through a slit in the side of this glass box and falls to the floor in lazy spirals. Click, click, K N $6^{1}/_{2}$, click, click, click, click, L N P $3^{1}/_{2}$, click, click, U N C $7^{3}/_{4}$. . . . The rat-tat-tat of these little blows spells out the state of mind with which the nation views the outlook for prosperity from one moment's flurry to the next; and outside the box the white tape runs through eager fingers.

It is a commonplace observation that the last few years have witnessed the development of a bull market in this country like no market the world has ever seen before. One phase of this market may be drawing near its end; one phase of this market may, in fact, have ended in a manner wholly satisfactory to the most impassioned pessimists before these words appear in print; the fact remains that the bull market of 1924 to 1929 is a phenomenon unmatched in the records of this country. It is possible to regard this market merely as another of those recurrent waves of speculative mania which sweep all nations periodically, but useless to look for its precise analogy in the McKinley boom of 1897, or the Northern Pacific wave of 1901, or the war flurry of 1915–16, or the postwar boom of 1919, for the reason that none of these markets remotely matched it in vigor or duration. As a rule, they lasted two years or three at most; they never succeeded in forcing trading on the New York Stock Exchange above three hundred and fifty million shares a year; and within reasonable limits they conformed respectfully to the scheme of behavior which the experts had charted for them in advance.

By comparison with these earlier waves of speculation, it should be noted of this last great rush that in 1929 it entered its fifth year; that time and again it confounded the experts and robbed the prophets of their honor; that after sixty months of sensational trading the average of fifty leading securities soared in February, 1929, two hundred and twenty-eight percent above their level in October, 1923; and that the volume of trading on the Stock Exchange increased so phenomenally as to smother the record of two hundred and eighty million shares in 1924, with a record of more than a billion shares between March 1, 1928, and March 1, 1929.

Tirelessly the brass rollers under the small glass domes of the stock tickers have pounded out new highs in railways, oils, and metals. Tirelessly the pools have thrown their resources behind new favorites, and the market has recovered from successive shocks. Tirelessly for many months a vast public has registered its faith that what goes up need not come down, at least not until it has provided a new set of tires for last summer's car, a closed-in sunroom for the back piazza, and at least one winter in Miami.

Thanks to the publication of a good many photographs in recent Sunday rotogravure sections, the market place that is the center of the nation's trading in securities is as familiar to the average man as the interior of Madison Square Garden with a prizefight in full swing. He knows that its walls are high and that they look down upon an ample floor left free for the battle of the bulls and bears. He knows that this floor is dotted with some thirty "posts" where stocks are bought and sold, each post ringed at its top with strips of paper fluttering like prayer-flags on a pole in a Tibetan monastery. He knows that on this floor three million shares change hands on an average day, that this is the place where prices are driven up or battered down by eager traders, and where his own small holdings must be sold when the day arrives for him to lump his loss or take his profit.

It is a scene that often figures in the daily papers and the moving pictures; and the traditional accounts which describe it as a great stone hall in which an apparently disorganized rabble mills its way excitedly from post to post through a shoe-high litter of its own discarded memoranda do it justice. Crowds that have formed as if by accident rotate for a moment around an unseen axis before they fall apart again. A dozen little disagreements coalesce suddenly into a major riot. There is the same panic of motion here as that produced by stirring up an ant-hill. Only, these ants have enormous voices. The high walls echo with the unbroken roar of five hundred bidders calling numbers full of noisy vowels. The blackboards crackle with the sharp staccato clicks of flapping numbers calling brokers to their telephones. Dead paper swirls on the floor like leaves in an October blow. And over the balustrade of the Visitors' Gallery, intent upon the pandemonium which exists beneath them, hang fascinated tourists from Riverside Drive, New England, and the Middle West, wondering whether the market is going up or going down, and picking out Mr. Morgan and Mr. Raskob more or less at random.

This is a scene of intense activity, but the impulses behind this activity are not local within these four Greek walls; they come from a thousand widely scattered towns and cities in a nation which did not really plumb the joys of a series of sudden spurts in American Can or Montgomery

Ward until 1926, and the pillars on the floor of the Exchange are simply their converging points.

Somewhere in Oregon lives a banker who owns one hundred shares of Magma Copper which he is willing to sell because the state of the market worries him. Somewhere in Massachusetts lives a doctor who has never owned a share of stock in an active life of sixty years but who is now in a mood for sudden action. For three years he has heard his neighbors boast of the killings they have made in this bull market, of General Motors bought for a song at 99 in 1925 and sold at 212 in time for Christmas, 1928—of Radio picked up casually at 88 in 1926 and sold three hundred glittering points above that mark in February, 1929—and his patience has been worn to the bone by this long vigil. Now a fresh triumph scored by his wife's brother in Imperial Oil convinces him that the time has come at last to discard the notion that it is too late in the day for a small investor to wring an honest penny from the market and present his claims for his own share in these vast mysterious profits. Of Magma Copper he knows only that it has been bought by the neighbor who snapped up Radio in 1926, that his wife's brother has a friend in St. Paul whose uncle has an inside tip, and that either copper or lead has been featured lately on the financial pages of his local paper. More than this, no doubt, would be needed for a complete grasp of the copper situation. But the iron is hot, the chance is there, and in a mood that is at last more eager than reluctant he enters a broker's office with an order for a hundred shares.

It is the initial phase of a transaction performed with the speed appropriate to such an act as the investment of new money in the industry of a dynamic nation. Within sixty seconds of the time when this late convert has appeared in the branch office of Jones & Co. in his home town with his first order, a clerk has written "Buy MMX 100" on a slip of yellow paper, a telegraph operator at his "bug" has transmitted the message to the main office of Jones & Co. in New York, an order clerk has extracted it from an incoming rush of business, and the telephone number of the floor-man of this company is flapping like a wounded crow on the giant blackboards of the Stock Exchange.

Thereafter, when he has hurried to his booth and received this message, which ought not take much more than another sixty seconds, the floor-man of Jones & Co. buffets his way to Post No. 28 and for ten seconds joins the milling crowd around this particular Mecca. "One hundred Magma at one thirty-seven and a quarter!" This is the voice of a broker commissioned, within the last two minutes, to sell one hundred shares for the banker in Oregon who has his doubts about the market. The floor-man of Jones & Co. calls out, "Take it!" The sale is made and the bargain sealed with a scribbled symbol on two bits of paper. Nobody asks for cash on one side or securities on the other. That will be adjusted later through the Clearing House. Two minutes, three thousand miles of telegraph wire, and a half-dozen shouted words are enough to link Oregon and Massachusetts once two total strangers have made their minds up to do business. From the crowd around Post No. 28 comes an attendant of the Stock Exchange on a gallop with a message for the ticker. The wires hum. And before this latest purchaser of copper stock in Massachusetts has had a chance to ask himself for the second time whether all this really was not rash and wouldn't it have been more statesmanlike to wait until tomorrow morning, the small brass drums under the round glass globes are inking themselves for another go at their strips of paper ribbon. . . . "Click, click, click, M M X, click, click, $7^1/_4$."

By how many pairs of eyes this latest bulletin from the front is read with interest there is no sure way of telling. Certainly it is safe to say, however, that during the last two years an incomparably greater audience has followed the ticker tape on its endless journey than has ever followed it before in any boom or at any time in the whole history of trading in this country since the first small company of frock-coated brokers met under a buttonwood tree near the site of the present Stock Exchange in 1790. For it is the most impressive fact about this market not that it set an endurance record or raised prices to bewildering levels, but that it succeeded in attracting to itself a great new horde of small investors who were never in this game before and have come out of it with six-passenger coupés or whitened hair. This has been a children's crusade, not an adventure for a few hard-boiled knights; and no historian of the years 1924 to 1929 can afford to ignore the evidence that the butcher and the baker and the candlestick-maker have been in this market on an unprecedented scale.

There is the direct evidence lent by the fact that the persistent orders of the small trader have created a phenomenal business for the "odd-lot houses" which handle securities in blocks of less than a hundred shares; as I write, The New York Times reports that odd-lot business is "at the highest level ever recorded" and that "the outstanding feature of this business is the heavy demand for lots of less than twenty-five shares."

There is the corroborative evidence of brokers' loans which increased from three billion dollars on February 1, 1927, to nearly seven billion dollars on February 1, 1929, to the dismay of the Federal Reserve Board.

There is the fact that brokerage firms which are members of the Stock Exchange have been forced to double the number of their branch offices since 1925 to handle the heavy rush of business, and that these branch offices have now invaded territory as remote from Wall Street as Steubenville, O., Independence, Kans., Amarillo, Tex., Gastonia, N.C., Storm Lake, Ia., Chickasha, Okla., and Shabbona, Ill.

There is the telltale evidence of stock reports being put on the radio with vespers, the official time, and chest-expansion exercises, as an indispensable item in the day's routine, and the phenomenal growth, meantime, of stock tables, market lists, and syndicated columns of successful inside tips in small-town newspapers which devoted this extra space to kitchen recipes even as late as 1926.

There is the fact, finally, that this new game of get-rich-quick has been played not only in the New York Stock Exchange, but played at the same break-neck pace in a score of local markets in every section of the country; that the Chicago Stock Exchange has multiplied by seventeen the amount of business it handled even as late as 1918; that the St. Louis Stock Exchange now deals in a million shares a year instead of eighty thousand as it did ten years ago, and that the Los Angeles Curb Exchange, which was not even in existence in the year 1927, handled no less than eighteen million shares in the year 1928.

There are still men left in the spring of 1929 who do not thumb their way straight to the stock news when they have had one fleeting glance at the first-page headlines in their evening papers, but the number of such men is smaller than in the spring of 1928; and the account-books of every brokerage firm in a broad nation show the names of school-teachers, seamstresses, barbers, machinists, necktie salesmen, gas-fitters, motormen, family cooks, and lexicographers who have taken their first dip in the market in the last two years. The ticker tape runs on. And to a greater extent than ever before in its history the whole country has been buying stocks, selling stocks, trading stocks, assessing profits, covering close margins with fresh capital, and following with increasing interest the broad line in the market-graphs that curves between the lowlands and the Himalayas. . . .

THE SUPER-CITY

The most significant transition taking place in the 1920's was the silent movement of people from the farms and small towns into the cities. The process of urbanization had begun in the nineteenth century, and though it lacked the drama and excitement of the frontier movement, it was far more influential in determining the character of twentieth-century

American life. By 1920, slightly more than half of the nation's population lived in communities of more than 2500, the Census Bureau definition of a city. During the decade, this movement accelerated, and by 1930, not only were 56.2 percent of the people residing in urban areas, but 44.6 percent lived in the ninety-six metropolitan areas which ranged in size from 100,000 up to New York's seven million. Sociologists were quick to realize the importance of this development, and when Herbert Hoover created a President's Research Committee on Social Trends in the fall of 1929, the chairman asked R. D. McKenzie, a professor of sociology at the University of Michigan, to survey the new super-cities. The selection below is taken from the conclusion of McKenzie's report.

R. D. McKENZIE, The Rise of Metropolitan Communities

It is now possible to take a bird's eye view of population movements in the United States as far as they are reflected in the growth and expansion of the metropolitan community. Fully one-half of the people of this country now live within an hour's motor journey of a city of 100,000 or more. Three-quarters of the national increase in population between 1920 and 1930 took place within the immediate orbits of these larger cities. The census classification of all incorporated places of 2,500 or more as urban is increasingly less significant than a classification based upon whether population is or is not contained within the sphere of influence of a metropolitan center. The trend toward the metropolitan community and the reaching out of such communities over an increasingly large expanse of territory are the outstanding phases of the recent "drift to the cities."

The censuses of 1910 and 1920 showed a concentration of population based largely upon the centralization of industry. In other words the population followed the factories. The census of 1930, with supplementary evidence now available, indicates that the factors involved in metropolitan growth during the past decade were primarily commercial and institutional, with industry playing a relatively smaller role. The metropolitan community, at least until the advent of the depression of 1929, offered an increasing variety of jobs as well as more steady employment. It also offered a wider variety of economic and cultural services. It took on more and more the aspects of a coherent economic and cultural state, more realistic in many ways than the existing political states.

R. D. McKenzie, "The Rise of Metropolitan Communities" in *Recent Social Trends in the United States* (2 volumes; New York, 1933), I, pp. 492-496, copyright, 1933. Reprinted by permission of the publisher, McGraw-Hill Book Company.

The super-community, or city region, is largely a product of modern means of communication, developed more extensively in local areas than throughout the nation as a whole. Assume that the boundaries of an ancient or medieval city were largely determined by the distance a man could walk in two hours. This would give a practicable radius of eight miles and a diameter of sixteen miles. The introduction of the motor car would at once multiply these limits at least six times, extending the practicable city radius to at least fifty miles. The case of the modern super-city is not quite so simple as this, since transportation by horse drawn stages, by steamboats where waterways were adjacent and by steam railways, extended the urban radius long before the coming of the automobile. But the illustration is pertinent. Measured in time rather than linear space the old boundaries of cities have shrunken and vast new areas have been brought within the city influence.

The super-community, therefore, absorbs varying numbers of separate local communities into its economic and cultural organization. Large cities everywhere are becoming conscious of themselves as centers of commercial provinces and are attempting to define and delineate their primary trade areas. The evidence at hand seems to indicate that the influence of the central city over these areas tends to diminish with distance outward. There is usually a line—not easy to determine since some influences of the central city are more potent and more far reaching than others—at which the territory of one center meets that of another. We can, in fact, draw a map tentatively alloting the entire territory of continental United States to a comparatively small number of super-cities.

These super-cities throughout the nation appear to be becoming more nearly uniform in their economic and institutional structure. The frontier type of city is gradually developing into a more mature type of metropolis. This is shown in physical structure—in the growth of skyscraper office buildings. It is shown also in the growing complexity of the industrial and occupational pattern of the larger cities throughout the nation—by the tendency toward wider distribution of talented or highly skilled persons in the more specialized occupations. This increasing diversity within the city and uniformity among the cities results in a higher degree of local autonomy. The regional city tends to become more self-sufficient. But this self-sufficiency is limited by the concentration of certain industries and of certain raw materials, and by a counter tendency toward a closer functional interrelationship of the metropolitan centers of the nation. Just as communities within a metropolitan region preserve a certain degree of independence and local identity, yet are closely bound within the economic and cultural network of the central city, so the regional communities themselves are independent in many things, yet are parts of a national urban system.

But while the role of the great city in the nation at large has been growing in importance and changing in nature, even more radical and important changes have taken place within the city itself. In the first place, every large city has experienced rapid shifts in its local population since the end of the World War. The suburban drift has not only increased in volume but has altered in character. The outward movement in recent years has been largely among the white collar classes, who have created a definite new problem by removing themselves to an increasing extent from the political city while remaining within the sphere of influence of the economic and cultural city. They have drawn after them a number of local institutions, business outlets and municipal services, creating a real *rus in urbe* in the suburban territories. Industry likewise has tended to migrate outward, not for the same reasons but because increasing congestion in the more central districts has hampered its activities and added to its production costs. The heavy industries go first and farthest; the lighter ones and those which are most dependent on proximity to their metropolitan customers do not go so soon or so far; but the tendency in nearly every case is centrifugal.

When individuals, businesses, and industries move out in this way, at the rate which has recently marked these migrations, they leave a partial vacuum. The general effect of this drift, coupled with the more intensive use of land brought about by large structural units, is to hasten the obsolescence of much of the older pattern of the city. This applies to practically every type of institution and service. Every large city is confronted on the one hand with the problem of increasing congestion in certain areas and, on the other, with that of revitalizing its blighted areas. The deteriorated districts are rarely rehabilitated by private enterprise, though in some cities, notably New York, blighted areas have been restored, at least partially, by the erection of high class apartment houses. But these areas are always in competition with newer subdivisions which offer a more inviting field for private enterprise. Usually lying close to the main business center of the city, they become the habitats of the vicious and criminal elements of the population. Without the economic incentive toward repair or replacement, buildings are allowed to deteriorate. Land values decline, assessments are lost to the city, transportation problems are aggravated by the fact that residence is further removed from business. This actual misuse and underuse of land creates a difficult situation for the city planner, the city assessor, the health department, the police department, the transportation managers and the housing and welfare agencies.

While the deteriorated areas are largely allowed to go to waste there is an intensive exploitation of certain other areas within the city and toward its periphery. There result problems of transportation and traffic which are among the gravest that confront any modern city. In some cities the growth of private transportation by motor car has tended to disorganize the mass transportation facilities originally existing and has at the same time created a new traffic problem. There are many intricate details and differences among cities in this field, which cannot be dealt with adequately in this chapter but will find their rightful place in the accompanying monograph. It may be pointed out here, however, that the loss of business by rapid transit lines to motor transportation has not been universal. Nearly everywhere the surface street car line has lost ground. In New York City, however, in normal times, the rapid transit facilities of all kinds have never been adequate to the demands put upon them.

Nearly every one of the new problems of great cities comes home sooner or later to the governmental agencies. The last decade has witnessed an unprecedented expansion of all types of municipal utilities and services. At the same time many of the governmental functions have failed to keep pace with the economic and cultural expansion of urban life. The multiplicity of separate governmental and taxation bodies in every large metropolitan aggregation constitutes one of the most serious difficulties confronting the metropolitan community today. Because city planning is by definition limited to the obsolescent political city it is now being rapidly superseded by regional planning. But regional planning on a scale commensurate with actual needs is thwarted by the large number of politically independent communities with which planning bodies have to deal.

The development of the new super-city points, therefore, to the need of some sort of super-metropolitan government. This problem and the steps already taken to cope with it were presented in the preceding section. It is quite apparent that the old procedure of annexation of surrounding territory by a central city is no longer a satisfactory solution. The spread of population under the influence of motor transport is far too rapid and too extensive to be dealt with adequately by annexation, even if annexation were not vigorously resisted by most of the outlying communities of most cities. Some plan of coordination of governmental functions must be developed before the political unity of the real functional metropolitan community can be achieved.

To sum up, the past decade has definitely witnessed the emergence of a new population and functional entity—the metropolitan community or super-city. So far as can be seen this new entity will characterize our national urban life for an indefinite time to come. The next decade may be expected to bring about further efforts to digest it into the economic, governmental, and cultural pattern of the nation.

THE OLD AMERICA

Although the city was becoming the dominant locale of American life in the 1920's, the small town was still a powerful force. Ranging in size from tiny crossroads with only a general store and a post office up to prosperous county seats, these communities were the preservers of the old America of the nineteenth century. They kept the faith, glorying in their Puritan virtues, their emphasis on the rural values of hard work and thrift, and their contempt for the city, with its alien population, sophisticated ways, and religious skepticism.

The city-dwellers, especially those who had recently escaped from what they felt was the prison of small-town conformity, delighted in ridiculing what H. L. Mencken called "the booboisie." In 1920, Sinclair Lewis published Main Street, a devastating critique of a small Minnesota town, and two years later he satirized the provincial businessman in Babbitt. All the bright young men of the twenties shared this feeling of disdain, and in 1922 Harold Stearns succeeded in having thirty of them collaborate in producing a composite portrait, as Henry May notes, "of a barren, neurotic, Babbitt-ridden society" under the title Civilization in the United States. Louis Raymond Reid, a New York journalist and free-lance writer, contributed an essay on the small town.

LOUIS RAYMOND REID, The Small Town

America is a nation of villagers, once remarked George Bernard Shaw in a moment of his most exclusive scorn for what he believed was our crude and naïve susceptibility to the modes and moods, to say nothing of the manners, of the professional patriots during that hectic period when Wilhelm was training to become the woodman of Amerongen. Now Shaw is the oracle of the Occident, and when he speaks there is no docile dog this side of Adelphi Terrace presumptuous enough to bark. At least there should not be; and in any event, neither history nor H. G. Wells records any spirited protest on America's part to the Shavian accusation.

From "The Small Town" by Louis Raymond Reid in Civilization in the United States, edited by Harold E. Stearns. Reprinted by permission of Harcourt, Brace & World, Inc.

Courtesy of the State Historical Society of Wisconsin. Photographer unknown.

Sinclair Lewis.

It was allowed to stand invulnerable and irrefutable. Of course, in our hearts, we know Shaw is right. We may for the moment be signifying *rus in urbe,* but between you and me and the chief copy-reader of the Marion (Ohio) *Star, in urbe* is a superfluous detail.

Show me a native New Yorker and I will show you something as extinct as a bartender. There are no native New Yorkers. All New Yorkers come from small towns and farms. Ask Dad, ask the Sunday editor, ask the census-taker—they know. And what is true of New York is true of Boston and Chicago. The big men, the notable men of the big cities, hail from the small towns, the Springfields, the Jacksons, the Jamestowns, George-towns, Charlestowns—yes, and from the Elizabeths and Charlottes—of the nation.

Under the circumstances any back-to-the-land movement in this country seems futile if not ridiculous. The land is still confident and capable of taking care of itself. It needs no aid from the city chaps and asks none. The Freudians are not deceived for a moment over the basis of a return-to-the-farm enterprise. They recognize it for what it is—a sentimental complex superinduced by the nervous hysteria of the city. But even the amazingly small proportion of the population that is not Freudian refuses to become influenced by the cry of the sentimentalists. Because it is keenly, though unpretentiously, aware of the genuinely rural state of its culture and civilization.

The civilization of America is predominantly the civilization of the small town. The few libertarians and cosmopolites who continue to profess to see a broader culture developing along the Atlantic seaboard resent this fact, though they scarcely deny it. They are too intelligent, too widened in vision to deny it. They cannot watch the tremendous growth and power and influence of secret societies, of chambers of commerce, of boosters' clubs, of the Ford car, of moving pictures, of talking-machines, of evangelists, of nerve tonics, of the *Saturday Evening Post,* of Browning societies, of circuses, of church socials, of parades and pageants of every kind and description, of family reunions, of pioneer picnics, of county fairs, of firemen's conventions without secretly acknowledging it. And they know, if they have obtained a true perspective of America, that there is no section of this vast political unit that does not possess—and even frequently boast—these unmistakably provincial signs and symbols. . . .

The basis, the underlying motive, of all cultural life in the small town is social. The intellectual never enters. It may try to get in but the doors are usually barred. There is practically no demand for the so-called intellectual magazines. Therefore, they are seldom placed on sale. But few daily papers outside of a radius of fifty miles are read. Plays which have exclusive appeal to the imagination or the intellect are presented to rows of empty seats. On the other hand, dramas teeming with primitive emotions and the familiar devices of hokum attract large audiences, provided the producing managers care to abide by the present excessive transportation rates. There is but little interest manifested in great world movements, such as the economic upheaval in Eastern Europe. Normalcy is, indeed, the watchword so far as intellectual development is concerned.

It is in the social atmosphere that the American village has its real *raison d'être.* Therein do we meet the characteristics that have stamped themselves indelibly upon American life. The thousand and one secret societies that flourish here have particularly fertile soil in the small towns.

Count all the loyal legionaries of all the chapters of all the secret societies between the Atlantic and Pacific oceans and you have a job suited only to the most irrepressible statistician. And the most loyal live in the small towns and villages of the United States. The choice is not limited. There are societies enough to suit all kinds of personalities and purses.

The Knights of Pythias, the Knights of the Maccabees, the Odd Fellows, the Elks, the Eagles, the Loyal Order of the Moose, the Modern Woodmen, the Masons with their elaborate subdivisions of Shriners and Knights Templar—all count their membership throughout the nation. And the women, jealous of their husbands' loyalty to various and complex forms of hocus-pocus, have organized auxiliary societies which, while not maintaining the secrecy that veils the fraternal orders, nevertheless build up a pretentious mystery intriguing to the male mind.

No town is a self-respecting town unless it can boast half a dozen of these societies. They are the fabric of which the basis of the social structure is built. They are the very essence of America. They dot the national landscape. Every city, as if to prove conclusively its provincial nature, displays one or more temples devoted to the rituals of fraternal organization.

Recently the South has revived the order of the Ku Klux Klan which flourished after the Civil War as a means of improving upon the orderly course of the law in dealing with the Negro race. Here is the apotheosis of a secret society, with its magnificent concealment of identity in a unique form of dress, its pretensions to 100 percent Americanism, its blatant proclamations of perpetuating the great and glorious traditions of the republic. The Negro has already organized to offset this propaganda. He knew that unless he could show secret orders of imposing strength he had no right even to the questionable heritage of habitation here. He would be outside the spirit of the times. He owed it to America, to "dear, crude America," to organize lodges and secret societies; and he has done so.

Undoubtedly the secret society plays a large part in the greatness of America. It has made the American class-conscious. It has made him recognize his own importance, his own right to the national distinction of good-fellowship. It provides him temporary surcease from domestic and business details, though there are countless numbers of men who join these orders to make business details, so far as they affect them, more significant.

The amazing prevalence of conventions in America is an outgrowth of the secret societies. Life to many 100 percent Americans is just one lodge convention after another. Held in a different city each year, a distinction that is industriously competed for, the convention has become a fixed fact in American cultural life. Here is the one occasion of the year when the serious diddle-daddle is laid aside, and refuge and freedom are sought in such amusements as the convention city can offer. The secret order convention has inspired the assembly of all kinds and descriptions of conventions—trade conventions, religious conventions, educational conventions—until there is no city in the land boasting a first-class hotel that does not at one time or another during the year house delegates with elaborate insignia and badges.

Probably the first parade held in America was that of a class-conscious fraternal organization eager to display its high standard of membership as well as a unique resplendence in elaborate regalia. The parade has continued an integral part of American life ever since. There is something of the vigor, the gusto and crudeness of America in a parade. It has come to represent life here in all its curious phases.

The parade had become an event of colourful significance when P. T. Barnum organized the "greatest show on earth." He decided to glorify it—in his dictionary "to glorify" really meant "to commercialize"—and once and for all associate it chiefly with the circus. He succeeded, mainly because the residents of the villages were receptive to the idea. They saw a bizarre relief from the monotony of existence. The farmers rolled down from the hills in their lumber-wagons and found an inarticulate joy, storekeepers closed shop and experienced a tumultuous freedom from the petty bickerings of trade, men and women renewed their youth, children were suddenly thrown into a very ecstasy of delight. Thus, the circus parade became part and parcel of American civilization.

And the precious and unique spirit created by the circus parade has been carried on in innumerable representations. Today America shelters parades of every conceivable enterprise. Firemen have a day in every small town of the land on which they joyously pull flower-laden hose-carts for the entertainment of their fellow-citizens. Bearing such labels as Alerts, Rescues, and Champion Hook and Ladder No. 1, they march proudly down Main Street—and the world goes hang. The volunteer firemen's organization is an institution peculiar to the American small town—an institution, too, that is not without class-consciousness. The rough-and-ready, comparatively illiterate young men form one group. The clerks, men engaged in the professions and social favourites compose another. This class is usually endowed by the wealthiest resident of the town, and its gratitude is expressed usually by naming the organization for the local Croesus.

The Elks parade, the Knights of Pythias parade, veterans of various wars parade, the Shriners and Knights Templar parade, prohibitionists parade, antiprohibitionists parade, politicians parade, women parade, babies parade —everybody parades in America. Indeed, America can be divided into two classes, those who parade and those who watch the parade. The parade is indelibly identified with the small town. It is also inalienably associated with the large city, composed, as it is, of small-town men. . . .

What offers more rustic charm and simplicity than a family reunion? Practically every family in the farming districts that claims an ancestral residence in this country of more than fifty years holds one annually. It is attended by the great and the near-great from the cities, by the unaffected relatives back home. Babies jostle great-grandparents. Large and perspiring women bake for days the cakes and pies to be consumed. The men of the house are foolishly helping in making the rooms and the front lawn ready. At last the reunion is at hand—a sentimental debauch, a grand gorging. Everybody present feels the poignancy of age. But while the heart throbs the stomach is working overtime. The law of compensation is satisfied. "A good time was had by all" finds another expression in the weekly paper, and the reunion becomes a memory.

At pioneer picnics one finds the family reunion on a larger scale. The whole township and county has for the time become related. It is the day of days, a sentimental tournament with handshaking as the most popular pastime. Organized in the rugged primitiveness of the early part of the 19th century by men who were first to settle in the vicinity, the pioneer picnic has been perpetuated, until today it is linked inalterably with America's development. It has weathered the passing of the nation from an agricultural to a great industrial commonwealth. It has stood the gaff of time. And so it goes on forever, a tradition of the small town and the farming community. While it has been divested almost entirely of its original purpose, it serves to bring the politicians in touch with the "peepul." Grandiloquent promises are made for a day from the rostrum by a battalion of "Honourables"—and forgotten both by the "Honourables" and the public intent upon dancing and walking aimlessly about the grounds. The politicians smile as they continue to preserve their heroic post, and the "peepul," satisfied that all is well with the world, turn to various gambling devices that operate under the hypocritical eye of the sheriff and to the strange dances that have crept up from the jungle, for it is a day filled with the eternal spirit of youth. There is ingenuous appeal in the fair samples of the yokelry present. There is a quiet force beneath the bovine expressions of the boys. The soul of America—an America glad to be alive—is being wonderfully and pathetically manifested. No shams, no superficialities, no self-conscious sophistication are met. Merely the sturdy quality of the true American civilization, picturesque and haunting in its primitiveness.

The county fair belongs in the same classification as the first-settler picnic. It is the annual relaxation by farmers and merchants from the tedious tasks of seeing and talking to the same people day after day. It offers them a measure of equality with the people in the city with their excursion boats, their baseball games, their park sports. And they make the most of their opportunity. They come to see and to be seen, to risk a few dollars on a horse race, to admire the free exhibitions in front of the side-shows, to watch with wide eyes the acrobatic stunts before the grand-stand, to hear the "Poet and the Peasant" overture by the band, proud and serious in a stand of its own.

Three or four days given to such pleasures naturally bestow a fine sense of illusion upon the visitors. They begin to believe that life has been specially ordered for them. They see through a glass lightly. They care not a whiff about the crowded excitements of the city. They have something infinitely more enjoyable than a professional baseball game or an excursion ride down the river. They have days of endless variety, of new adventures, of new thoughts. They, too, know that America cannot go wrong so long as they continue to find illusion. And they are correct. They may not suspect that American culture is crude. They do know, however, that it is dear. They should worry.

Against such a background have the flavour and essence of American life been compounded. Their influence has extended in all directions, in all walks of industry. They have left their impress upon the character of the country, upon the mob and the individual. Sentimental attachment to the old ties, to boyhood ideals and traditions remains potent though a little concealed by the mask, be it affected or real, of sophistication. It is the voice of a new land, of a vigorous and curious nationalism that is being exerted. There obviously cannot be among such a naturally healthy people a supercilious contempt for sentiment. We may laugh a little haughtily at the amazing susceptibility of folks to the extravagant eloquence of itinerant evangelists. We may look on an "old home week" with a touch of urban disdain. We may listen to the band concert on a Saturday night in the Court House Square with a studied indifference. We may assume an attrac-tive weariness in watching the promenaders on Main Street visit one ice-cream emporium after another. But deep down in our hearts is a feeling of invincible pride in the charming homeliness, the youthful vitality, the fine simplicity, yes, and the sweeping pathos of these aspects of small-town civilization.

2 / THE 1930'S:
CHALLENGE AND RESPONSE

INTRODUCTION

The twenties ended with the great crash. The panic in the stock market was a sign that the boom had ended, and for the next three years the economy moved steadily downward. Factories cut their work-week, then closed their doors; farmers watched the already low prices for their crops decline until some struck out blindly against the bankers who foreclosed on their mortgaged land; men out of work saw their savings melt away as they tried month after month to find jobs that would help them feed their families and regain the self-respect they lost on the breadlines. The bitterest blow was to the American psyche. The nation had not known a severe depression since the 1890's, and the prosperity of the twenties had led millions to believe that want and deprivation were things of the past. People who believed that a new era of affluence had arrived were ill-equipped to weather the harsh realities of the depression.

In the White House, Herbert Hoover struggled valiantly with the economic disaster. He did not, as Democrats later charged, start the depression, nor did he sit idly by while people starved. Though hampered by a rigid ideology, he did commit the federal government to action, creating the Reconstruction Finance Corporation to save failing businesses, loaning money to the states and cities for relief, and instituting large-scale public works to create jobs for the unemployed. Hoover's tragedy was his inability to go beyond these limited measures and embrace a full-scale program of relief and recovery. An inept political leader, he was never able to make the American people believe in him, and so despite his good intentions and good deeds, he became the scapegoat for the economic catastrophe.

Franklin D. Roosevelt took over at the lowest ebb, at a time when the economy had slowed to a virtual standstill and the banks were collapsing under the strain. Still relatively unknown to the American people, his credentials were not impressive. He had served as Assistant Secretary of the Navy under Wilson, and then had run unsuccessfully for the vice-presidency in 1920 only to be buried under the Harding landslide. His crippling attack of polio in 1921 changed his life. Displaying great courage, he fought his way back from a life of invalidism, and though he would never walk unaided again, he set his eyes on the presidency. In 1928, Al Smith talked him into running for the governorship of New York to bolster the Democratic ticket, and though Smith failed to carry the state, Roosevelt won a stunning victory. He was a good though not outstanding governor, reacting belatedly but with vigor to the problems of the depression. His greatest virtues were political. He combined a flair for the dramatic with a shrewd knowledge of men and measures. Most of all, he had the rare ability to project his own unshakeable confidence in himself and to transmit an infectious faith that the nation could weather and endure the trials of the depression.

Once President, Roosevelt launched the New Deal, which lasted for five hectic years. In treating this momentous upheaval, historians often speak of two New Deals, one of relief and recovery in 1933 and one of reform beginning in 1935. Such a division is artificial and misleading. In his summary of Roosevelt's achievements, William Leuchtenburg uses the much sounder description, reconstruction, which suggests the fundamental unity of all Roosevelt did. Relief, recovery, and reform were all bound up together in a heroic effort to restore a fallen America and ensure that it would not collapse again.

The programs were varied, ranging from the business-oriented National Recovery Administration to the social engineering of the Tennessee Valley Authority. A bewildering array of committees, bureaus, and agencies appeared and disappeared, some achieving genuine progress, others failing completely. Some New Deal measures were purely temporary, like the WPA (Works Progress Administration), designed simply to provide work relief for the unemployed, while others, such as the Social Security Act, marked a reform of enduring significance.

By 1936, the New Deal was substantially complete. Nearly every reform of real importance had been proposed before Congress adjourned in the fall of 1935, and the remaining years were to be spent in perfecting and consolidating the earlier efforts. Roosevelt's triumphal reelection in 1936 was the popular response of gratitude for these achievements, not a mandate for a further wave of reform. For the President, the most serious problem was the Supreme Court, which had begun striking down early New Deal measures in 1935. After the election Roosevelt challenged the Court, and though he finally forced the judges to accept the New Deal, he aroused such fierce opposition in Congress and the nation at large that he spent the remainder of his second term using his energies to defend his previous accomplishments and thus failed to open up new avenues of social and economic reform.

The debate over the effectiveness of the New Deal, heated in the 1930's, still rages on. In many ways, Roosevelt and his aides were most successful in areas where they were most bitterly criticized by contemporaries and did least well in fulfilling their avowed objectives. The business community, after a brief honeymoon in 1933, turned on Roosevelt savagely, accusing him of betraying his own class, of assuming dictatorial powers, of leading the nation to the threshold of socialism. Ironically, it was the business community that benefited most from the New Deal. Roosevelt's greatest achievement was saving capitalism and the free enterprise system from its own excesses. He used the power of the federal government to repair a damaged economy and make it healthy again, adding safeguards against a future breakdown. Far from being a revolutionary, Roosevelt acted in a profoundly conservative cause.

But in other ways, Roosevelt failed. As Professor Leuchtenburg points out, he never achieved the promised return to prosperity in peacetime—the economy only reached full recovery after the outbreak of World War II. Moreover, he did least for those who needed most, the "forgotten man" that he promised to aid at the outset. The New Deal marked the development of "interest-group" politics. Those who were organized made their needs known in Washington and thus gained governmental favor. Labor unions, farm organizations, business groups—these were the prime beneficiaries of the New Deal. Those who lacked organization had no way to influence governmental action. And so the sharecroppers, the Negroes, and the unskilled laborers remained the forgotten men and women in American society, helped indirectly by many New Deal programs, but never singled out for special assistance. Thus, as Professor Leuchtenburg concludes, the Roosevelt reconstruction was only a halfway revolution. And yet even this was a major gain for the American people. Roosevelt and his aides had begun to tackle the fundamental problems of the new America that first became apparent in the twenties, and if they did not resolve them, at least they made a beginning.

INTERPRETATION

Professor William E. Leuchtenburg, a political historian at Columbia University, provides an astute and remarkably balanced appraisal of the New Deal of Franklin D. Roosevelt. This is the final chapter of Professor Leuchtenburg's book on this subject.

WILLIAM E. LEUCHTENBURG,
The Roosevelt Reconstruction: Retrospect

In eight years, Roosevelt and the New Dealers had almost revolutionized the agenda of American politics. "Mr. Roosevelt may have given the wrong answers to many of his problems," concluded the editors of *The Economist*. "But he is at least the first President of modern America who has asked the right questions." In 1932, men of acumen were absorbed to an astonishing degree with such questions as prohibition, war debts, and law enforcement. By 1936, they were debating social security, the Wagner Act, valley authorities, and public housing. The thirties witnessed a rebirth of issues politics, and parties split more sharply on ideological lines than they had in many years past. "I incline to think that for years up to the present juncture thinking Democrats and thinking Republicans had been divided by an imaginary line," reflected a Massachusetts congressman in 1934. "Now for the first time since the period before the Civil War we find vital principles at stake." Much of this change resulted simply from the depression trauma, but much too came from the force of Roosevelt's personality and his use of his office as both pulpit and lectern. "Of course you have fallen into some errors—that is human," former Supreme Court Justice John Clarke wrote the President, "but you have put a new face upon the social and political life of our country."

Franklin Roosevelt recreated the modern Presidency. He took an office which had lost much of its prestige and power in the previous twelve years and gave it an importance which went well beyond what even Theodore Roosevelt and Woodrow Wilson had done. Clinton Rossiter has observed: "Only Washington, who made the office, and Jackson, who remade it, did more than Roosevelt to raise it to its present condition of strength, dignity, and independence." Under Roosevelt, the White House became the focus of all government—the fountainhead of ideas, the initiator of action, the representative of the national interest.

Roosevelt greatly expanded the President's legislative functions. In the nineteenth century, Congress had been jealous of its prerogatives as the lawmaking body, and resented any encroachment on its domain by the Chief Executive. Woodrow Wilson and Theodore Roosevelt had broken new ground in sending actual drafts of bills to Congress and in using devices like the caucus to win enactment of measures they favored. Franklin Roosevelt made such constant use of these tools that he came to assume a legislative role not unlike that of a prime minister. He sent special messages to Congress, accompanied them with drafts of legislation prepared by his assistants, wrote letters to committee chairmen or members of Congress to urge passage of the proposals, and authorized men like Corcoran to lobby as presidential spokesmen on the Hill. By the end of Roosevelt's tenure in the White House, Congress looked automatically to the Executive for guidance; it expected the administration to have a "program" to present for consideration.

Roosevelt's most important formal contribution was his creation of the Executive Office of the President on September 8, 1939. Executive Order 8248, a "nearly unnoticed but none the less epoch-making event in the history of American institutions," set up an Executive Office staffed with six administrative assistants with a "passion for anonymity." In 1939, the President not only placed obvious agencies like the White House Office in the Executive Office but made the crucial decision to shift the Bureau of the Budget from the Treasury and put it under his wing. In later years, such pivotal agencies as the Council of Economic Advisers, the National Security Council, and the Central Intelligence Agency would be moved into the Executive Office of the President. Roosevelt's decision, Rossiter has concluded, "converts the Presidency into an instrument of twentieth-century government; it gives the incumbent a sporting chance to stand the strain and fulfill his constitutional mandate as a one-man branch of our three-part government; it deflates even the most forceful arguments, which are still raised occasionally, for a plural executive; it assures us that the Presidency will survive the advent of the positive state. Executive Order 8248 may yet be judged to have saved the Presidency from paralysis and the Constitution from radical amendment."

Roosevelt's friends have been too quick to concede that he was a poor administrator. To be sure, he found it difficult to discharge incompetent aides, he procrastinated about decisions, and he ignored all the canons of sound administration by giving men overlapping assignments and creating a myriad of agencies which had no clear relation to the regular departments of government. But if the test of good administration is not an impeccable organizational chart but creativity, then Roosevelt must be set down not merely as a good administrator but as a resourceful innovator. The new agencies he set up gave a spirit of excitement to Washington that the routinized old-line departments could never have achieved. The President's refusal to proceed through channels, however vexing at times to his subordinates, resulted in a competition not only among men but among ideas, and encouraged men to feel that their own beliefs might win the day. "You would be surprised, Colonel, the remarkable ideas that have been turned loose just because men have felt that they can get a hearing," one senator confided.* The President's "procrastination" was his own way both of arriving at a sense of national consensus and of reaching a decision by observing a trial by combat among rival theories. Periods of indecision —as in the spring of 1935 or the beginning of 1938—were inevitably followed by a fresh outburst of new proposals.

Most of all, Roosevelt was a successful administrator because he attracted to Washington thousands of devoted and highly skilled men. Men who had been fighting for years for lost causes were given a chance: John Collier, whom the President courageously named Indian Commissioner; Arthur Powell Davis, who had been ousted as chief engineer of the Department of the Interior at the demand of power interests; old conservationists like Harry Slattery, who had fought the naval oil interests in the Harding era. When Harold Ickes took office as Secretary of the Interior, he looked up Louis Glavis—he did not even know whether the "martyr" of the Ballinger-Pinchot affair was still alive—and appointed him to his staff.

The New Dealers displayed striking ingenuity in meeting problems of governing. They coaxed salmon to climb ladders at Bonneville; they sponsored a Young Choreographers Laboratory in the WPA's Dance Theatre; they gave the pioneer documentary film maker Pare Lorentz the opportunity to create his classic films *The Plow That Broke the Plains* and *The River*. At the Composers Forum-Laboratory of the Federal Music Project, William Schuman received his first serious hearing. In Arizona, Father Berard Haile of St. Michael's Mission taught written Navajo to the Indians. Roosevelt, in the face of derision from professional foresters and prairie states' governors, persisted in a bold scheme to plant a mammoth "shelterbelt" of parallel rows of trees from the Dakotas to the Panhandle. In all, more than two hundred million trees were planted—cottonwood and willow, hackberry and cedar, Russian olive and Osage orange; within six years, the President's visionary windbreak had won over his former critics. The spirit behind such innovations generated a new excitement about the

---

*Elbert Thomas to Colonel E. LeRoy Bourne, Jan. 6, 1934, Elbert Thomas MSS., Box 23.

potentialities of government. "Once again," Roosevelt told a group of young Democrats in April, 1936, "the very air of America is exhilarating."

Roosevelt dominated the front pages of the newspapers as no other President before or since has done. "Frank Roosevelt and the NRA have taken the place of love nests," commented Joe Patterson, publisher of the tabloid New York *Daily News.* At his very first press conference, Roosevelt abolished the written question and told reporters they could interrogate him without warning. Skeptics predicted the free and easy exchange would soon be abandoned, but twice a week, year in and year out, he threw open the White House doors to as many as two hundred reporters, most of them representing hostile publishers, who would crowd right up to the President's desk to fire their questions. The President joshed them, traded wisecracks with them, called them by their first names; he charmed them by his good-humored ease and impressed them with his knowledge of detail. To a degree, Roosevelt's press conference introduced, as some observers claimed, a new institution like Britain's parliamentary questioning; more to the point, it was a device the President manipulated, disarmingly and adroitly, to win support for his program. It served too as a classroom to instruct the country in the new economics and the new politics.

Roosevelt was the first president to master the technique of reaching people directly over the radio. In his fireside chats, he talked like a father discussing public affairs with his family in the living room. As he spoke, he seemed unconscious of the fact that he was addressing millions. "His head would nod and his hands would move in simple, natural, comfortable gestures," Frances Perkins recalled. "His face would smile and light up as though he were actually sitting on the front porch or in the parlor with them." Eleanor Roosevelt later observed that after the President's death people would stop her on the street to say "they missed the way the President used to talk to them. They'd say 'He used to talk to me about my government.' There was a real dialogue between Franklin and the people," she reflected. "That dialogue seems to have disappeared from the government since he died."

For the first time for many Americans, the federal government became an institution that was directly experienced. More than state and local governments, it came to be the government, an agency directly concerned with their welfare. It was the source of their relief payments; it taxed them directly for old age pensions; it even gave their children hot lunches in school. As the role of the state changed from that of neutral arbiter to a "powerful promoter of society's welfare," people felt an interest in affairs in Washington they had never had before.

Franklin Roosevelt personified the state as protector. It became commonplace to say that people felt toward the President the kind of trust they would normally express for a warm and understanding father who comforted them in their grief or safeguarded them from harm. An insurance man reported: "My mother looks upon the President as someone so immediately concerned with her problems and difficulties that she would not be greatly surprised were he to come to her house some evening and stay to dinner." From his first hours in office, Roosevelt gave people the feeling that they could confide in him directly. As late as the Presidency of Herbert Hoover, one man, Ira Smith, had sufficed to take care of all the mail the White House received. Under Roosevelt, Smith had to acquire a staff of fifty people to handle the thousands of letters written to the President each week. Roosevelt gave people a sense of membership in the national community. Justice Douglas has written: "He was in a very special sense the people's President, because he made them feel that with him in the White House they shared the Presidency. The sense of sharing the Presidency gave even the most humble citizen a lively sense of belonging."

When Roosevelt took office, the country, to a very large degree, responded to the will of a single element: the white, Anglo-Saxon, Protestant property-holding class. Under the New Deal, new groups took their place in the sun. It was not merely that they received benefits they had not had before but that they were "recognized" as having a place in the commonwealth. At the beginning of the Roosevelt era, charity organizations ignored labor when seeking "community" representation; at the end of the period, no fund-raising committee was complete without a union representative. While Theodore Roosevelt had founded a lily-white Progressive party in the South and Woodrow Wilson had introduced segregation into the federal government, Franklin Roosevelt had quietly brought the Negro into the New Deal coalition. When the distinguished Negro contralto Marion Anderson was denied a concert hall in Washington, Secretary Ickes arranged for her to perform from the steps of Lincoln Memorial. Equal representation for religious groups became so well accepted that, as one priest wryly complained, one never saw a picture of a priest in a newspaper unless he was flanked on either side by a minister and a rabbi.

The devotion Roosevelt aroused owed much to the fact that the New Deal assumed the responsibility for guaranteeing every American a minimum standard of subsistence. Its relief programs represented an advance over the barbaric predepression practices that constituted a difference not in degree but in kind. One analyst wrote: "During the ten years between 1929 and 1939 more progress was made in public welfare and relief than in the three hundred years after this country was first settled." The Roosevelt administration gave such assistance not as a matter of charity but of right. This system of social rights was written into the Social Security Act. Other New Deal legislation abolished child labor in interstate commerce and, by putting a floor under wages and a ceiling on hours, all but wiped out the sweatshop.

Roosevelt and his aides fashioned a government which consciously sought to make the industrial system more humane and to protect workers and their families from exploitation. In his acceptance speech in June, 1936, the President stated: "Governments can err, Presidents do make mistakes, but the immortal Dante tells us that divine justice weighs the sins of the cold-blooded and the sins of the warm-hearted in different scales.

"Better the occasional faults of a Government that lives in a spirit of charity than the constant omission of a Government frozen in the ice of its own indifference." Nearly everyone in the Roosevelt government was caught up to some degree by a sense of participation in something larger than themselves. A few days after he took office, one of the more conservative New Deal administrators wrote in his diary: "This should be a Gov't of humanity."

The federal government expanded enormously in the Roosevelt years. The crisis of the depression dissipated the distrust of the state inherited from the eighteenth century and reinforced in diverse ways by the Jeffersonians and the Spencerians. Roosevelt himself believed that liberty in America was imperiled more by the agglomerations of private business than by the state. The New Dealers were convinced that the depression was the result not simply of an economic breakdown but of a political collapse; hence, they sought new political instrumentalities. The reformers of the 1930's accepted almost unquestioningly the use of coercion by the state to achieve reforms. Even Republicans who protested that Roosevelt's policies were snuffing out liberty voted overwhelmingly in favor of coercive measures.

This elephantine growth of the federal government owed much to the fact that local and state governments had been tried in the crisis and found wanting. When one magazine wired state governors to ask their views, only one of the thirty-seven who replied announced that he was willing to have the states resume responsibility for relief. Every time there was a rumored cutback of federal spending for relief, Washington was besieged by delegations of mayors protesting that city governments did not have the resources to meet the needs of the unemployed.

Even more dramatic was the impotence of local governments in dealing with crime, a subject that captured the national imagination in a decade of kidnapings and bank holdups. In September, 1933, the notorious bank robber John Dillinger was arrested in Ohio. Three days later, his confederates released him from jail and killed the Lima, Ohio, sheriff. In January, 1934, after bank holdups at Racine, Wisconsin, and East Chicago, Indiana, Dillinger was apprehended in Tucson, Arizona, and returned to the "escape-proof" jail of Crown Point, Indiana, reputedly the strongest county prison in the country. Within two days he had bluffed his way out with a wooden gun he had whittled and had driven off in the sheriff's car. While five thousand law officers pursued him, he stopped for a haircut in a barber shop, bought cars, and had a home-cooked Sunday dinner with his family in his home town. When he needed more arms, he raided the police station at Warsaw, Indiana.

Dillinger's exploits touched off a national outcry for federal action. State and local authorities could not cope with gangs which crossed and re-crossed jurisdictional lines, which were equipped with Thompson sub-machine guns and high-powered cars, and which had a regional network of informers and fences in the Mississippi Valley. Detection and punishment of crime had always been a local function; now there seemed no choice but to call in the federal operatives. In July, 1934, federal agents shot down Dillinger outside a Chicago theater. In October, FBI men killed Pretty Boy Floyd near East Liverpool, Ohio; in November, they shot Baby Face Nelson, Public Enemy No. 1, near Niles Center, Illinois. By the end of 1934, the nation had a new kind of hero: the G-man Melvin Purvis and the chief of the Division of Investigation of the Department of Justice, J. Edgar Hoover. By the end of that year, too, Congress had stipulated that a long list of crimes would henceforth be regarded as federal offenses, including not only kidnaping but holding up a bank insured by the Federal Deposit Insurance Corporation. The family of a kidnaped victim could call in the federal police simply by phoning National 7117 in Washington.

Under the New Deal, the federal government greatly extended its power over the economy. By the end of the Roosevelt years, few questioned the right of the government to pay the farmer millions in subsidies not to grow crops, to enter plants to conduct union elections, to regulate business enterprises from utility companies to air lines, or even to compete directly with business by generating and distributing hydroelectric power. All of these powers had been ratified by the Supreme Court, which had even held that a man growing grain solely for his own use was affecting interstate commerce and hence subject to federal penalties. The President, too, was well on his way to becoming "the chief economic engineer," although this was not finally established until the Full Employment Act of 1946. In 1931, Hoover had hooted that some people thought "that by some legerdemain we can legislate ourselves out of a world-wide depression." In the Roosevelt era, the conviction that government both should and could act to forestall future breakdowns gained general acceptance. The New Deal left a large legacy of antidepression controls—securities regulation, banking reforms, unemployment compensation—even if it could not guarantee that a subsequent administration would use them.

In the 1930's, the financial center of the nation shifted from Wall Street to Washington. In May, 1934, a writer reported: "Financial news no longer originates in Wall Street." That same month, *Fortune* commented on a revolution in the credit system which was "one of the major historical events of the generation." "Mr. Roosevelt," it noted, "seized the Federal Reserve without firing a shot." The federal government had not only broken down the old separation of bank and state in the Reserve system but had gone into the credit business itself in a wholesale fashion under the aegis of the RFC, the Farm Credit Administration, and the housing agencies. Legislation in 1933 and 1934 had established federal regulation of Wall Street for the first time. No longer could the New York Stock Exchange operate as a private club free of national supervision. In 1935, Congress leveled the mammoth holding-company pyramids and centralized yet more authority over the banking system in the federal government. After a tour of the United States in 1935, Sir Josiah Stamp wrote: "Just as in 1929 the whole country was 'Wall Street-conscious' now it is 'Washington-conscious.' "

Despite this encroachment of government on traditional business prerogatives, the New Deal could advance impressive claims to being regarded as a "savior of capitalism." Roosevelt's sense of the land, of family, and of the community marked him as a man with deeply ingrained conservative traits. In the New Deal years, the government sought deliberately, in Roosevelt's words, "to energize private enterprise." The RFC financed business, housing agencies underwrote home financing, and public works spending aimed to revive the construction industry. Moreover, some of the New Deal reforms were Janus-faced. The NYA, in aiding jobless youth, also served as a safety valve to keep young people out of the labor market. A New Deal congressman, in pushing for public power projects, argued that the country should take advantage of the sea of "cheap labor" on the relief rolls. Even the Wagner Act and the movement for industrial unionism were motivated in part by the desire to contain "unbalanced and radical" labor groups. Yet such considerations should not obscure the more important point: that the New Deal, however conservative it was in some respects and however much it owed to the past, marked a radically new departure. As Carl Degler writes: "The conclusion seems inescapable that, traditional as the words may have been in which the New Deal expressed itself, in actuality it was a revolutionary response to a revolutionary situation."

Not all of the changes that were wrought were the result of Roosevelt's own actions or of those of his government. Much of the force for change came from progressives in Congress, or from nongovernmental groups like the C.I.O., or simply from the impersonal agency of the depression itself. Yet, however, much significance one assigns the "objective situation," it is difficult to gainsay the importance of Roosevelt. If, in Miami in February, 1933, an assassin's bullet had been true to its mark and John Garner rather than Roosevelt had entered the White House the next month, or if the Roosevelt lines had cracked at the Democratic convention in 1932 and Newton Baker had been the compromise choice, the history of America in the thirties would have been markedly different.

At a time when democracy was under attack elsewhere in the world, the achievements of the New Deal were especially significant. At the end of 1933, in an open letter to President Roosevelt, John Maynard Keynes had written: "You have made yourself the trustee for those in every country who seek to mend the evils of our condition by reasoned experiment within the framework of the existing social system. If you fail, rational change will be gravely prejudiced throughout the world, leaving orthodoxy and revolution to fight it out." In the next few years, teams of foreigners toured the TVA, Russians and Arabs came to study the shelterbelt, French writers taxed Léon Blum with importing "Rooseveltism" to France, and analysts characterized Paul Van Zeeland's program in Belgium as a "New Deal." Under Roosevelt, observed a Montevideo newspaper, the United States had become "as it was in the eighteenth century, the victorious emblem around which may rally the multitudes thirsting for social justice and human fraternity."

In their approach to reform, the New Dealers reflected the tough-minded, hard-boiled attitude that permeated much of America in the thirties. In 1931, the gangster film *Public Enemy* had given the country a new kind of hero in James Cagney: the aggressive, unsentimental tough guy who deliberately assaulted the romantic tradition. It was a type whose role in society could easily be manipulated; gangster hero Cagney of the early thirties was transformed into G-man hero Cagney of the later thirties. Even more representative was Humphrey Bogart, creator of the "private eye" hero, the man of action who masks his feelings in a calculated emotional neutrality. Bogart, who began as the cold desperado Duke Mantee of *Petrified Forest* and the frightening Black Legionnaire, soon turned up on the right side of anti-Fascist causes, although he never surrendered the pose of noninvolvement. This fear of open emotional commitment and this admiration of toughness ran through the vogue of the "Dead End Kids," films like *Nothing Sacred,* the popularity of the St. Louis Cardinals' spike-flying Gas House Gang, and the "hard-boiled" fiction of writers like James Cain and Dashiell Hammett.

Unlike the earlier Progressive, the New Dealer shied away from being thought of as sentimental. Instead of justifying relief as a humanitarian measure, the New Dealers often insisted it was necessary to stimulate purchasing power or to stabilize the economy or to "conserve manpower." The justification for a better distribution of income was neither "social justice" nor a "healthier national life," wrote Adolf Berle. "It remained for the hard-boiled student to work out the simple equation that unless the national income was pretty widely diffused there were not enough customers to keep the plants going." The reformers of the thirties abandoned—or claimed they had abandoned—the old Emersonian hope of reforming man and sought only to change institutions. This meant that they did not seek to "uplift" the people they were helping but only to improve their economic position. "In other words," Tugwell stated bluntly, "the New Deal is attempting to do nothing to *people,* and does not seek at all to alter their way of life, their wants and desires."

Reform in the 1930's meant *economic* reform; it departed from the Methodist-parsonage morality of many of the earlier Progressives, in part because much of the New Deal support, and many of its leaders, derived from urban immigrant groups hostile to the old Sabbatarianism. While the progressive grieved over the fate of the prostitute, the New Dealer would have placed Mrs. Warren's profession under a code authority. If the archetypical progressive was Jane Addams singing "Onward, Christian Soldiers," the representative New Dealer was Harry Hopkins betting on the horses at Laurel Race Track. When directing FERA in late 1933, Hopkins announced: "I would like to provide orchestras for beer gardens to encourage people to sit around drinking their beer and enjoying themselves. It would be a great unemployment relief measure." "I feel no call to remedy evils," Raymond Moley declared. "I have not the slightest urge to be a reformer. Social workers make me very weary. They have no sense of humor."

Despite Moley's disclaimer, many of the early New Dealers like himself and Adolf Berle did, in fact, hope to achieve reform through regeneration: the regeneration of the businessman. By the end of 1935, the New Dealers were pursuing a quite different course. Instead of attempting to evangelize the Right, they mobilized massive political power against the power of the corporation. They relied not on converting industrial sinners but in using sufficient coercion. New Dealers like Thurman Arnold sought to ignore "moral" considerations altogether; Arnold wished not to punish wrongdoers but to achieve price flexibility. His "faith" lay in the expectation that "fanatical alignments between opposing political principles may disappear and a competent, practical, opportunistic governing class may rise to power." With such expectations, the New Dealers frequently had little patience with legal restraints that impeded action. "I want to assure you," Hopkins told the NYA Advisory Committee, "that we are not afraid of exploring anything within the law, and we have a lawyer who will declare anything you want to do legal."

In the thirties, nineteenth-century individualism gave ground to a new emphasis on social security and collective action. In the twenties, America hailed Lindbergh as the Lone Eagle; in the thirties, when word arrived that Amelia Earhart was lost at sea, the *New Republic* asked the government to prohibit citizens from engaging in such "useless" exploits. The NRA sought to drive newsboys off the streets and took a Blue Eagle away from a company in Huck Finn's old town of Hannibal, Missouri, because a fifteen-year-old was found driving a truck for his father's business. Josef Hofmann urged that fewer musicians become soloists, Hollywood stars like Joan Crawford joined the Screen Actors Guild, and Leopold Stokowski canceled a performance in Pittsburgh because theater proprietors were violating a union contract. In New York in 1933, after a series of meetings in Heywood Broun's penthouse apartment, newspapermen organized the American Newspaper Guild in rebellion against the disspiriting romanticism of Richard Harding Davis. "We no longer care to develop the individual as a unique contributor to a democratic form," wrote the mordant Edgar Kemler. "In this movement each individual sub-man is important, not for his uniqueness, but for his ability to lose himself in the mass, through his fidelity to the trade union, or cooperative organization, or political party."

The liberals of the thirties admired intellectual activity which had a direct relation to concrete reality. Stuart Chase wrote of one government report: "This book is live stuff—wheelbarrow, cement mixer, steam dredge, generator, combine, power-line stuff; library dust does not gather here." If the poet did not wish to risk the suspicion that his loyalties were not to the historic necessities of his generation, wrote Archibald MacLeish, he must "soak himself not in books" but in the physical reality of "by what organization of men and railroads and trucks and belts and bookentries the materials of a single automobile are assembled." The New Dealers were fascinated by "the total man days per year for timber stand improvement," and Tugwell rejoiced in the "practical success" of the Resettlement Administration demonstrated by "these healthy collection figures." Under the Special Skills Division of the RA, Greenbelt was presented with inspirational paintings like *Construction Sewers, Concrete Mixer,* and *Shovel at Work.* On one occasion, in attempting to mediate a literary controversy, the critic Edmund Wilson wrote: "It should be possible to convince Marxist critics of the importance of a work like 'Ulysses' by telling them that it is a great piece of engineering—as it is." In this activist world of the New Dealers, the aesthete and the man who pursued a life of contemplation, especially the man whose interests centered in the past, were viewed with scorn. In Robert Sherwood's *The Petrified Forest,* Alan Squier, the ineffectual aesthete, meets his death in the desert and is buried in the petrified forest where the living turn to stone. He is an archaic type for whom the world has no place.

The new activism explicitly recognized its debt to Dewey's dictum of "learning and doing" and, like other of Dewey's ideas, was subject to exaggeration and perversion. The New Deal, which gave unprecedented authority to intellectuals in government, was, in certain important respects, anti-intellectual. Without the activist faith, perhaps not nearly so much would have been achieved. It was Lilienthal's conviction that "there is almost nothing, however fantastic, that (given competent organization) a team of engineers, scientists, and administrators cannot do today" that helped make possible the success of TVA. Yet the liberal activists grasped only a part of the truth; they retreated from conceptions like "tragedy," "sin," "God," often had small patience wth the force of tradition, and showed little understanding of what moved men to seek meanings outside of political experience. As sensitive a critic as the poet Horace Gregory could write, in a review of the works of D. H. Lawrence: "The world is moving away from Lawrence's need for personal salvation; his 'dark religion' is not a substitute for economic planning." This was not the mood of all men in the thirties—not of a William Faulkner, an Ellen Glasgow— and many of the New Dealers recognized that life was more complex than some of their statements would suggest. Yet the liberals, in their desire to free themselves from the tyranny of precedent and in their ardor for social achievement, sometimes walked the precipice of superficiality and philistinism.

The concentration of the New Dealers on public concerns made a deep mark on the sensibility of the 1930's. Private experience seemed self-indulgent compared to the demands of public life. "Indeed the public world with us has *become* the private world, and the private world has become the public," wrote Archibald MacLeish. "We live, that is to say, in a revolutionary time in which the public life has washed in over the dikes of private existence as sea water breaks over into the fresh pools in the spring tides till everything is salt." In the thirties, the Edna St. Vincent Millay whose candle had burned at both ends wrote the polemic *Conversation at Midnight* and the bitter "Epitaph for the Race of Men" in *Wine From These Grapes*.

The emphasis on the public world implied a specific rejection of the values of the 1920's. Roosevelt dismissed the twenties as "a decade of debauch," Tugwell scored those years as "a decade of empty progress, devoid of contribution to a genuinely better future," Morris Cooke deplored the "gilded-chariot days" of 1929, and Alben Barkley saw the twenties as a "carnival" marred by "the putrid pestilence of financial debauchery." The depression was experienced as the punishment of a wrathful God visited on a nation that had strayed from the paths of righteousness. The fire that followed the Park Avenue party in Thomas Wolfe's *You Can't Go Home Again*, like the suicide of Eveline at the end of John Dos Passos' *The Big Money*, symbolized the holocaust that brought to an end a decade of hedonism. In an era of reconstruction, the attitudes of the twenties seemed alien, frivolous, or—the most cutting word the thirties could visit upon a man or institution—"escapist." When Morrie Ryskind and George Kaufman, authors of the popular *Of Thee I Sing,* lampooned the government again in *Let 'em Eat Cake* in the fall of 1933, the country was not amused. The New York *Post* applauded the decision of George Jean Nathan and his associates to discontinue the *American Spectator:* "Nihilism, dadaism, smartsetism—they are all gone, and this, too, is progress." One of H. L. Mencken's biographers has noted: "Many were at pains to write him at his new home, telling him he was a sophomore, and those writing in magazines attacked him with a fury that was suspect because of its very violence."*

Commentators on the New Deal have frequently characterized it by that much-abused term "pragmatic." If one means by this that the New Dealers carefully tested the consequences of ideas, the term is clearly a misnomer. If one means that Roosevelt was exceptionally anti-ideological in his approach to politics, one may question whether he was, in fact, any more "pragmatic" in this sense than Van Buren or Polk or even "reform" Presidents like Jackson and Theodore Roosevelt. The "pragmatism" of the New Deal seemed remarkable only in a decade tortured by ideology, only in contrast to the rigidity of Hoover and of the Left.

The New Deal was pragmatic mainly in its skepticism about utopias and final solutions, its openness to experimentation, and its suspicion of the dogmas of the Establishment. Since the advice of economists had so often been wrong, the New Dealers distrusted the claims of orthodox theory— "All this is perfectly terrible because it is all pure theory, when you come down to it," the President said on one occasion—and they felt free to try new approaches. Roosevelt refused to be awed by the warnings of economists and financial experts that government interference with the "laws" of the economy was blasphemous. "We must lay hold of the fact that economic laws are not made by nature," the President stated. "They are made by human beings." The New Dealers denied that depressions were inevitable events that had to be borne stoically, most of the stoicism to be displayed by the most impoverished, and they were willing to explore novel ways to make the social order more stable and more humane. "I am for experimenting . . . in various parts of the country, trying out schemes which are supported by reasonable people and see if they work," Hopkins told a conference of social workers. "If they do not work, the world will not come to an end."

Hardheaded, "anti-utopian," the New Dealers nonetheless had their Heavenly City: the greenbelt town, clean, green, and white, with children

* William Manchester, *Disturber of the Peace* (New York, 1951), p. 258.

playing in light, airy, spacious schools; the government project at Long view, Washington, with small houses, each of different design, colored roofs, and gardens of flowers and vegetables; the Mormon villages of Utah that M. L. Wilson kept in his mind's eye—immaculate farmsteads on broad, rectangular streets; most of all, the Tennessee Valley, with its model town of Norris, the tall transmission towers, the white dams, the glistening wire strands, the valley where "a vision of villages and clean small factories has been growing into the minds of thoughtful men."* Scandinavia was their model abroad, not only because it summoned up images of the countryside of Denmark, the beauties of Stockholm, not only for its experience with labor relations and social insurance and currency reform, but because it represented the "middle way" of happy accommodation of public and private institutions the New Deal sought to achieve. "Why," inquired Brandeis, "should anyone want to go to Russia when one can go to Denmark?"

Yet the New Deal added up to more than all of this—more than an experimental approach, more than the sum of its legislative achievements, more than an antiseptic utopia. It is true that there was a certain erosion of values in the thirties, as well as a narrowing of horizons, but the New Dealers inwardly recognized that what they were doing had a deeply moral significance however much they eschewed ethical pretensions. Heirs of the Enlightenment, they felt themselves part of a broadly humanistic movement to make man's life on earth more tolerable, a movement that might someday even achieve a co-operative commonwealth. Social insurance, Frances Perkins declared, was "a fundamental part of another great forward step in that liberation of humanity which began with the Renaissance."

Franklin Roosevelt did not always have this sense as keenly as some of the men around him, but his greatness as a President lies in the remarkable degree to which he shared the vision. "The new deal business to me is very much bigger than anyone yet has expressed it," observed Senator Elbert Thomas. Roosevelt "seems to really have caught the spirit of what one of the Hebrew prophets called the desire of the nations. If he were in India today they would probably decide that he had become Mahatma— that is, one in tune with the infinite." Both foes and friends made much of Roosevelt's skill as a political manipulator, and there is no doubt that up to a point he delighted in schemes and stratagems. As Donald Richberg later observed: "There would be times when he seemed to be a Chevalier Bayard, *sans peur et sans reproche,* and times in which he would seem to be the apotheosis of a prince who had absorbed and practiced all the teachings of Machiavelli." Yet essentially he was a moralist who wanted

---

* Tugwell, *Battle for Democracy,* p. 22.

to achieve certain humane reforms and instruct the nation in the principles of government. On one occasion, he remarked: "I want to be a *preaching President*—like my cousin." His courtiers gleefully recounted his adroitness in trading and dealing for votes, his effectiveness on the stump, his wicked skill in cutting corners to win a point. But Roosevelt's importance lay not in his talents as a campaigner or a manipulator. It lay rather in his ability to arouse the country and, more specifically, the men who served under him, by his breezy encouragement of experimentation, by his hopefulness, and—a word that would have embarrassed some of his lieutenants—by his idealism.

The New Deal left many problems unsolved and even created some perplexing new ones. It never demonstrated that it could achieve prosperity in peacetime. As late as 1941, the unemployed still numbered six million, and not until the war year of 1943 did the army of the jobless finally disappear. It enhanced the power of interest groups who claimed to speak for millions, but sometimes represented only a small minority. It did not evolve a way to protect people who had no such spokesmen, nor an acceptable method for disciplining the interest groups. In 1946, President Truman would resort to a threat to draft railway workers into the Army to avert a strike. The New Deal achieved a more just society by recognizing groups which had been largely unrepresented—staple farmers, industrial workers, particular ethnic groups, and the new intellectual-administrative class. Yet this was still a halfway revolution; it swelled the ranks of the bourgeoisie but left many Americans—share-croppers, slum dwellers, most Negroes—outside of the new equilibrium.

Some of these omissions were to be promptly remedied. Subsequent Congresses extended social security, authorized slum clearance projects, and raised minimum-wage standards to keep step with the rising price level. Other shortcomings are understandable. The havoc that had been done before Roosevelt took office was so great that even the unprecedented measures of the New Deal did not suffice to repair the damage. Moreover, much was still to be learned, and it was in the Roosevelt years that the country was schooled in how to avert another major depression. Although it was war which freed the government from the taboos of a balanced budget and revealed the potentialities of spending, it is conceivable that New Deal measures would have led the country into a new cycle of prosperity even if there had been no war. Marked gains had been made before the war spending had any appreciable effect. When recovery did come, it was much more soundly based because of the adoption of the New Deal program.

Roosevelt and the New Dealers understood, perhaps better than their critics, that they had come only part of the way. Henry Wallace remarked:

"We are children of the transition—we have left Egypt but we have not yet arrived at the Promised Land." Only five years separated Roosevelt's inauguration in 1933 and the adoption of the last of the New Deal measures, the Fair Labor Standards Act, in 1938. The New Dealers perceived that they had done more in those years than had been done in any comparable period in American history, but they also saw that there was much still to be done, much, too, that continued to baffle them. "I believe in the things that have been done," Mrs. Roosevelt told the American Youth Congress in February, 1939. "They helped but they did not solve the fundamental problems. . . . I never believed the Federal government could solve the whole problem. It bought us time to think." She closed not with a solution but with a challenge: "Is it going to be worth while?"

"This generation of Americans is living in a tremendous moment of history," President Roosevelt stated in his final national address of the 1940 campaign.

"The surge of events abroad has made some few doubters among us ask: Is this the end of a story that has been told? Is the book of democracy now to be closed and placed away upon the dusty shelves of time?

"My answer is this: All we have known of the glories of democracy— its freedom, its efficiency as a mode of living, its ability to meet the aspirations of the common man—all these are merely an introduction to the greater story of a more glorious future.

"We Americans of today—all of us—we are characters in the living book of democracy.

"But we are also its author. It falls upon us now to say whether the chapters that are to come will tell a story of retreat or a story of continued advance."

THE GREAT DEPRESSION

Unemployment was the single most important manifestation of the depression throughout the 1930's. The number of men out of jobs increased steadily until Roosevelt came into office, and though it dropped some after 1933, there were still nearly ten million unemployed at the end of the decade. Behind the cold statistics lay the human problem—the families with inadequate food, the frustration of young men fresh out of high school or college with no jobs available, the deadening experience of men spending day after day in idleness in a culture that had always stressed the nobility of toil.

From the beginning, local authorities tried to meet the more obvious human needs with relief. At first private charities, then city and state governments used their resources in an effort to stem privation. By the end of 1931, these bodies had exhausted their funds. President Hoover believed that it was immoral for the federal government to engage directly in relief payments. But finally he agreed that it would be ethical for the government to loan money to the states for welfare purposes, and in 1932 Congress passed the Emergency Relief Act, making $300 million available to the states to relieve suffering. Yet even this sum was not enough. In June, 1932, a ragged army of World War I veterans marched on Washington to request the bonus Congress had promised servicemen in the twenties. Though this pathetic group posed no threat to the established order, President Hoover ordered troops to drive the Bonus Army from the shanties they had set up along the banks of the Potomac. And throughout the nation, as this report in September, 1942, in Fortune magazine makes clear, the problem was approaching a critical point.

THE EDITORS OF FORTUNE, No One Has Starved

Dull mornings last winter the sheriff of Miami, Florida, used to fill a truck with homeless men and run them up to the county line. Where the sheriff of Fort Lauderdale used to meet them and load them into a second truck

From "No One Has Starved," Fortune, V (September, 1932), pp. 19, 21-22, 28. Reprinted by permission of the editors of Fortune.

and run them up to *his* county line. Where the sheriff of Saint Lucie's would meet them and load them into a third truck and run them up to *his* county line. Where the sheriff of Brevard County would *not* meet them. And whence they would trickle back down the roads to Miami. To repeat.

It was a system. And it worked. The only trouble was that it worked too well. It kept the transients transient and it even increased the transient population in the process. But it got to be pretty expensive, one way or another, if you sat down and figured it all out—trucks and gas and time and a little coffee . . .

That was last winter.

Next winter there will be no truck. And there will be no truck, not because the transients will have disappeared from Miami: if anything, there will be more blistered Fords with North Dakota licenses and more heelworn shoes with the Boston trade-mark rubbed out next winter than there were last. But because the sheriff of Miami, like the President of the U. S., will next winter think of transients and unemployed miners and jobless mill workers in completely different terms.

The difference will be made by the Emergency Relief Act. Or rather by the fact that the Emergency Relief Act exists. For the Act itself with its $300,000,000 for direct relief loans to the states is neither an adequate nor an impressive piece of legislation. But the passage of the Act, like the green branch which young Mr. Ringling used to lay across the forks of the Wisconsin roads for his circus to follow, marks a turning in American political history. And the beginning of a new chapter in American unemployment relief. It constitutes an open and legible acknowledgement of government responsibility for the welfare of the victims of industrial unemployment. And its ultimate effect must be the substitution of an ordered, realistic, and intelligent relief program for the wasteful and uneconomic methods (of which the Miami truck is an adequate symbol) employed during the first three years of the depression.

There can be no serious question of the failure of those methods. For the methods were never seriously capable of success. They were diffuse, unrelated, and unplanned. The theory was that private charitable organizations and semipublic welfare groups, established to care for the old and the sick and the indigent, were capable of caring for the casuals of a world-wide economic disaster. And the theory in application meant that social agencies manned for the service of a few hundred families, and city shelters set up to house and feed a handful of homeless men, were compelled by the brutal necessities of hunger to care for hundreds of thousands of families and whole armies of the displaced and the jobless. And to depend for their resources upon the contributions of communities no longer able to contribute, and upon the irresolution and vacillation of state Legislatures and municipal assemblies long since in the red on their annual budgets. The result was the picture now presented in city after city and state after state—heterogeneous groups of official and semi-official and unofficial relief agencies struggling under the earnest and untrained leadership of the local men of affairs against an inertia of misery and suffering and want they are powerless to overcome.

But the psychological consequence was even worse. Since the problem was never honestly attacked as a national problem, and since the facts were never frankly faced as facts, people came to believe that American unemployment was relatively unimportant. They saw little idleness and they therefore believed there was little idleness. It is possible to drive for blocks in the usual shopping and residential districts of New York and Chicago without seeing a breadline or a food station or a hungry mob or indeed anything else much more exciting than a few casuals asleep on a park bench. And for that reason, and because their newspapers played down the subject as an additional depressant in depressing times, and because they were bored with relief measures anyway, the great American public simply ignored the whole thing. They would still ignore it today were it not that the committee hearings and the Congressional debate and the Presidential veto of relief bills this last June attracted their attention. And that the final passage of the Emergency Relief and Construction Act of 1932 has committed their government and themselves to a policy of affirmative action which compels both it and them to know definitely and precisely what the existing situation is.

It should be remarked at this point that nothing the federal government has yet done or is likely to do in the near future constitutes a policy of *constructive* action. Unemployment basically is not a social disease but an industrial phenomenon. The natural and inevitable consequence of a machine civilization is a lessened demand for human labor. (An almost total elimination of human labor in plowing, for example, is now foreseeable.) And the natural and inevitable consequence of a lessened demand for human labor is an increase of idleness. Indeed the prophets of the machine age have always promised an increase of idleness, under the name of leisure, as one of the goals of industry. A constructive solution of unemployment therefore means an industrial solution—a restatement of industrialism which will treat technological displacement not as an illness to be cured but as a goal to be achieved—and achieved with the widest dispensation of benefits and the least incidental misery.

But the present relief problem as focused by the federal Act is not a problem of ultimate solutions but of immediate palliatives. One does not talk architecture while the house is on fire and the tenants are still inside. The question at this moment is the pure question of fact. Having decided

Courtesy of the State Historical Society of Wisconsin.

Dispensing fish at a relief station, 1935.

at last to face reality and do something about it, what is reality? How many men are unemployed in the U. S.? How many are in want? *What are the facts?*

The following minimal statements may be accepted as true—with the certainty that they underestimate the real situation:

(1) Unemployment has steadily increased in the U. S. since the beginning of the depression and the rate of increase during the first part of 1932 was more rapid than in any other depression year.

(2) The number of persons totally unemployed is now at least 10,000,000.

(3) The number of persons totally unemployed next winter will, at the present rate of increase, be 11,000,000.

(4) Eleven millions unemployed means better than one man out of every four employable workers.

(5) This percentage is higher than the percentage of unemployed British workers registered under the compulsory insurance laws (17.1 percent in May, 1932, as against 17.3 percent in April and 18.4 percent in January) and higher than the French, the Italian, and the Canadian percentages, but lower than the German (43.9 percent of trade unionists in April, 1932) and the Norwegian.

(6) Eleven millions unemployed means 27,500,000 whose regular source of livelihood has been cut off.

(7) Twenty-seven and a half millions without regular income includes the families of totally unemployed workers alone. Taking account of the numbers of workers on part time, the total of those without adequate income becomes 34,000,000 or better than a quarter of the entire population of the country.

(8) Thirty-four million persons without adequate income does not mean 34,000,000 in present want. Many families have savings. But savings are eventually dissipated and the number in actual want tends to approximate the number without adequate income. How nearly it approximates it now or will next winter no man can say. But it is conservative to estimate that the problem of next winter's relief is a problem of caring for approximately 25,000,000 souls. . . .

But it is impossible to think or to act in units of 25,000,000 human beings. Like the casualty lists of the British War Office during the Battle of the Somme, they mean nothing. They are at once too large and too small. A handful of men and women and children digging for their rotten food in the St. Louis dumps are more numerous, humanly speaking, than all the millions that ever found themselves in an actuary's column. The 25,000,000 only become human in their cities and their mill towns and their mining villages. And their situation only becomes comprehensible in terms of the relief they have already received.

That is to say that the general situation can only be judged by the situation in the particular localities. But certain generalizations are possible. Of which the chief is the broad conclusion that few if any of the industrial areas have been able to maintain a minimum decency level of life for their unemployed. Budgetary standards as set up by welfare organizations, public and private, after years of experiment have been discarded. Food only, in most cases, is provided and little enough of that. Rents are seldom paid. Shoes and clothing are given in rare instances only. Money for doctors and dentists is not to be had. And free clinics are filled to overflowing. Weekly allowances per family have fallen as low as $2.39 in New York with $3 and $4 the rule in most cities and $5 a high figure. And even on these terms funds budgeted for a twelve-month period have been exhausted in three or four. While city after city has been compelled to abandon a part of its dependent population. "We are merely trying to prevent hunger and exposure," reported a St. Paul welfare head last May. And the same sentence would be echoed by workers in other cities with such additions as were reported at the same time from Pittsburgh where a cut of 50 percent was regarded as "inevitable," from Dallas where Mexicans and Negroes were not given relief, from Alabama where discontinuance of relief in mining and agricultural sections was foreseen, from New Orleans where no new applicants were being received and 2,500 families in need of relief were receiving none, from Omaha where two-thirds of the cases receiving relief were to be discontinued, from Colorado where the counties had suspended relief for lack of funds . . . from Scranton . . . from Cleveland . . . from Syracuse . . .

. . . the depression, along with its misery, has produced its social curiosities, not the least of which is the wandering population it has spilled upon the roads. Means of locomotion vary but the objective is always the same—somewhere else. No one has yet undertaken to estimate the number of hitchhikers whose thumbs jerk onward along the American pike, nor the number of spavined Fords dragging destitute families from town to town in search of a solvent relative or a generous friend. But the total migratory population of the country has been put at 600,000 to 1,000,000. The Pacific Coast, the Southwest, and the Atlantic South are the habitat of the larger groups. Los Angeles once had over 70,000 with a daily influx of 1,500 more while the state of California reported an increase of 311.8 percent in the monthly average of meals served to homeless men in early 1931 as compared with early 1929. And 365 vagrant boys running from fourteen to twenty and including college students, high school students, and eighth-graders applied to the Salt Lake Salvation Army and the Salt Lake County Jail for shelter between May 15 and June 15, 1932. Many of them were homeless, destitute children of families broken up by unemployment. And save for the fact that almost all of them were traveling

Refugee families near Holtville, California, 1937.

alone or with one companion, and that most of them wanted work, they suggested with an uncomfortable accuracy the vagrant children who haunted the Russian railway stations after the October Revolution.

The presence of these wandering groups is curious and significant. It has long been recognized that the population of the U. S. was becoming increasingly migratory in character. But it was not until the depression that the meaning of the phenomenon was made clear. When millions of people have no relation to the land and are able at the same time to find cheap transportation, the effect of an economic crisis is not to fix them in one place but to drive them elsewhere. And the consequence, as regards these groups, is a complete failure of local relief. The destitute families of the Fords and the homeless men of the flat cars are entitled to relief in no city. As the history of the Bonus Expeditionary Force after its ouster from Washington makes clear. . . .

FACING THE CRISIS

"First of all," Franklin Roosevelt declared in his Inaugural Address on March 4, 1933, "let me assert my firm belief that the only thing we have to fear is fear itself—nameless, unreasoning, unjustified terror. . . ." There was good reason for fear. The banking system of the nation was on the edge of collapse. Withdrawal of deposits by panic-stricken people had led to the closing of banks in 38 states, and that morning the new governor of New York closed the banks in his state, thereby crippling the national economy. The President responded the next day by declaring a national bank holiday and calling Congress into special session. When the legislators convened on March 9, the President presented an Emergency Banking Act which they passed in record time. On the evening of March 12, Roosevelt spoke to the nation on the radio in his first fireside chat to explain what he had done. His rich, melodious voice informed an estimated sixty million anxious listeners that the government had examined the banks of the country, and that those that were sound would reopen the next day. Thus reassured, the people greeted the reopening of the banks by depositing far more money than they withdrew, and the crisis passed.

For the next five weeks, Roosevelt bombarded Congress with messages requesting legislation. By early May, Congress had responded to Roosevelt's prods by going off the gold standard, legalizing the sale of beer for the first time since prohibition had begun, and creating the Civilian Conservation Corps to take idle young men off the streets of the nation's cities and put them to work in the forests. On May 7, the President reported to the people again over the radio.

FRANKLIN D. ROOSEVELT, *Second Fireside Chat*

On a Sunday night a week after my Inauguration I used the radio to tell you about the banking crisis and the measures we were taking to meet it. I think that in that way I made clear to the country various facts that might

Samuel Rosenman, ed., *The Public Papers and Addresses of Franklin D. Roosevelt: The Year of Crisis* (New York, Random House, 1938), pp. 160-165, 167-168. Reprinted by permission of the publisher.

otherwise have been misunderstood and in general provided a means of understanding which did much to restore confidence.

Tonight, eight weeks later, I come for the second time to give you my report; in the same spirit and by the same means to tell you about what we have been doing and what we are planning to do.

Two months ago we were facing serious problems. The country was dying by inches. It was dying because trade and commerce had declined to dangerously low levels; prices for basic commodities were such as to destroy the value of the assets of national institutions such as banks, savings banks, insurance companies, and others. These institutions, because of their great needs, were foreclosing mortgages, calling loans, refusing credit. Thus there was actually in process of destruction the property of millions of people who had borrowed money on that property in terms of dollars which had an entirely different value from the level of March, 1933. That situation in that crisis did not call for any complicated consideration of economic panaceas or fancy plans. We were faced by a condition and not a theory.

There were just two alternatives: The first was to allow the foreclosures to continue, credit to be withheld and money to go into hiding, thus forcing liquidation and bankruptcy of banks, railroads and insurance companies and a recapitalizing of all business and all property on a lower level. This alternative meant a continuation of what is loosely called "deflation," the net result of which would have been extraordinary hardships on all property owners and, incidentally, extraordinary hardships on all persons working for wages through an increase in unemployment and a further reduction of the wage scale.

It is easy to see that the result of this course would have not only economic effects of a very serious nature, but social results that might bring incalculable harm. Even before I was inaugurated I came to the conclusion that such a policy was too much to ask the American people to bear. It involved not only a further loss of homes, farms, savings and wages, but also a loss of spiritual values—the loss of that sense of security for the present and the future so necessary to the peace and contentment of the individual and of his family. When you destroy these things you will find it difficult to establish confidence of any sort in the future. It was clear that mere appeals from Washington for confidence and the mere lending of more money to shaky institutions could not stop this downward course. A prompt program applied as quickly as possible seemed to me not only justified but imperative to our national security. The Congress, and when I say Congress I mean the members of both political parties, fully understood this and gave me generous and intelligent support. The members of Congress realized that the methods of normal times had to be replaced in the emergency by measures which were suited to the serious and pressing requirements of the moment. There was no actual surrender of power, Congress still retained its constitutional authority, and no one has the slightest desire to change the balance of these powers. The function of Congress is to decide what has to be done and to select the appropriate agency to carry out its will. To this policy it has strictly adhered. The only thing that has been happening has been to designate the President as the agency to carry out certain of the purposes of the Congress. This was constitutional and in keeping with the past American tradition.

The legislation which has been passed or is in the process of enactment can properly be considered as part of a well-grounded plan.

First, we are giving opportunity of employment to one-quarter of a million of the unemployed, especially the young men who have dependents, to go into the forestry and flood-prevention work. This is a big task because it means feeding, clothing and caring for nearly twice as many men as we have in the regular army itself. In creating this civilian conservation corps we are killing two birds with one stone. We are clearly enhancing the value of our natural resources, and we are relieving an appreciable amount of actual distress. This great group of men has entered upon its work on a purely voluntary basis; no military training is involved and we are conserving not only our natural resources, but our human resources. One of the great values to this work is the fact that it is direct and requires the intervention of very little machinery.

Second, I have requested the Congress and have secured action upon a proposal to put the great properties owned by our Government at Muscle Shoals to work after long years of wasteful inaction, and with this a broad plan for the improvement of a vast area in the Tennessee Valley. It will add to the comfort and happiness of hundreds of thousands of people and the incident benefits will reach the entire Nation.

Next, the Congress is about to pass legislation that will greatly ease the mortgage distress among the farmers and the home owners of the Nation, by providing for the easing of the burden of debt now bearing so heavily upon millions of our people.

Our next step in seeking immediate relief is a grant of half a billion dollars to help the States, counties and municipalities in their duty to care for those who need direct and immediate relief.

The Congress also passed legislation authorizing the sale of beer in such States as desired it. This has already resulted in considerable reemployment and incidentally has provided much-needed tax revenue.

We are planning to ask the Congress for legislation to enable the Government to undertake public works, thus stimulating directly and indirectly the employment of many others in well-considered projects.

Further legislation has been taken up which goes much more fundamentally into our economic problems. The Farm Relief Bill seeks by the use of several methods, alone or together, to bring about an increased return to farmers for their major farm products, seeking at the same time to prevent in the days to come disastrous overproduction which so often in the past has kept farm commodity prices far below a reasonable return. This measure provides wide powers for emergencies. The extent of its use will depend entirely upon what the future has in store.

Well-considered and conservative measures will likewise be proposed which will attempt to give to the industrial workers of the country a more fair wage return, prevent cut-throat competition and unduly long hours for labor, and at the same time encourage each industry to prevent overproduction.

Our Railroad Bill falls into the same class because it seeks to provide and make certain definite planning by the railroads themselves, with the assistance of the Government, to eliminate the duplication and waste that is now resulting in railroad receiverships and continuing operating deficits.

I am certain that the people of this country understand and approve the broad purposes behind these new governmental policies relating to agriculture and industry and transportation. We found ourselves faced with more agricultural products than we could possibly consume ourselves and with surpluses which other Nations did not have the cash to buy from us except at prices ruinously low. We found our factories able to turn out more goods than we could possibly consume, and at the same time we were faced with a falling export demand. We found ourselves with more facilities to transport goods and crops than there were goods and crops to be transported. All of this has been caused in large part by a complete lack of planning and a complete failure to understand the danger signals that have been flying ever since the close of the World War. The people of this country have been erroneously encouraged to believe that they could keep on increasing the output of farm and factory indefinitely and that some magician would find ways and means for that increased output to be consumed with reasonable profit to the producer.

Today we have reason to believe that things are a little better than they were two months ago. Industry has picked up, railroads are carrying more freight, farm prices are better, but I am not going to indulge in issuing proclamations of over-enthusiastic assurance. We cannot ballyhoo ourselves back to prosperity. I am going to be honest at all times with the people of the country. I do not want the people of this country to take the foolish course of letting this improvement come back on another speculative wave. I do not want the people to believe that because of unjustified optimism we can resume the ruinous practice of increasing our crop output and our factory output in the hope that a kind Providence will find buyers at high prices. Such a course may bring us immediate and false prosperity but it will be the kind of prosperity that will lead us into another tailspin.

It is wholly wrong to call the measures that we have taken Government control of farming, industry, and transportation. It is rather a partnership between Government and farming and industry and transportation, not partnership in profits, for the profits still go to the citizens, but rather a partnership in planning, and a partnership to see that the plans are carried out.

Let me illustrate with an example. Take the cotton-goods industry. It is probably true that 90 percent of the cotton manufacturers would agree to eliminate starvation wages, would agree to stop long hours of employment, would agree to stop child labor, would agree to prevent an overproduction that would result in unsalable surpluses. But, what good is such an agreement if the other 10 percent of cotton manufacturers pay starvation wages, require long hours, employ children in their mills and turn out burdensome surpluses? The unfair 10 percent could produce goods so cheaply that the fair 90 percent would be compelled to meet the unfair conditions. Here is where Government comes in. Government ought to have the right and will have the right, after surveying and planning for an industry, to prevent, with the assistance of the overwhelming majority of that industry, unfair practices and to enforce this agreement by the authority of Government. The so-called antitrust laws were intended to prevent the creation of monopolies and to forbid unreasonable profits to those monopolies. That purpose of the antitrust laws must be continued, but these laws were never intended to encourage the kind of unfair competition that results in long hours, starvation wages and overproduction.

The same principle applies to farm products and to transportation and every other field of organized private industry.

We are working toward a definite goal, which is to prevent the return of conditions which came very close to destroying what we call modern civilization. The actual accomplishment of our purpose cannot be attained in a day. Our policies are wholly within purposes for which our American Constitutional Government was established 150 years ago.

I know that the people of this country will understand this and will also understand the spirit in which we are undertaking this policy. I do not deny that we may make mistakes of procedure as we carry out the policy. I have no expectation of making a hit every time I come to bat. What I seek is the highest possible batting average, not only for myself but for the team. Theodore Roosevelt once said to me: "If I can be right 75 percent of the time I shall come up to the fullest measure of my hopes." . . .

To you, the people of this country, all of us, the members of the Congress and the members of this Administration, owe a profound debt of gratitude. Throughout the depression you have been patient. You have granted us wide powers; you have encouraged us with a widespread approval of our purposes. Every ounce of strength and every resource at our command we have devoted to the end of justifying your confidence. We are encouraged to believe that a wise and sensible beginning has been made. In the present spirit of mutual confidence and mutual encouragement we go forward.

LAUNCHING THE NRA

On June 16, exactly 100 days after it had convened, Congress adjourned. The Hundred Days had seen an historic outpouring of legislation; Congress had enacted 15 major administration proposals. The most significant was the National Industrial Recovery Act which sought to coordinate the efforts of American industry to get back on its feet. Passed by Congress in early June, the legislation created a National Recovery Administration (NRA) charged with overseeing the drafting of production codes in all major segments of American industry. Drawing on the experience of the War Industries Board during World War I, the government hoped that businessmen would give up their usual fierce competition to pull together toward recovery. The basic aim was to control production and stabilize prices as a first step toward prosperity, while at the same time protecting workers by fixing minimum wages and maximum hours of labor.

Roosevelt appointed Hugh Johnson, a profane, dynamic business executive who had served on the War Industries Board, to administer NRA. Disappointed at the slow process of writing codes, Johnson convinced Roosevelt in mid-July of the necessity of mounting a mammoth public campaign to pressure American industry into cooperating. On July 24, Roosevelt called on the American people to join in the NRA crusade.

FRANKLIN D. ROOSEVELT, *Third Fireside Chat*

Last Autumn, on several occasions, I expressed my faith that we can make possible by democratic self-discipline in industry general increases in wages and shortening of hours sufficient to enable industry to pay its own workers enough to let those workers buy and use the things that their labor produces. This can be done only if we permit and encourage co-operative action in industry, because it is obvious that without united action a few selfish men in each competitive group will pay starvation wages and insist on long hours of work. Others in that group must either follow suit or close up shop. We have seen the result of action of that kind in the continuing descent into the economic hell of the past four years.

There is a clear way to reverse that process: If all employers in each competitive group agree to pay their workers the same wages—reasonable wages—and require the same hours—reasonable hours—then higher wages and shorter hours will hurt no employer. Moreover, such action is better for the employer than unemployment and low wages, because it makes more buyers for his product. That is the simple idea which is the very heart of the Industrial Recovery Act.

On the basis of this simple principle of everybody doing things together, we are starting out on this nationwide attack on unemployment. It will succeed if our people understand it—in the big industries, in the little shops, in the great cities and in the small villages. There is nothing complicated about it and there is nothing particularly new in the principle. It goes back to the basic idea of society and of the Nation itself that people acting in a group can accomplish things which no individual acting alone could even hope to bring about. . . .

In war, in the gloom of night attack, soldiers wear a bright badge on their shoulders to be sure that comrades do not fire on comrades. On that principle, those who cooperate in this program must know each other at a glance. That is why we have provided a badge of honor for this purpose, a simple design with a legend, "We do our part," and I ask that all those who join with me shall display that badge prominently. It is essential to our purpose.

Already all the great, basic industries have come forward willingly with proposed codes, and in these codes they accept the principles leading to mass reemployment. But, important as is this heartening demonstration, the

Samuel Rosenman, ed., *The Public Papers and Addresses of Franklin D. Roosevelt: The Year of Crisis* (New York, Random House, 1938), pp. 298-299, 301-303. Reprinted by permission of the publisher.

richest field for results is among the small employers, those whose contribution will be to give new work for from one to ten people. These smaller employers are indeed a vital part of the backbone of the country, and the success of our plan lies largely in their hands.

Already the telegrams and letters are pouring into the White House— messages from employers who ask that their names be placed on this special Roll of Honor. They represent great corporations and companies, and partnerships and individuals. I ask that even before the dates set in the agreements which we have sent out, the employers of the country who have not already done so—the big fellows and the little fellows—shall at once write or telegraph to me personally at the White House, expressing their intentions of going through with the plan. And it is my purpose to keep posted in the post office of every town, a Roll of Honor of all those who join with me.

I want to take this occasion to say to the twenty-four Governors who are now in conference in San Francisco, that nothing thus far has helped in strengthening this great movement more than their resolutions adopted at the very outset of their meeting, giving this plan their instant and unanimous approval, and pledging to support it in their States.

To the men and women whose lives have been darkened by the fact or the fear of unemployment, I am justified in saying a word of encouragement because the codes and the agreements already approved, or about to be passed upon, prove that the plan does raise wages, and that it does put people back to work. You can look on every employer who adopts the plan as one who is doing his part, and those employers deserve well of everyone who works for a living. It will be clear to you, as it is to me, that while the shirking employer may undersell his competitor, the saving he thus makes is made at the expense of his country's welfare.

While we are making this great common effort there should be no discord and dispute. This is no time to cavil or to question the standard set by this universal agreement. It is time for patience and understanding and cooperation. The workers of this country have rights under this law which cannot be taken from them, and nobody will be permitted to whittle them away but, on the other hand, no aggression is now necessary to attain those rights. The whole country will be united to get them for you. The principle that applies to the employers applies to the workers as well, and I ask you workers to cooperate in the same spirit.

When Andrew Jackson, "Old Hickory," died, someone asked, "Will he go to Heaven?" and the answer was, "He will if he wants to." If I am asked whether the American people will pull themselves out of this depression, I answer, "They will if they want to." The essence of the plan is a universal limitation of hours of work per week for any individual by common consent, and a universal payment of wages above a minimum, also by common consent. I cannot guarantee the success of this nationwide plan, but the people of this country can guarantee its success. I have no faith in "cure-alls" but I believe that we can greatly influence economic forces. I have no sympathy with the professional economists who insist that things must run their course and that human agencies can have no influence on economic ills. One reason is that I happen to know that professional economists have changed their definition of economic laws every five or ten years for a very long time, but I do have faith, and retain faith, in the strength of the common purpose, and in the strength of unified action taken by the American people.

That is why I am describing to you the simple purposes and the solid foundations upon which our program of recovery is built. That is why I am asking the employers of the Nation to sign this common covenant with me—to sign it in the name of patriotism and humanity. That is why I am asking the workers to go along with us in a spirit of understanding and of helpfulness.

GOVERNMENT BY COMMITTEE

Franklin Roosevelt's gifts and techniques as an administrator, as Professor Leuchtenburg notes, have been the subject of considerable controversy among historians. The President never liked neat tables of organization; he preferred to give his chief associates vague and overlapping jurisdictions so that he could always retain control of the final decisions. But even if Roosevelt had been a master of order and efficiency, the sudden proliferation of governmental agencies and bureaus that was characteristic of the New Deal would have given him great difficulty.

In the summer of 1933, he created an Executive Council in an effort to coordinate the work of economic recovery. This group, which was simply an enlarged Cabinet, proved too cumbersome, so in November he replaced it with a National Emergency Council, which consisted of several cabinet members and the heads of the more important independent agencies. In

1934, as Roosevelt's relations with Hugh Johnson became more strained, he charged the Council with the job of overseeing the NRA, and in September, when Johnson finally resigned, he replaced him with Donald Richberg, who was also the director of the National Emergency Council. The following exchange between Roosevelt and Richberg occurred during the National Emergency Council meeting on December 11, 1934.

Minutes of the National Emergency Council

Mr. Richberg: Mr. President, at the last meeting, the question came up of finding out the number of interdepartmental committees, how many were alive, how many were inactive, and how they were related. The effort to get the information has been a rather staggering one. Up to date, we have found that there are 124 interdepartmental committees, boards and commissions, which have 224 interdepartmental subcommittees, making a total of 348 interdepartmental arrangements. We have prepared some charts simply as an indication of the size and complexity of this problem and for the further handling of it. I will just give an example of one group. Here, in the overlapping of functions, there are 22 functions carried on by 44 interdepartmental committees directly concerned with foreign trade matters. I give just an example of the charting of that particular group.

President Roosevelt: Say that again, just as to foreign trade.

Mr. Richberg: There are 22 functions carried on by 44 interdepartmental committees. Obviously, there is a great deal of overlapping. The foreign trade work is carried on by 27 bureaus of 20 departments and independent establishments. I point this out particularly because it is a good illustration of activities very closely related that should be coordinated and tied together.

In addition to those committees, there are not listed here 12 other committees which have related functions, such as the Central Statistical Board, the Natural Resources Board, and others. That is one group and there are other groups which I will simply point out in passing, such as that concerned with the various problems of economic security and another concerned with public works; here is a chart of the agencies concerned with planning in general; here is a group concerned with public health, general administration, and financial problems; here is another group concerned with the subject of procurement. You may even observe by a mere glance

Lester G. Seligman and Elmer E. Cornwell, Jr., eds., *New Deal Mosaic: Roosevelt Confers with his National Emergency Council, 1933-1936* (Eugene, Ore., 1965), pp. 355-357. Reprinted by permission of University of Oregon Books.

the size of that particular group which includes 78 interdepartmental sub-committees, as to which there are possible duplications. When it comes to statistics, there is far from coordination in that work. We have a very large group concerned with transportation problems, and there is another on science advisory problems. It has been actually impossible to chart these in any way that would be fundamentally effective. These groupings are not those which would probably be permanent. The purpose of trying to chart them is to bring forward the absolute necessity of trying to co-ordinate these committees into certain fundamental groups which could then be created as subcommittees of this Council and then be connected, through the Council, with the general functions of the Administration. A great many of these exist off by themselves at the present time. They are not connected with any particular group. They have no function with any single agency. They do not report anywhere. They have been created to take care of problems, and a great many of them have been forgotten. A great many of them were at work, but the product of the work does not land anywhere. We could go into greater detail with this but I think that may be sufficient.

President Roosevelt: The majority of these are inherited. These organizations have been growing up for years and years.

Mr. Richberg: The great mass of them are very old. Some have been created to meet vital necessities. In order to get at the problem it is suggested that a committee of the Council make a thorough study of this information which we have obtained for the purpose of recommending to the Council necessary reorganization, consolidation, and abolition of committees with a view to preventing overlapping and duplication. In that connection, Mr. President, I make the suggestion that there are primarily concerned here these departments, going through the list: State, Treasury, Agriculture, Interior, Commerce, and Labor. The other four departments are not so frequently involved in these interdepartmental committees; but if you are going to attempt to coordinate these groups I should think very clearly those six departments should be represented upon any committee charged with that object, as they will be constantly working with those six departments. The committee could be organized by including a direct representative such as an assistant secretary.

President Roosevelt: In other words, we have three hundred forty-two now and you want the three hundred forty-third?

Mr. Richberg: Yes, to eliminate the 342! (Laughter) One large boa constrictor to swallow all the others!

Mr. Jones*: How many have been added in this administration?

* Jesse H. Jones, Chairman, Reconstruction Finance Corporation.

Mr. Richberg: I don't know as we have that. There is an enormous amount of confusion because we had committees reporting which other departments denied existed although they were supposed to be on them. My thought, Mr. President, is that if a committee could be created on which I would suggest possibly that somebody from the National Emergency Council—my office—should act as executive head, as we have gathered the material and we can furnish it and save a great deal of labor. This committee could then eliminate a great many simply by saying that their functions had ceased to exist, and could coordinate a great many, and leave some that would be brought back to the Council with the question as to the desirability of continuing them.

ROOSEVELT'S PHILOSOPHY OF REFORM

At this same meeting of the National Emergency Council on December 11, 1934, Roosevelt disclosed his own personal views on several key New Deal measures. He indicated his dissatisfaction with the existing relief program and outlined an approach that would see fruition in 1935 as the Works Progress Administration (WPA). He then spoke at length on housing and the Tennessee Valley Authority (TVA), which was under increasing fire from private public utilities on grounds that its electric power operations were destroying competition.

Minutes of the National Emergency Council

President Roosevelt: I have three things down here. Donald [Richberg] suggested I might outline to you certain policies. We have a great many people working, and no one person knows what the other person is doing, except myself — right here, nowhere else in the government—as to the

Lester G. Seligman and Elmer E. Cornwell, Jr., eds., *New Deal Mosaic: Roosevelt Confers with his National Emergency Council*, 1933-1936 (Eugene, Ore., 1965), pp. 365-370. Reprinted by permission of University of Oregon Books.

coordination of the public works program, the relief program, and the housing program, insofar as new legislation goes; and nobody knows exactly what is going to be done until the third of January. We are seeking to cut down relief in this sense; there are only two schools of thought, one school represented by a number of very worthy persons who believe we should adopt the dole system in this country because it would cost less. We have somewhere around five million people on relief in the United States today, on the subsistence basis; we can save a great deal of money by just giving them cash or market baskets on Saturday night, thereby destroying morale at the saving of a large sum of money. That is out of the window; we are not going to adopt that policy. The policy is going to be to eliminate that form of relief all we possibly can. That means the adoption of the alternative, which is furnishing work instead of the dole. We are working on that at the present time.

As a part of that work program we come to the question of the housing program. The easiest way is to explain it, once more, in words of one syllable. There are in this country about 120,000,000 people. The government is doing something for three groups of that 120,000,000 people in the way of housing. The richest group for whom we are doing something are people who have borrowing capacity. That is to say, they have either jobs with incomes that go with jobs, or at least form a class of sufficient wealth in the community for banks and other lending agencies to lend money to them. For various reasons, banks and other lending agencies have shown a disinclination to come forward as fast as we hoped they would. We, therefore, have tried to stimulate lending by private agencies through the establishment of the Housing Administration. The Housing Administration has made very great progress—excellent progress. It has operated through the system of the guaranteeing of a percentage of the loan; in other words, the insurance method. They have been lending money so far under Title I of the Housing Act to people—I think I am right, Jim* and Dan‡—with average income of about $2,750 a year. In almost every case, those people already have their own homes and they are borrowing money to improve their existing homes. People in this country with an average of $2,750 a year income are rich people. They are far above the average in respect to income; and we are doing a fine job for them.

Next come the people a little lower down the scale, but people who still have borrowing capacity—some form of security to offer to private capital. Those are the people who already had their homes or their farms.

---

*James A. Moffett, Federal Housing Administration
‡ Daniel W. Bell, Acting Director of the Budget

Bill Myers* and John Fahey‡ are looking after their wants. In other words, the Farm Credit Administration is extending government credit or the credit of the federal farm banks or federal home loan banks is being extended to people who already have property. They are extending it in the form of loans or in the form of reduced interest rates on existing mortgages. Those people come into a lower income group in almost all cases than the people who go to Jim Moffett. There may be 10,000,000 men, women, and children who have taken advantage of the Housing Administration; there might be another 10,000,000 people, or possibly 15,000,000— perhaps 20,000,000 people—who would take advantage of the Farm Credit Administration or the Home Owners' Loan organization. That is about 30,000,000 people in this country.

Below them is the largest mass of the American population—people who have not got enough, either in earning capacity or in security in the form of tangibles, to go either to Moffett or Fahey or Myers. Those are the people who are living—most of them—in un-American surroundings and conditions. They cannot be helped by the Housing, the Farm Credit, or the Home Loan; they are too poor. They cannot go to a bank or a building and loan association or to a private money lender and get money to improve their living conditions. The question comes up, are we licked in trying to help them in their living conditions? A good many real estate people consider we are; and they say the government should not help them. We say, "Will private capital help them?" They say, "No, it can't, but we don't want the government to help them." Are we licked in trying to help these people—forty million of them, men, women, and children? Their answer is, "Yes, we are licked; we must not do anything to help them, because we might interfere with private capital." The answer is, "No, we are not licked! We are going to help them!" I am telling you quite a lot about policies; we are going to help those forty million people by giving them better houses—a great many of them, all we possibly can. Hence, there is no conflict whatsoever in the government's housing program—never was. They fall into entirely different social groups. The program of building houses has nothing to do with the Housing Administration, nothing to do with the Farm Credit, nothing to do with the Home Owners' Loan. It is an entirely separate proposition and will have entirely separate handling. And, incidentally, we will kill two birds with one stone; we are going to provide better housing, and put a lot of people to work.

I think it is clear to everybody and there will be no further question about any conflict, because there is no conflict. Then we come down to

---

* William I. Myers, Governor, Farm Credit Administration
‡ Chairman, Federal Home Loan Bank Board

another thing—TVA and electric power. There have been two confusions of thought, perhaps among some members of the administration and certainly in the public mind. I will also set it out in words of one syllable. TVA is not an agency of the government. It was not initiated or organized for the purpose of selling electricity. This is a side function. Am I right on that, Arthur*?

There is a much bigger situation behind the Tennessee Valley Authority. If you will read the message on which the legislation was based you will realize that we are conducting a social experiment that is the first of its kind in the world, as far as I know, covering a convenient geographical area—in other words, the watershed of a great river. The work proceeds along two lines, both of which are intimately connected—the physical land and water and soil end of it, and the human side of it. It proceeds on the assumption that we are going to the highest mountain peak of the Tennessee Watershed and we are going to take an acre of land up there and say, "What should this land be used for, and is it being badly used at the present time?" And a few feet farther down we are going to come to a shack on the side of the mountain where there is a white man of about as fine stock as we have in this country who, with his family of children, is completely uneducated—never had a chance, never sees twenty-five or fifty dollars in cash a year, but just keeps body and soul together—manages to do that—and is the progenitor of a large line of children for many generations to come. He certainly has been forgotten, not by the Administration, but by the American people. They are going to see that he and his children have a chance, and they are going to see that the farm he is using is classified, and if it is not proper for him to farm it, we are going to give him a chance on better land. If he should use it, we are going to try to bring him some of the things he needs, like schools, electric lights, and so on. We are going to try to prevent soil erosion, and grow trees, and try to bring in industries. It is a tremendous effort with a very great objective. As an incident to that it is necessary to build some dams. And when you build a dam as an incident to this entire program, you get probably a certain amount of water power development out of it. We are going to try to use that water power to its best advantage.

Insofar as competition goes with other companies—private companies— it comes down to a very simple proposition. There has been, again, a confusion of thought. The power people—not the people who are running the operating companies but the people who have cornered the control of those operating companies in large financial groups called holding com-

---

* Dr. Arthur E. Morgan, Chairman, Tennessee Valley Authority

panies—have been talking about the attack on utility securities. There is a perfectly clear distinction well expressed by an effort made the other day in New York to get the insurance company to join with the holding companies in opposing the government program. I think it was Mr. Ecker of the Metropolitan who, on being asked to join in the attack, was told that the security bonds—the utility bonds—of the Metropolitan would be jeopardized, made the perfectly simple answer that the large insurance companies, like the savings banks, if you go through their portfolios of securities that make up their resources against policies, those portfolios will show a very large number of utility bonds; but in every case of the larger companies and the savings banks those bonds are bonds of operating companies. In other words, they represent money that was put into the actual development. It is a pretty fair guess that ninety-nine and a half percent of the bonds of all the operating company utilities in the United States are worth at least a hundred cents on the dollar today. They are absolutely all right. The only utility securities which are all wrong are the securities of holding companies, which securities represent no cash invested in electrical development itself. They represent merely financial transactions, and therefore, it is a perfectly safe position for anybody to take that the government program does not jeopardize in any way the securities of honest operating companies. If every operating utility company was concerned only with making the interest on its bonds and a reasonable profit on its stock, they could reduce their rates per kilowatt hour to the household users of power throughout the United States and survive, making a good living and an honest profit. Those reduced rates would almost immediately stop the rush of municipalities to put in their own plants. It is a perfectly simple proposition. There is hardly a municipality in the United States where 3¢ power is possible for the existing private companies, that would seek to put in its own municipal plant if they could get 3¢ power. And in most parts of the United States, the private company can give 3¢ power and make a substantial profit on their investment.

THE CONSTITUTIONAL CONFLICT

Franklin Roosevelt received a massive vote of confidence in the fall Con-
gressional elections of 1934 when the people returned a Congress with
the heaviest Democratic majorities the party had ever enjoyed. But in early
1935, the Supreme Court, composed of four conservative justices, three
liberals, and two moderates, began to challenge the New Deal. In January,
the Court invalidated the petroleum section of the NIRA, and then in
March the justices barely upheld the government's repudiation of the
gold clause in redeeming federal bonds. The most significant decision came
on May 27, 1935. The year before, the Schechter brothers, wholesale
poultry dealers in Brooklyn, had been found guilty of selling diseased
chickens in violation of the NRA's Live Poultry Code. They appealed the
decision in what the press quickly dubbed the "sick chicken" case. The
Court ruled unanimously in favor of the Schechter brothers. The opinion,
written by Chief Justice Hughes, denied that the depression emergency
justified the delegation of unlimited power to the President to regulate
American business. Hughes harked back to the Knight case of 1895 in sug-
gesting that the commerce clause of the Constitution limited federal
regulatory powers to goods actually in transit between states, thereby
apparently undermining the Constitutional basis of much of the New Deal.
   The decision was announced on Monday; two days later, at his regular
press conference, the President dodged comment on the Schechter case.
But on Friday morning he called a special press conference. Instead of the
usual light banter and give-and-take with reporters, Roosevelt spoke with-
out interruption for an hour and twenty-five minutes, analyzing every
aspect of the Court's decision and pointing out its impact on the New Deal.

FRANKLIN D. ROOSEVELT, the 209th Press Conference

. . . Now, coming down to the decision itself. What are the implications?
For the benefit of those of you who haven't read it through I think I can
put it this way: the implications of this decision are much more important

Samuel Rosenman, ed., *Public Papers of Franklin D. Roosevelt: The Court Disapproves*
(New York, Random House, 1938), pp. 205-207, 208-210, 218-219. Reprinted by permission
of the publisher.

than almost certainly any decision of my lifetime or yours, more important than any decision probably since the Dred Scott case, because they bring the country as a whole up against a very practical question. That is in spite of what one gentleman said in the paper this morning, that I resented the decision. Nobody resents a Supreme Court decision. You can deplore a Supreme Court decision, and you can point out the effect of it. You can call the attention of the country to what the implications are as to the future, what the results of that decision are if future decisions follow this decision.

Now take the decision itself. In the Schechter case the first part of it states the facts in the case, which you all know. Then it takes up the code itself and it points out that the code was the result of an Act of Congress. It mentions in passing that the Act of Congress was passed in a great emergency and that it sought to improve conditions immediately through the establishing of fair practices, through the prevention of unfair practices. It then goes on in general and says that even though it was an emergency, it did not make any difference whether it was an emergency or not, it was unconstitutional because it did not set forth very clearly, in detail, definitions of the broad language which was used in the Act. In fact, it says that it makes no difference what kind of emergency this country ever gets into, an Act has to be constitutional. Of course, it might take a month or two of delay to make an Act constitutional and then you wouldn't know whether it was constitutional or not—you would have to do the best you could.

Now, they have pointed out in regard to this particular Act that it was unconstitutional because it delegated certain powers which should have been written into the Act itself. And then there is this interesting language that bears that out. It is on page eight.

> We are told that the provisions of the statute authorizing the adoption of the codes must be viewed in the light of the grave national crisis with which Congress was confronted. Undoubtedly, the conditions to which power is addressed are always to be considered when the exercise of power is challenged. Extraordinary conditions may call for extraordinary remedies. But the argument necessarily stops short of an attempt to justify action which lies outside the sphere of constitutional authority. Extraordinary conditions do not create or enlarge constitutional power.

Of course, that is a very interesting implication. Some of us are old enough to remember the war days—the legislation that was passed in April, May and June of 1917. Being a war, that legislation was never brought before the Supreme Court. Of course, as a matter of fact, a great deal of that legislation was far more violative of the strict interpretation of the Constitution than any legislation that was passed in 1933. All one has to do is to go back and read those war acts which conferred upon the Executive far greater power over human beings and over property than anything that was done in 1933. But the Supreme Court has finally ruled that extraordinary conditions do not create or enlarge constitutional power! It is a very interesting statement on the part of the Court. . . .

Let's put the decision in plain lay language in regard to at least the dictum of the Court and never mind this particular sick chicken or whatever they call it. That was a question of fact, but of course the Court in ruling on the question of fact about these particular chickens said they were killed in New York and sold and probably eaten in New York, and therefore it was probably intrastate commerce. But of course the Court does not stop there. In fact the Court in this decision, at least by dictum—and remember that dictum is not always followed in the future—has gone back to the old Knight case in 1885 [sic], which in fact limited any application of interstate commerce to goods in transit—nothing else!

Since 1885 the Court in various decisions has enlarged on the definition of interstate commerce—railroad cases, coal cases and so forth and so on. It was clearly the opinion of the Congress before this decision and the opinion of various attorneys-general, regardless of party, that the words "interstate commerce" applied not only to an actual shipment of goods but also to a great many other things that affected interstate commerce. . . .

The whole tendency over these years has been to view the interstate commerce clause in the light of present-day civilization. The country was in the horse-and-buggy age when that clause was written and if you go back to the debates on the Federal Constitution you will find in 1787 that one of the impelling motives for putting in that clause was this: There wasn't much interstate commerce at all—probably 80 or 90 percent of the human beings in the thirteen original States were completely self-supporting within their own communities.

They got their own food, their own clothes; they swapped or bought with any old kind of currency, because we had thirteen different kinds of currency. They bought from their neighbors and sold to their neighbors. However, there was quite a fear that each of the thirteen States could impose tariff barriers against each other and they ruled that out. They would not let the States impose tariff barriers, but they were afraid that the lawyers of that day would find some other method by which a State could discriminate against its neighbors on one side or the other, or discriminate in favor of its neighbors on one side or the other. Therefore, the interstate commerce clause was put into the Constitution with the general objective of preventing discrimination by one of these Sovereign States against another Sovereign State.

They had in those days no problems relating to employment. They had no problems relating to the earning capacity of people—what the man in Massachusetts earned, what his buying power was. Nobody had ever thought of what the wages were or the buying capacity in the slave-holding States of the South. There were no social questions in those days. The question of health on a national basis had never been discussed. The question of fair business practices had never been discussed. The word was unknown in the vocabulary of the Founding Fathers. The ethics of the period were very different from what they are today. If one man could skin a fellow and get away with it, why, that was all right.

In other words, the whole picture was a different one when the interstate commerce clause was put into the Constitution from what it is now. Since that time, because of the improvement in transportation, because of the fact that, as we know, what happens in one State has a good deal of influence on the people in another State, we have developed an entirely different philosophy.

The prosperity of the farmer does have an effect on the manufacturer in Pittsburgh. The prosperity of the clothing worker in the city of New York has an effect on the prosperity of the farmer in Wisconsin, and so it goes. We are interdependent—we are tied in together. And the hope has been that we could, through a period of years, interpret the interstate commerce clause of the Constitution in the light of these new things that have come to the country. It has been our hope that under the interstate commerce clause we could recognize by legislation and by judicial decision that a harmful practice in one section of the country could be prevented on the theory that it was doing harm to another section of the country. That was why the Congress for a good many years, and most lawyers, have had the thought that in drafting legislation we could depend on an interpretation that would enlarge the Constitutional meaning of interstate commerce to include not only those matters of direct interstate commerce, but also those matters which indirectly affect interstate commerce.

The implication, largely because of what we call obiter dicta in this opinion, the implication of this opinion is that we have gone back, that the Supreme Court will no longer take into consideration anything that indirectly may affect interstate commerce. That hereafter they will decide the only thing in interstate commerce over which they can permit the exercise of Federal jurisdiction is goods in transit plus, perhaps, a very small number of transactions which would directly affect goods in transit. . . .

And so we are facing a very, very great national nonpartisan issue. We have got to decide one way or the other. I don't mean this summer or winter or next fall, but over a period, perhaps, of five years or ten years we have got to decide: whether we are going to relegate to the forty-eight States practically all control over economic conditions—not only State economic conditions but national economic conditions; and along with that whether we are going to relegate to the States all control over social and working conditions throughout the country regardless of whether those conditions have a very definite significance and effect in other States outside of the individual States. That is one side of the picture. The other side of the picture is whether in some way we are going to turn over or restore to—whichever way you choose to put it—turn over or restore to the Federal Government the powers which exist in the national Governments of every other Nation in the world to enact and administer laws that have a bearing on, and general control over, national economic problems and national social problems.

That actually is the biggest question that has come before this country outside of time of war, and it has to be decided. And, as I say, it may take five years or ten years.

This N.R.A. decision—if you accept the obiter dicta and all the phraseology of it—seems to be squarely on the side of restoring to the States forty-eight different controls over national economic and social problems. This is not a criticism of the Supreme Court's decision; it is merely pointing out the implications of it.

THE CHAMPION CAMPAIGNER

Roosevelt's counterattack against the Supreme Court marked the beginning of a Second Hundred Days. Throughout the long summer of 1935, the President bombarded Congress with messages for a series of vital legislative programs. When the weary Congressmen and Senators finally adjourned in late August, they had enacted Social Security, adopted the Wagner Act to guarantee collective bargaining for American labor unions, established work relief through the WPA, and passed banking and taxation measures that transformed the American economic structure.

This burst of reform legislation led to new attacks on Roosevelt's leadership. Businessmen, originally part of the New Deal coalition in the depths of the depression, now became bitterly critical; in 1935, disaffected Democrats joined with wealthy conservatives to found the Liberty League to spearhead the drive against Roosevelt. But the leaderless Republican Party was forced to settle for the little-known and lackluster Kansas governor, Alfred Landon, as its presidential candidate. Though Landon was willing to accept much of the New Deal, he was unable to shake the magnetic hold Roosevelt had established over the American people. When the Democratic National Convention met in Philadelphia in July, 1936, the delegates quickly renominated the President, and then, as columnist Raymond Clapper describes it, submitted in exultation to the Roosevelt magic.

RAYMOND CLAPPER, Watching the World

No one who was at the Philadelphia convention will easily forget the night at Franklin Field, which revealed Roosevelt, not merely the good political showman, but a master ripened into the fullness of his powers. It is not probable that many of us who were there shall experience anything like it again.

After a week of cheap, tinhorn ballyhoo which never rose above the level of a shoddy political war dance, a new spirit of dignity seemed to settle over the convention scene as it moved from the turbulent hall out into the evening calmness under the open sky.

Probably 100,000 persons were there, undoubtedly the largest political audience ever assembled in this country. In nearly 20 years of political reporting, I have never in any political meeting observed quite the atmosphere which dominated this night. The audience was not noisy, wild, nor hysterical, but it was sympathetic—deeply so, I should say. It listened. It seemed to understand.

Undoubtedly the arrangements contributed toward creating this mood. Instead of a brassy band blaring out "Hail, Hail, the Gang's All Here," the Philadelphia Symphony Orchestra played the final movement of a Tschaikowsky symphony. Imagine warming up a political meeting with a symphony concert. At first it seemed a foolish mistake. You can't pep up a political audience on Tschaikowsky.

Then beside the director's stand a small, white, doll-like figure appeared, Lily Pons, the Metropolitan Opera Company's little songbird. She bared her tiny throat to that vast crowd, to whom she must have appeared no larger than a snowflake, and sang the "Song of the Lark." One hundred thousand people sat in breathless enchantment. In that vast ocean of people gathered for a political hurrah, there was not the faintest stirring, not a sound save the muffled clicking of telegraph instruments in the press box. When she finished, dozens of political writers were on their feet joining in the deafening applause. Something had happened to that audience. It had been lifted, not to a cheap political emotional pitch, but to something finer. It was ready for Roosevelt.

He entered the arena, not to some raucous thumping air, but to the symphony orchestra's stately stringing of "Pomp and Circumstance."

Preliminaries were dispatched quickly and then Roosevelt spoke. It was his moment. It was now or never. This was the flood tide of his opportunity.

With a voice never more confident, never more commanding, never warmer in its sympathy, Roosevelt played upon his audience with one of the most skillful political addresses of our time. It was more than a feat of showmanship. It was a work of art which all of the political instincts of the Roosevelt dynasty were summoned to aid.

Economic royalists . . . We have conquered fear . . . Privileged princes of new economic dynasties . . . The spirit of 1776 . . . The flag and the Constitution stand for democracy, not tyranny; for freedom, not subjection; and against dictatorship by mob rule and the overprivileged alike. . . . The enemy within our gates . . . We cannot afford to accumulate a deficit in the books of human fortitude. . . . Divine justice weighs the sins of the cold-blooded and the sins of the warm-hearted in different scales. . . . This generation of Americans has a rendezvous with destiny . . . It is a war for the survival of democracy. I am enlisted for the duration.

Each word was loaded with the subtle power of suggestion, designed to sap the force of every attack from his opponents. Like the fathers of 1776, he was fighting not political royalists but economic royalists. Memories of his battle against fear and panic in March, 1933, were awakened as if to recapture once more the mood in which the nation hailed him as its deliverer. The Republican Party promises to restore the people's liberties. Roosevelt declares war for the survival of democracy. His mistakes are those of a warm heart. They will be judged leniently.

But the master's superb touch was still to come. As he finished, standing there with his mother and family around him, the strains of "Auld Lang

Courtesy of the State Historical Society of Wisconsin. Photographer unknown.

Franklin D. Roosevelt, 1936.

Syne" floated out over the audience. There was a pause. "I'd like to hear 'Auld Lang Syne' again," the President said. The audience joined in, these thousands, and Roosevelt, as old friends who had fought through the crisis together. Still a third time it was repeated. As a political theme song, it will be a hard one to beat.

In a moment Roosevelt was gone. The audience stood in its tracks for quite some time, as if still under the spell, and then quietly began to leave.

ROOSEVELT ATTACKS THE SUPREME COURT

Though Roosevelt won reelection by a triumphal majority in 1936, he still faced a serious roadblock in the Supreme Court. The justices had voided the AAA, the New Deal's effort to help American farmers, and the President now feared that the Court would throw out the Wagner Act, Social Security, and the other reform measures passed in 1935. Though many of his advisers favored a Constitutional amendment that would cut the ground away from the conservative justices, Roosevelt settled on a more devious approach. On February 5, 1937, without any prior notice, he sent Congress an elaborate plan to reorganize the federal judiciary. Commenting on the advanced ages of many of the Supreme Court justices and the backlog of cases awaiting decision, he asked for legislation that would allow him to appoint additional judges for each man over seventy. Thus under the guise of improving efficiency, Roosevelt planned to pack the Court with men sympathetic to the New Deal.

The President was not prepared for the hostile reception his message received in Congress. Conservatives viewed Roosevelt as attacking the handiwork of the Founding Fathers; liberals who sympathized with Roosevelt's objective were dismayed by his tactics. As the criticism mounted, Roosevelt appealed once again to the American people in a fireside chat on the evening of March 9, 1937.

FRANKLIN D. ROOSEVELT, *Fireside Chat*

. . . I hope that you have reread the Constitution of the United States in these past few weeks. Like the Bible, it ought to be read again and again.

It is an easy document to understand when you remember that it was called into being because the Articles of Confederation under which the original thirteen States tried to operate after the Revolution showed the need of a National Government with power enough to handle national problems. In its Preamble, the Constitution states that it was intended to form a more perfect Union and promote the general welfare; and the powers given to the Congress to carry out those purposes can best be described by saying that they were all the powers needed to meet each and every problem which then had a national character and which could not be met by merely local action.

But the framers went further. Having in mind that in succeeding generations many other problems then undreamed of would become national problems, they gave to the Congress the ample broad powers "to levy taxes . . . and provide for the common defense and general welfare of the United States."

That, my friends, is what I honestly believe to have been the clear and underlying purpose of the patriots who wrote a Federal Constitution to create a National Government with national power, intended as they said, "to form a more perfect union . . . for ourselves and our posterity."

For nearly twenty years there was no conflict between the Congress and the Court. Then, in 1803, Congress passed a statute which the Court said violated an express provision of the Constitution. The Court claimed the power to declare it unconstitutional and did so declare it. But a little later the Court itself admitted that it was an extraordinary power to exercise and through Mr. Justice Washington laid down this limitation upon it. He said: "It is but a decent respect due to the wisdom, the integrity and the patriotism of the Legislative body, by which any law is passed, to presume in favor of its validity until its violation of the Constitution is proved beyond all reasonable doubt."

But since the rise of the modern movement for social and economic progress through legislation, the Court has more and more often and more and more boldly asserted a power to veto laws passed by the Congress and by State Legislatures in complete disregard of this original limitation, which I have just read.

Samuel Rosenman, ed., *Public Papers of Roosevelt: The Constitution Prevails* (New York, Macmillan 1941), pp. 124-129. Reprinted by permission of the editor.

In the last four years the sound rule of giving statutes the benefit of all reasonable doubt has been cast aside. The Court has been acting not as a judicial body, but as a policy-making body.

When the Congress has sought to stabilize national agriculture, to improve the conditions of labor, to safeguard business against unfair competition, to protect our national resources, and in many other ways to serve our clearly national needs, the majority of the Court has been assuming the power to pass on the wisdom of these Acts of the Congress—and to approve or disapprove the public policy written into these laws.

That is not only my accusation. It is the accusation of most distinguished Justices of the present Supreme Court. I have not the time to quote to you all the language used by dissenting Justices in many of these cases. But in the case holding the Railroad Retirement Act unconstitutional, for instance, Chief Justice Hughes said in a dissenting opinion that the majority opinion was "a departure from sound principles," and placed "an unwarranted limitation upon the commerce clause." And three other Justices agreed with him.

In the case holding the Triple A unconstitutional, Justice Stone said of the majority opinion that it was a "tortured construction of the Constitution." And two other Justices agreed with him.

In the case holding the New York Minimum Wage Law unconstitutional, Justice Stone said that the majority were actually reading into the Constitution their own "personal economic predilections," and that if the legislative power is not left free to choose the methods of solving the problems of poverty, subsistence and health of large numbers in the community, then "government is to be rendered impotent." And two other Justices agreed with him.

In the face of these dissenting opinions, there is no basis for the claim made by some members of the Court that something in the Constitution has compelled them regretfully to thwart the will of the people.

In the face of such dissenting opinions, it is perfectly clear that, as Chief Justice Hughes has said: "We are under a Constitution but the Constitution is what the Judges say it is."

The Court, in addition to the proper use of its judicial functions, has improperly set itself up as a third House of the Congress—a super-legislature, as one of the Justices has called it—reading into the Constitution words and implications which are not there, and which were never intended to be there.

We have, therefore, reached the point as a Nation where we must take action to save the Constitution from the Court and the Court from itself. We must find a way to take an appeal from the Supreme Court to the

Constitution itself. We want a Supreme Court which will do justice under the Constitution—not over it. In our Courts we want a government of laws and not of men.

I want—as all Americans want—an independent judiciary as proposed by the framers of the Constitution. That means a Supreme Court that will enforce the Constitution as written—that will refuse to amend the Constitution by the arbitrary exercise of judicial power—amendment, in other words, by judicial say-so. It does not mean a judiciary so independent that it can deny the existence of facts which are universally recognized.

How then could we proceed to perform the mandate given us? It was said in last year's Democratic platform, and here are the words, "If these problems cannot be effectively solved within the Constitution, we shall seek such clarifying amendment as will assure the power to enact those laws, adequately to regulate commerce, protect public health and safety, and safeguard economic security." In other words, we said we would seek an amendment only if every other possible means by legislation were to fail.

When I commenced to review the situation with the problem squarely before me, I came by a process of elimination to the conclusion that short of amendments the only method which was clearly constitutional, and would at the same time carry out other much needed reforms, was to infuse new blood into all our Courts. We must have men worthy and equipped to carry out impartial justice. But, at the same time, we must have Judges who will bring to the Courts a present-day sense of the Constitution—Judges who will retain in the Courts the judicial functions of a court, and reject the legislative powers which the Courts have today assumed.

It is well for us to remember that in forty-five out of the forty-eight States of the Union Judges are chosen not for life but for a period of years. In many states Judges must retire at the age of seventy. Congress has provided financial security by offering life pensions at full pay for Federal Judges on all Courts who are willing to retire at seventy. In the case of Supreme Court Justices that pension is $20,000 a year. But all Federal Judges, once appointed, can, if they choose, hold office for life, no matter how old they may get to be.

What is my proposal? It is simply this: Whenever a Judge or Justice of any Federal Court has reached the age of seventy and does not avail himself of the opportunity to retire on a pension, a new member shall be appointed by the President then in office, with the approval, as required by the Constitution, of the Senate of the United States.

That plan has two chief purposes. By bringing into the Judicial system a steady and continuing stream of new and younger blood, I hope, first, to make the administration of all Federal justice, from the bottom to the top, speedier and, therefore, less costly; secondly, to bring to the decision of social and economic problems younger men who have had personal experience and contact with modern facts and circumstances under which average men have to live and work. This plan will save our national Constitution from hardening of the judicial arteries.

The number of Judges to be appointed would depend wholly on the decision of present Judges now over seventy, or those who would subsequently reach the age of seventy.

If, for instance, any one of the six Justices of the Supreme Court now over the age of seventy should retire as provided under the plan, no additional place would be created. Consequently, although there never can be more than fifteen, there may be only fourteen, or thirteen, or twelve. And there may be only nine.

There is nothing novel or radical about this idea. It seeks to maintain the Federal bench in full vigor. It has been discussed and approved by many persons of high authority ever since a similar proposal passed the House of Representatives in 1869.

Why was the age fixed at seventy? Because the laws of many states, and the practice of the Civil Service, the regulations of the Army and Navy, and the rules of many of our universities and of almost every great private business enterprise, commonly fix the retirement age at seventy years or less.

The statute would apply to all the Courts in the Federal system. There is general approval so far as the lower Federal courts are concerned. The plan has met opposition only so far as the Supreme Court of the United States itself is concerned. But, my friends, if such a plan is good for the lower courts it certainly ought to be equally good for the highest Court from which there is no appeal.

Those opposing this plan have sought to arouse prejudice and fear by crying that I am seeking to "pack" the Supreme Court and that a baneful precedent will be established.

What do they mean by the words "packing the Supreme Court"?

Let me answer this question with a bluntness that will end all honest misunderstanding of my purposes.

If by that phrase "packing the Court" it is charged that I wish to place on the bench spineless puppets who would disregard the law and would decide specific cases as I wished them to be decided, I make this answer— that no President fit for his office would appoint, and no Senate of honorable men fit for their office would confirm, that kind of appointees to the Supreme Court.

But if by that phrase the charge is made that I would appoint and the Senate would confirm Justices worthy to sit beside present members of the Court who understand modern conditions—that I will appoint Justices who will not undertake to override the judgment of the Congress on legislative policy—that I will appoint Justices who will act as Justices and not as legislators—if the appointment of such Justices can be called "packing the Court," then I say that I, and with me the vast majority of the American people, favor doing just that thing—now.

Is it a dangerous precedent for the Congress to change the number of the Justices? The Congress has always had, and will have, that power. The number of Justices has been changed several times before—in the Administrations of John Adams and Thomas Jefferson—both of them signers of the Declaration of Independence—in the Administrations of Andrew Jackson, Abraham Lincoln and Ulysses S. Grant.

I suggest only the addition of Justices to the bench in accordance with a clearly defined principle relating to a clearly defined age limit. Fundamentally, if in the future, America cannot trust the Congress it elects to refrain from abuse of our Constitutional usages, democracy will have failed far beyond the importance to democracy of any kind of precedent concerning the Judiciary. . . .

A LIBERAL DISSENTS

The Senate Judiciary Committee began hearings on the President's reorganization plan in mid-March. While the hearings were in progress, the Court released a series of decisions upholding key New Deal measures, including the Wagner Act and Social Security, with moderate Justice Owen J. Roberts voting with the new liberal majority. Despite this victory, Roosevelt continued to press for adoption of his judicial reform. His sharpest opposition came from a Montana Democrat, Senator Burton Wheeler, who appeared before the Senate committee on March 22. His testimony, together with the letter from Chief Justice Hughes which Wheeler read to the committee, proved to be decisive.

The debate in the Senate dragged on until July, when the death of Majority Leader Joseph Robinson of Arkansas, who had been leading the fight for the administration, caused Roosevelt to give up the struggle. Congress eventually passed a bill to improve court procedures, but Roosevelt's request for six new justices was quietly shelved. Although from this time forward the Court no longer opposed New Deal measures, Roosevelt never again commanded the loyalty and support of Congress he had enjoyed in the past. The New Deal had ended.

BURTON WHEELER, *Reorganization of the Federal Judiciary*

Senator Wheeler: Mr. Chairman and members of the Committee on the Judiciary: It is with some reluctance that I appear here this morning. I have only appeared because of the insistence of many of my colleagues who are opposed to the bill which is pending before you to increase the Supreme Court membership by six. I want it to be understood at the outset that anything I may say is not said because of the fact that I have any unfriendly feeling toward the President. On the contrary, my relations with the President of the United States during his term of office have been exceedingly friendly, perhaps more friendly than those of some other members of this committee. I supported him when he was first a candidate. I supported him in the preprimary campaign. I was one of the first members of the United States Senate to openly come out for his nomination. I traveled from one end of this country to the other making speeches for him in the preprimary campaign. I went to the city of Chicago 10 days in advance of the convention and worked for his nomination. There has never at any time been anything but the most cordial relations between us.

I have felt compelled to disagree with him at times. I disagreed with him on the N.R.A. I disagreed with him because of the fact that I did not want to delegate the powers of the Congress of the United States to the corporate interests of this country, in order that they might regulate themselves and fix prices contrary to the provisions of the Sherman antitrust law. I felt that act would be used to raise prices to the farmers of this country, and I felt that the benefits that labor might receive from it would be more than offset by the detriments which labor would receive and that the farmers of this country would receive at the hands of these monopolistic interests.

"Reorganization of the Federal Judiciary," *Hearings before the Senate Judiciary Committee*, 75th Congress, 1st Session (Washington, Government Printing Office, 1937), pp. 485-488, 498-499.

The Supreme Court of the United States held that law unconstitutional. I submit that there is not a lawyer of any learning or intelligence in this country but who would have to agree with the decision of the Supreme Court of the United States in that case.

I voted against the President on the so-called McCarran amendment, which sought to allow the W.P.A., or whatever it was at the time, to pay the prevailing wage scale to relief workers. I voted against him on the soldiers' bonus, and voted to override his veto. I disagreed with him with reference to the remonetization of silver. Notwithstanding those disagreements, I have always had and have at the present time a very high regard for the President.

I regret to have to disagree with him on this fundamental issue which confronts the Congress of the United States and the people of the United States at this time. I think I might say to the members of this committee that this proposal is not new to me. It may be new to many of the members of the committee. I appreciate the fact that the administration did not take into its confidence any of the members of the Committee on the Judiciary or the leaders among either the Democrats or Progressives; but a proposal was submitted to me at the last session of Congress to increase the Supreme Court. The proposal was not made to me by the President of the United States, and was made probably without his knowledge or consent, but it was made by men who were close advisers to the President and who are now working day and night to see that this proposal is enacted into law. I said to these young men at that time that I was opposed to it; that I thought it was wrong in principle, and that the American public would never stand for it.

And so I was shocked and surprised when I picked up the paper one day when I was in New York, not visiting the economic royalists, but visiting with people who were investigating economic royalists—the railroads of this country—and read the President's message to Congress and the proposed bill accompanying that message.

I might say to you at the outset that I have been severe in my criticism of some of the decisions of the Supreme Court. I have not agreed with the Court in many instances. I did not agree with it in the child-labor decision. I did not agree with it in the first income-tax decision. If you will pardon the suggestion, I think I have tried as many cases as most members of this committee, because for 20 years or more I was engaged extensively in the trial of cases, both defending and prosecuting in civil and criminal cases. I have had many courts decide against me, but I never for one moment entertained the idea that, because the court did not agree with me on what I thought was the needs of the times, that court should be increased in number with members who held my political and economic views.

So I say I was shocked when I read the message of the President of the United States and the letter accompanying it written by the Attorney General. I thought it was a serious reflection upon all the members of the Supreme Court, including one of the greatest liberals in the United States upon that Court, Mr. Justice Brandeis. I submit to you that there is no greater liberal and never has been a greater liberal upon the Supreme Court, with the possible exception of the late Justice Oliver Wendell Holmes. I have sat at the feet of those two men for many years and agreed with their policies, their economic and their judicial views. And to say that those two men, because of their age, had ceased to keep pace with the times, seemed to me to be extremely unkind, to say the least. I do not believe that age has anything to do with liberalism.

I do not know when this administration first became adverse to old men. My late colleague, Senator Walsh, when he was appointed Attorney General of the United States was 74 years of age. Carter Glass, who was offered a position in the Cabinet of the present administration, was one of the "elder statesmen" of this country. Senator Norris, Senator Borah, and Senator Johnson have been among the forward looking men in this country, and certainly it cannot be said of them that they have not had a vision that kept in touch with human affairs and the needs of the times.

I thought it was a reflection upon the Court when it was stated that the Court was behind in its work, and when it was very strongly intimated, if not stated in so many words, that such a condition resulted from the age of the members of the Court. I thought it was a reflection upon the Justices to say that this Court had been remiss in its duty in not hearing the appeals of litigants in this country.

I was not familiar with the details, but I went immediately, or had my office staff go immediately to the Attorney General's report, and there I found in the Solicitor General's report a statement to the effect that the Court was not behind in its work and, in addition to that, that the disposition of cases and of writs of certiorari was, in substance, in accordance with the best practices.

I likewise went to another great authority, a man who has been a great student of the Supreme Court. In fact, I went to two men. One was Mr. Felix Frankfurter, professor of law at Harvard University, alleged by many people to be the intimate and close adviser of the President. I went to a book which was written by him and Professor James Landis, in which they pointed out that any improvement of the Supreme Court is not to be had by adding to the membership of that Court.

It was only after the Attorney General of the United States came before this committee, as I understood from the newspapers without reading his testimony, and repeated the charges that he had previously made that I went to the only source in this country that could know exactly what the facts were and that better than anyone else, to see if it was possible to refute the reflection that had been made upon the Court and upon the integrity of those individuals who constitute that Court.

And I have here now a letter by the Chief Justice of the Supreme Court, Mr. Charles Evans Hughes, dated March 21, 1937, written by him and approved by Mr. Justice Brandeis and Mr. Justice Van Devanter. Let us see what these gentlemen say about it. The letter reads as follows:

Supreme Court of the United States
Washington, D. C., March 21, 1937

Hon. Burton K. Wheeler,
United States Senate, Washington, D. C.

My Dear Senator Wheeler:

In response to your inquiries, I have the honor to present the following statement with respect to the work of the Supreme Court:

1. The Supreme Court is fully abreast of its work. When we rose on March 15 (for the present recess) we had heard argument in cases in which certiorari had been granted only 4 weeks before—February 15.

During the current term, which began last October and which we call "October term, 1936", we have heard argument on the merits in 150 cases (180 numbers) and we have 28 cases (30 numbers) awaiting argument. We shall be able to hear all these cases, and such others as may come up for argument, before our adjournment for the term. There is no congestion of cases upon our calendar.

This gratifying condition has obtained for several years. We have been able for several terms to adjourn after disposing of all cases which are ready to be heard. . . .

But to say that you want to put six new men on the Supreme Court at this time for the purpose of meeting the needs of the time—well, I just want to talk about the needs of the time for a little bit. The needs of the time have not changed, in my judgment, with reference to child labor; the needs of the time have not changed with reference to price-fixing; the needs of the time have not changed with reference to minimum wages and hours, from what they were 20 years ago; because, if we had tried to do some of these things then, we would not be faced with the conditions with which we are faced today. After all, when you talk about the needs of the time, it is a very shifting idea. It is like shifting sands.

Perhaps one of the reasons why I feel so keenly about this matter is because of the war hysteria which I went through in my own State. If we had had a President of the United States and a Congress of the United States at that time who would have put 6 men upon the Supreme Court or 9 or 10 men upon the Supreme Court to meet what a lot of superpatriots thought were the needs of the time during that period, you would have suspended the Bill of Rights, and I would have probably been—I do not know where. But I had the legislature of my State come within one vote of condemning me, when I was United States attorney, because I would not prosecute cases that should not have been prosecuted under the law. We had a State council of defense, composed of labor leaders and farm leaders, and yet they condemned me because of the fact that I was doing my duty.

Needs of the time? I have suffered for my liberalism as perhaps few of you have suffered. I have not just become a liberal since I have taken office in Washington. I want to say right now—and you gentlemen know it as well as I do—that a lot of these official liberals around here, who have been leading the New Deal movement, and are now leading it, are now seeking fat jobs from the "economic royalists" to go to work in the caves of Wall Street. It is sickening to me to see some of these people who call themselves liberals.

Now, I do not want to see the liberal principles for which I have been fighting frittered away by any stop gap or expedient legislation. I am not going to see it happen if I can prevent it. If you put six men upon the Supreme Bench, what assurance can you have that the legislation which you pass will be affirmed by them? I voted against Mr. Chief Justice Hughes. He has been one of the most liberal members of that Court. I voted against Justice Stone because I thought he was a reactionary, and he has been one of the most liberal members of that Court. All the liberals voted for Mr. Justice Roberts. He turned out to be one of the more conservative members. . . .

I want to say to you liberals, and to you who call yourselves liberals or progressives, that if you put six new men on the Supreme Court of the United States, you are going to do more to hurt the liberal cause and the labor cause in the United States, in my judgment, than anything else that could possibly happen. You will turn back the wheels of progress. You are going to discredit the liberal movement and the labor movement in this country. You are going to discredit the Democratic Party. I say to you in closing that if you want to destroy the President of the United States, I know of no better way than to vote to give him six new judges and let him place them upon that Court.

3 / WORLD WAR II: SEARCH FOR A BETTER WORLD

INTRODUCTION

The First World War had witnessed the emergence of the United States as a world leader, but in the years that followed, the American people tried their best to escape their new role. There was never any question of returning to the isolationism of the nineteenth century; the United States was too deeply involved in international affairs to withdraw entirely. But the nation did refuse to assume the responsibilities that go with world leadership. The United States was the wealthiest country on earth in the 1920's, and though bankers and businessmen aggressively expanded American economic interests abroad, Congress raised rather than lowered the tariff, Republican Presidents insisted on repayment of the war debt, and in 1933 Franklin Roosevelt sabotaged the London World Economic Conference, preferring narrow economic nationalism to broader international efforts to fight the depression. In regard to security, the United States was equally disdainful. Rejecting the League of Nations in 1919, America refused to cooperate in efforts in the 1920's to strengthen the machinery of collective security. The sole American contribution to the cause of world peace was the Kellogg-Briand Pact, the treaty that piously outlawed war as an instrument of national policy, but carefully avoided any mention of how to deal with a nation that violated this pledge. The chief result was to usher in a new age of undeclared war.

In the 1920's, when the world was at peace and times were good, the American estrangement was mild and tentative; in the 1930's, depression and the increasing likelihood of war led to a more active rejection of international affairs. The reality of economic deprivation and unemployment made events overseas seem remote and of little personal consequence in the depression years. As domestic conditions improved in the mid-1930's, Mussolini's aggression in Ethiopia, Japan's invasion of China, and Hitler's demonic call for a greater Third Reich that would spread across most of Europe alarmed many Americans and intensified their desire to stay aloof. Fearful of a repetition of the sequence of events that preceded American entry into World War I, Congress passed neutrality legislation to prevent Americans from selling arms, loaning money, or traveling on the ships of nations at war. In early 1938, only the active intervention of President Roosevelt blocked consideration of a constitutional amendment which called for a nationwide referendum before Congress could declare war.

By the end of the decade, public opinion was slowly changing. Hitler's brutal conquest of Czechoslovakia, carried out in utter disregard of his pledges at Munich, shocked the American people. In the summer of 1939, they became increasingly concerned as Hitler made demands on Poland, negotiated a secret deal with Russia to avoid a two-front war, and then on September 1, let loose his Panzer divisions on the Polish plains to begin World War II. When the Nazis won victory after victory, overrunning Poland in four weeks, seizing Norway by a daring amphibious operation, and then driving the British off the continent and defeating France in a brilliant and overpowering display of armed force, Americans belatedly realized that a triumphant Nazi Germany threatened the security that they had so long taken for granted. If England fell and Germany gained control of the British Navy, the Atlantic could become the highway for an invasion of the Western Hemisphere. Under Roosevelt's gentle prodding, the nation responded to the danger. The President, acting on his own, gave Britain 50 destroyers to guard the flow of supplies across the submarine-infested Atlantic; Congress passed the Lend-Lease Act in March, 1941, authorizing the transfer of war matériel to all nations fighting against Germany and appropriating $7 million to pay the costs. When Hitler invaded Russia in the summer of 1941, Roosevelt, once he was convinced the Soviets had a chance of resisting successfully, extended Lend-Lease aid, and thus began the strange alliance that proved to be the key to Hitler's eventual defeat. By fall, American destroyers were helping to convoy supplies halfway across the Atlantic, and Congress had repealed virtually all the restraints in the Neutrality Act. America was fully committed to the defeat of Nazi Germany, but it took a final push from Japan on December 7, 1941 to end the pretense of neutrality and bring the United States all the way into World War II.

The war, as Gaddis Smith points out in his interpretive analysis, was viewed by the American people and conducted by their leaders as an all-out effort against a completely wicked and evil foe. Peace, according to the prevailing psychology, could only be achieved through the total destruction of the Axis powers. So intent were Americans on winning the war that they failed to prepare for the peace that would follow, beyond a naïve and idealistic movement to create a new world organization to replace the discredited League of Nations. Few realized that the shape of the postwar world was already being determined by the course of the war. The Russian victories in the East permitted the Soviets to create a cluster of satellites from the Baltic to the Adriatic; the occupation of France and Holland and Britain's exhaustion ensured the end of colonial empire and the emergence of a multitude of new nations in Asia, the Middle East, and Africa after the war. Even the seemingly unimportant refusal by Franklin

Roosevelt to accept Charles De Gaulle as an equal was destined to have a significant impact on the future of Europe. The leaders only dimly realized how important their wartime decisions were in influencing the future peace, but in retrospect it is clear that policies arrived at casually and often in haste by Churchill, Stalin, and Roosevelt at Tehran and Yalta gave rise to problems that would plague the world for decades to come.

The tragedy of American diplomacy during World War II lies in its misguided realism. Intent on avoiding the idealism that had undermined Wilson's efforts at peace in 1919, a pragmatic Franklin Roosevelt set out to achieve realistic goals. Instead of a peace without victory, he planned to destroy the enemy's capacity to wage war; instead of a sprawling and discordant peace conference likely to produce an inconclusive treaty, he wanted to restrict peacemaking to the Big Three who alone had the power to enforce a comprehensive settlement. Yet Roosevelt never seemed to realize that he was as much a prisoner of his illusions as Wilson had ever been. Sure of his own power of persuasion, he accepted Stalin as a loyal partner and failed to question Soviet motives; skeptical of British imperialism, he disregarded Churchill's blunt call for a return to a balance of power. And though he alone of the Big Three sensed the surging nationalism that was to transform China into a great power, he placed undue reliance on the leadership of Chiang Kai-shek. And so when he suffered a massive cerebral hemorrhage on April 12, 1945, he died still cherishing his vision of the Big Three ushering in a new age of lasting peace. Unlike Wilson, he was at least spared the anguish of witnessing the betrayal of his dream. New leaders and another generation of Americans had to deal with the problems created by the disintegration of the wartime alliance and the onset of the Cold War.

INTERPRETATION

The selection that follows is the first chapter in American Diplomacy During the Second World War, 1941-1945 *by Gaddis Smith. Professor Smith, a specialist in diplomatic history at Yale University, surveys the nature of wartime diplomacy, concentrating on the conflicting attitudes of Roosevelt, Churchill, and Stalin regarding the problems of war and peace.*

GADDIS SMITH, *The Nature of Wartime Diplomacy*

In the first half of the twentieth century man approximately doubled his population, quadrupled his industrial production, and radically altered the form of government over most of the earth. He also increased a thousand-fold his power to kill. Chronic, dangerous instability was the result. World security depended as never before on international cooperation, but suspicion and hostility were the rule between states. Some nations longed for peace but prepared fearfully for war. Other nations gloried in the use of force because amoral leaders preferred to steal what they were unable to build in peace.

At first the United States considered itself blessedly immune from the world's violence and suffering. In 1914 President Woodrow Wilson urged unconditional neutrality as the way to safety during the European war. Neutrality was impossible; the United States joined the war and tipped the balance of opposing forces sufficiently to bring about the military defeat of Germany and an armistice in November 1918. Wilson then said that the unconditional acceptance by all nations of the ideals of altruism, democracy, and the League of Nations was the only way to secure lasting peace. The American people, however, denounced the League of Nations, and other countries felt that idealism was scant protection against the economic and political chaos of the time. By 1936 the League was dying, and the American Congress was busy passing laws designed to preserve absolute isolation when the next war, ominously visible on the horizon, swept over Europe.

War broke out in 1939 when Great Britain and France declared war on Germany for invading Poland. Germany and Soviet Russia, in cynical col-

Gaddis Smith, *American Diplomacy During the Second World War, 1941-1945* (New York, 1965), pp. 1-19. Copyright, 1965 by John Wiley & Sons, Inc. Reprinted by permission of the publisher.

lusion, divided Poland and the Baltic states. Hitler soon struck to the west. Italy, stabbing France in the back, joined her Nazi ally. In June 1940 France fell. Hitler dominated western Europe and was planning to invade Great Britain. In Asia Japan intensified her war against China, entered into formal anti-American alliance with Germany and Italy, and prepared to extend her conquests.

American public opinion changed before the spectacle of unchecked Nazi aggression. President Franklin D. Roosevelt won support for military and naval preparedness and material aid to Great Britain. The United States became the "arsenal of democracy." Congress put aside the neutrality laws and passed the lend-lease program in March 1941. Three months later Hitler attacked Russia. Americans forgot their dislike for the Soviet state and extended aid. Roosevelt claimed that his aim was to keep the United States out of war, but by late 1941 the American people realized that the higher aim of checking Axis aggression might soon make entry into war inevitable. On the Atlantic the American navy was skirmishing with German U-boats. In the Pacific Japan might strike at any moment against the tightening web of American economic warfare. The blow came at Pearl Harbor, December 7, 1941. The United States was at war with Japan. Germany and Italy immediately declared war on the United States. The period of equivocal undeclared war was over.

Repeatedly and without success the United States had tried various unconditional approaches to peace and security: neutrality in 1914, idealism in 1918, isolation in the 1930's. Now the nation sought security by the unconditional defeat of the enemy. Since the enemy's existence was deemed the only significant cause of insecurity, men now assumed that a world consistent with American ideals and interests would emerge once the Axis powers were destroyed. Freed from enslavement and the fear of Axis aggression, all nations would embrace American ideals of democracy and peaceful conduct. If a misguided ally—Great Britain, for example— showed a tendency to stray from these ideals, a little friendly diplomatic persuasion would be sufficient to return her to the paths of righteousness. Absolute victory was achieved after four years and some effort had been made to change the behavior of allies, but Americans discovered in sorrow that peace was still unsecured. At the moment of victory in 1945 American leaders were on the verge of the realization that there were no unconditional solutions and that final, complete security in the twentieth century was unattainable.

The first diplomatic objective on the road to unconditional victory was coordination of the American, British, and Russian efforts. This was the task of the three heads of government: President Roosevelt, Prime Minister Winston S. Churchill, and Premier Josef V. Stalin. While the Big

Three at the summit decided grand strategy and ambiguously discussed fundamental objectives of the war, their subordinates bargained to allocate materials, provide shipping, build bases, assign troops, and develop new weapons. The great decisions were tied to the outcome of the lesser and all required international negotiation. Diplomacy, instead of retiring to the sidelines until the fighting was over, became indispensable to every aspect of the war and thus to the life of the United States.

In December 1941 the potential power of the United States was great, but the immediate outlook was disastrous, far more disastrous than the American public realized. The navy was crippled; the army was an expanding swarm of civilians without sufficient equipment, training, or experienced officers; and industry was only partially converted from peacetime production. Germany controlled western Europe and her armies were wintering deep in Russia. Who dared predict that Russia could withstand the onslaught through another summer? Elsewhere German armies seemed on the verge of driving the British from Egypt and taking the vital Suez Canal. At any moment Franco in Spain might snatch Gibraltar. Hitler could then close the Mediterranean, dominate North Africa and the Middle East while choking the United Kingdom with a cordon of submarines in the Atlantic. The western hemisphere would be directly threatened. In Asia and the Pacific the only limit to Japan's wave of conquest was her own decision not to move beyond certain lines. Half of China, the Philippines, Indochina, Burma, Malaya, the Netherlands East Indies, and scores of smaller island groups were in her grasp. Would she seize India, Australia, Siberia, Hawaii? What could stop her? Anything was conceivable.

Fortunately, American diplomacy responded less to the immediate military peril, which might have been paralyzing, than to an optimistic view of the nation's historical experience and to the buoyantly confident personality of the commander-in-chief, Franklin D. Roosevelt. Americans later were to be led astray by too much optimism, but, on the dark morrow of Pearl Harbor, optimism enabled men to begin planning for victory. Notwithstanding the pain and humiliation of retreat in the Pacific, attention was turned first to coordinating strategy for the defeat of Germany. This priority was maintained on the sound assumption that Germany without Japan would be as strong as ever, whereas Japan without Germany could not long stand alone.

The remembered experience of the First World War exercised a profound effect on the diplomacy of European strategy. Americans had misleading and rather happy memories. In the summer of 1918 large numbers of American troops faced the enemy for the first time. By November the war was over. Admittedly, circumstances were now radically different, but the experience of 1918 combined with a natural optimism led Americans to favor a strategy of direct attack as soon as possible (preferably 1942 but certainly 1943) across the Channel on the center of German power.

The favored strategy of Great Britain, also based in large measure on experience of the First War, was totally different. From the autumn of 1914 until the summer of 1918, while the United States remained neutral or in a state of preparation, Great Britain and France had seen an entire generation of young manhood die in the stinking trenches of the western front. For four years gains and losses were measured in yards, casualties in millions. Now, twenty-five years later, France was conquered and Britain, having narrowly rescued her small army at Dunkirk, stood alone in Europe. What Englishman could advocate a deliberate return to the horrors of the continent before all other methods of attacking the enemy had been exhausted and victory assured? Certainly not Churchill, who had in the First War been a leading, if unsuccessful, critic of the stationary slaughter of the trenches. In the Second War Churchill, expressing his own and his nation's convictions, argued tirelessly against a premature frontal attack. By no means all of his alternative proposals were adopted, but he did succeed in postponing the main attack until Anglo-American strength was overwhelming. Until that attack came, in June 1944, the competition between the two strategies—the massive direct assault versus shifting operations on the periphery—was a central theme in Anglo-American diplomacy to which all other issues were in some way related.

Russia, the third great ally, had only one possible strategy: maximum defensive pressure against Germany while urging the United States and Great Britain to open the second front in Europe without delay and simultaneously hoping that Japan, a neutral in the Russo-German war, would not attack in Siberia. The keynote of Russian diplomacy was surly suspicion compounded from Marxist-Leninist-Stalinist theories, Russia's warped memory and interpretation of events since 1917, and anticapitalist propaganda which Soviet leaders no doubt had come themselves to believe. According to the Russian view, the capitalist nations had sought to strangle the Soviet Union at birth from 1917 to 1920, but having failed had sought in the 1930's to save their own necks by turning Hitler against Russia. Current Anglo-American friendliness was, in Soviet eyes, the product of fear and the mask to a continuing hope that Russia would bleed to death. Postponement of the second front in Europe was simply an expression of this hope.

British and American leaders were angered and hurt by the Soviet calumny, but they differed in their opinions of how to deal with it. The British were relatively unruffled and stoical. Russian suspicions were a fact of life to the British. Russian demands for an immediate second front were understandable, but must be firmly refused until the time was ripe. The idea that Russia might make a separate peace with Germany, as at Brest-Litovsk in 1918, if she did not receive full satisfaction from the West was dismissed by the British as nonsense. Similarly, the British argued that Russian cooperation or the lack of it in the postwar world would depend on the power structure at the time and not on fanciful Russian gratitude for favors which the West could not afford to grant.

The American attitude toward Russia was not monolithic, but the dominant view, to which President Roosevelt subscribed, was conciliatory, indulgent, and tinged with the vague fear that an unappeased Russia might make a separate peace. Roosevelt and his closest advisers were far readier than the British to meet Russian demands, to see an element of truth in Russian distortion of the past, and to insist that the way to win Russian trust was to begin by trusting, and making every possible allowance for Russian unpleasantness. Furthermore, Americans proclaimed time and again that the final peace of the world depended not on the balance of power but on the closest possible cooperation with Russia. That cooperation could and must be assured while the war was still in progress. In short, Americans were pessimistic concerning what Russia might do if her wishes were not met, but they were essentially optimistic in their belief that Western attitudes could shape Russian behavior both during and after the war. The ramifications of this Anglo-American-Soviet interplay appear everywhere in the diplomacy of the war. They affected the debate over grand strategy and they touched such questions as shipping and allocation of supplies. They lay behind the formulation of war aims for Europe, for Asia, and for the nature of the United Nations. In that interplay can be found some of the origins of the Cold War.

American optimism extended to the war against Japan. This segment of the conflict remained second priority until the day of victory in Europe, but it absorbed an increasing amount of diplomatic energy and military resources. The ocean war on the Pacific was an American show and required few diplomatic arrangements, but on the mainland of Asia diplomacy encountered its most complicated, difficult, and frustrating task: the support of China. Of all the allies of the United States, China excited the highest hopes and ultimately provided the most crushing disappointment. The reasons are embedded in both Chinese and American history as well as in the hard realities of geography and military power during the war. Had the China of Chiang Kai-shek conformed to the romantic image cherished widely in the United States all would have been well. According to this image, which had flourished since the early nineteenth century,

China was yearning and able to follow in the ways of its one benefactor and friend, the United States. If China could only be freed from the bondage of foreign oppression, an efficient, modern democracy would emerge. The Japanese occupation was a serious obstacle on this road to freedom, but, according to American illusion, the full moral support of the United States plus whatever equipment could be spared would bring ultimate triumph and a united, independent China, one of the four great powers (along with the United States, Russia, and Britain) upon whose permanent friendship the peace of the world would depend.

Such was the dream. Before long it became a nightmare. First, as in other areas of war, came the conflict of basic strategies. Naturally, Chiang Kai-shek considered that the center of the war was in China and that he should receive as much American support as he needed in order to preserve his position against the Communists and other domestic foes and then defeat the Japanese. For the United States, however, world strategy placed China fourth in line as a recipient of supplies: behind Anglo-American operations in Europe, behind Russia, and behind the naval war in the Pacific; and at no time was the United States willing to see its limited aid to China used for any purpose except the waging of war against Japan. Next came the problem of geography and logistics. Because Japan soon controlled all the land and water routes into China, every ton of supplies had to be transported first to northeastern India and then flown "over the Hump" at astronomical expense. For equal expenditure the United States could deliver hundreds of tons of supplies to England for every ton delivered in China. Last and most important was the relationship of the irreconcilable conflict between Chiang's government and the Communists. Few Americans could comprehend the murderous bitterness of this antagonism or why the Chinese could not forget their differences, like good Democrats and Republicans in the United States, in the patriotic struggle against Japan. Throughout the war and for more than a year afterward, it was American policy to seek to unify the Chinese factions. Seldom has an effort been so futile.

But in the days after Pearl Harbor none of these dismal facts about China was understood. Roosevelt, his advisers, and the American people looked forward to a triumphant partnership. Thus, in every quarter of the globe American diplomacy, sustained by an optimistic reading of the past and an unreal attitude toward the present, began its wartime tasks.

A factor that influenced the style and results of American wartime diplomacy as much as the nation's optimistic interpretation of the past was the personality of President Roosevelt. He took crucial diplomatic negotiations more completely into his own hands than any president before or since. One way to examine Roosevelt's qualities as a diplomat is to compare him with Woodrow Wilson. There was nothing cheerful about Wilson's solemn crusade of Christian good against the forces of evil. Roosevelt, in contrast, always gave the appearance of a happy man, sometimes to the point of an unbecoming and inappropriate frivolity. Wilson found it hard to like the individuals with whom he was forced to deal; Roosevelt's first instinct was to like everybody. Wilson was solitary; Roosevelt loved the crowd, huge parties, the feeling of presiding over a numerous family.

Associates found both Wilson and Roosevelt difficult to work with, but for different reasons. Wilson enjoyed admitting that he had a "one track mind." For long periods he would concentrate on a single issue and ignore others of equal importance. Roosevelt's mind, in contrast, was trackless. He would dabble in a dozen questions simultaneously and acquire a superficial acquaintance with thousands of details in which Wilson would have had no interest. Subordinates found it difficult to keep Roosevelt's mind focused for long on any one problem. He loved to ramble and he seldom studied deeply.

Wilson was stubborn and opinionated; his dislike for advice that did not conform with his own conclusions often became dislike for the adviser. Roosevelt, on the other hand, had a compulsion to be liked. In dealing with others he would feign agreement with an opinion rather than produce disappointment. In domestic politics this habit of trying to please everyone caused confusion but no lasting harm. When Roosevelt's final views on an issue emerged, the man who had been misled could resign. Many did.

But this Rooseveltian technique had doleful results when applied to international affairs, where all the favorable conditions that Roosevelt enjoyed at home were missing. Disagreements in domestic affairs were over means, not basic objectives. All Americans desired a healthy economy, an end to unemployment, and a broadening of security among the whole population. There were no disagreements that could not be faced and thrashed out by reasonable men of good will. But how different the conduct of international affairs, especially in the emergency conditions of a world war. The nations in uneasy coalition against the Axis disagreed not only on the means of winning the war, but also on fundamental objectives for the future. Differences were too profound to be dissolved by geniality, and disgruntled allies, unlike subordinates, could not be ignored. Roosevelt either forgot these truths, or else believed that his power to make friends was so irresistible that all opposition could be charmed out of existence. He was wrong.

There was another unfortunate connection between domestic politics and Roosevelt's diplomacy. As the most successful American politician of the century, Roosevelt had a superb sense of how much support he could command for his domestic programs. But in his understanding of what the people would accept in foreign affairs he was timid and unsure. Often he shied away from problems that needed to be confronted—Russian treatment of Poland, for example—because he feared that publicity might lose votes. He overestimated the strength of isolationism and underestimated the ability of the American people to absorb bad news and undertake new responsibility. As a result Roosevelt sometimes gave the public a falsely optimistic picture of our diplomacy, especially in regard to Russia and China. He also gave the Russians the impression that the United States would probably withdraw into partial isolation after victory and that Russia, therefore, need not worry about American opposition to her postwar ambitions in Europe.

Two further traits of Roosevelt's character should be noted. The President had a small boy's delight in military and naval problems. Under the Constitution he was commander-in-chief of the armed forces and he set out to give practical as well as theoretical meaning to the title. Much of his time was spent in close consultation with military and naval authorities. Usually, he took the advice of the chiefs of staff, but on occasion he made important military decisions independently. Roosevelt's fascination with strategy and tactics intensified the American emphasis on military objectives to the neglect of those long-range political conditions to which military operations should always be subordinate. For example, in 1944 and 1945 Roosevelt concentrated so hard on the military objective of bringing Russia into the war against Japan that he seriously weakened American bargaining power in the settlement of permanent political objectives in Europe and Asia.

Finally, Roosevelt, unlike Wilson, was a pragmatist who lived in a world in which good and bad were somewhat mixed. He had no qualms about further blending of the two, and for settling by way of compromise for the best that seemed available. Roosevelt was no metaphysician losing sleep by wondering if evil means could contaminate a worthy end. He was more inclined to act and let the historians worry about the philosophical problems involved in his behavior. The historian must conclude, however, that much of Roosevelt's diplomacy fails of justification even on its own terms. Too often the means were questionable and the results worse.

Roosevelt's character produced the worst results in his diplomacy with Stalin; with Churchill the best. Churchill and Roosevelt enjoyed the closest personal and official relationship that has ever existed between an American president and the head of another government. It was not, however, a relationship of equality. Roosevelt had the power and Churchill the ideas. Churchill, acutely aware of the British Empire's dependence on the

United States, kept Roosevelt informed and entertained with an almost daily stream of incomparably lucid and persuasive letters and telegrams. Frequently, he traveled to meet Roosevelt in Washington, at Hyde Park, or in Canada. Roosevelt never went to Churchill in Great Britain, although both Roosevelt and Churchill did meet Stalin on or near his home ground. Churchill's sincere liking for Roosevelt, his understanding of the President's character, and above all the range and penetration of his intellect served the British Empire and the Anglo-American cause well. No other man could have won Roosevelt's approval to such a large measure of British policy. But sometimes Roosevelt and his advisers did refuse Churchill's requests. On those occasions Churchill gave way with a grace that was as uncharacteristic of his past political behavior as it was serviceable for the preservation of the even tenor of Anglo-American relations.

Roosevelt's personal relations with Stalin were the least effective aspect of his diplomacy. The President met Stalin's displays of temper, suspicion, and churlish obstructionism with redoubled efforts at conciliation. Early in the war he tried to please Stalin by an implied promise of an immediate second front, and later he remained silent in the face of barbarous Soviet conduct in Poland. Sometimes he tried to win Stalin's confidence by ridiculing Churchill and hinting at a Soviet-American alignment against British colonialism. In personal relations and in diplomacy it is unwise and dangerous to pretend to denounce a proven friend in order to ingratiate oneself with a third party. Churchill bore the humiliation manfully; Stalin was not fooled. He listened to Roosevelt's chatter, said little himself, and coolly pushed the Soviet advantage in Europe and Asia without regard to the idealistic principles of political liberty to which Russia, as one of the United Nations, had subscribed. Stalin acted on the assumption, which Roosevelt's words and behavior amply confirmed, that the United States would raise no effective opposition to hostile Russian expansion. By the time Roosevelt's policy was reversed after the war, the Russian position had been consolidated, and the lines of the Cold War drawn.

The results of Roosevelt's personal diplomatic contact with the proud and haughty leaders who ranked just below the triumvirate, Chiang Kai-shek of China and Charles de Gaulle of France, were poor. Chiang and de Gaulle were similar in many ways. Each claimed to represent a great power suffering from temporary adversity; each was quick to resent the slightest reflection on his personal prestige or the sovereign prerogatives of his nation. Roosevelt, however, treated the two leaders in opposite fashion, acting more in terms of his preconceived notions about France and China than the actual situation. The President was an infatuated captive of the myth that China under Chiang Kai-shek was one of the world's great powers and deserved to be treated as such. He even toyed with the idea of giving Chiang a voice in the settlement of European affairs. No amount of evidence concerning Chiang's maladministration, the disunity of the country, the strength of the opposition, or the inefficiency of the Kuomintang armies appeared capable of shaking Roosevelt's illusion, at least until the closing months of the war.

For modern France, in contrast, Roosevelt had acquired an attitude of contempt as extreme as his admiration for China. He considered France a source of decay in the world, a politically and socially sick nation which by laying down before Hitler and giving way to the Japanese in Indochina had forfeited the right to be respected. Roosevelt saw de Gaulle as a pompous adventurer who represented only a clique of followers and who secretly intended to assume the dictatorship of his country after the liberation. Ultimately, Roosevelt's attitudes led to severe friction with France and to bitter misunderstandings on the part of the American people when Chiang Kai-shek collapsed so ignominiously in his civil war with the Communists.

———————————

Although wartime diplomacy, pervasively influenced by the personality of President Roosevelt, dealt principally with military operations, one overriding question was always present: what kind of world did each of the three major allies desire after the war? Each power sought, first of all, a victory that would prevent recurrence of a war as catastrophic as the one in which the world was then involved. American leaders gradually developed among themselves some broad ideas on how this might be done, but they believed that their objectives could best be achieved if specific discussions concerning the future were postponed until the fighting was over. Assuming that no postwar problem could be as important or difficult as the defeat of the Axis and that there would be time enough after victory to make detailed arrangements, they were insensitive to the way in which the conduct of war can prejudice the results.

From the American point of view, there were several ways that the goal of postwar security might be sought. Isolation had failed and was now discredited, more thoroughly than Roosevelt realized. A unilateral armed *Pax Americana* in which every threat to security was instantaneously smashed by the exercise of the superior force of the United States was technically worth considering, but was not politically or morally tolerable. A *Pax Anglo-Americana* in which the United States and Great Britain together ran the world had appeal for some Americans, and briefly for President Roosevelt, but it, too, was not feasible. Roosevelt until 1944 favored a peace secured by the armed cooperation of "the Four Policemen": the United States, Russia, China, and Great Britain—in that order of importance. Little countries would be required to keep quiet and take orders. This concept had numerous flaws. A power vacuum would be left in western Europe where, according to Roosevelt, neither Germany nor France would again be factors in world politics. This would be especially dangerous if Roosevelt's assumption of an identity of interest between Russia and the West proved unfounded. In Asia there was considerable doubt whether the Chiang Kai-shek regime in China could survive, much less serve as a policeman for others. In addition, the outcry of small nations at being herded about by the great powers would be too loud to ignore in the United States and Great Britain, countries which prided themselves on respecting the rights of others.

Churchill felt that Roosevelt intended to relegate Great Britain to a position of undeserved and unrealistic inferiority while encouraging the disintegration of the British Empire, a development which Churchill resisted with skill and energy. The Prime Minister's own program for securing the peace was equally objectionable to most Americans. Churchill, a strong believer in the traditional British reliance on the balance of power, assumed that the fate of Europe still determined the fate of the world; that there was a basic conflict of interest between Russia and the West; that these differences should be faced openly and realistically; that western Europe had to be rehabilitated as quickly as possible with France and eventually Germany rejoining the continent's power structure; that the United States ought to cooperate with Britain in rebuilding Europe and be prepared, if necessary, to oppose Russian ambitions. Churchill believed that colonial peoples should receive increased self-government, but that the imperial powers should continue to exercise responsibility for their colonies in the interests of world stability.

Roosevelt abandoned the concept of "the Four Policemen" in favor not of Churchill's balance of power program but in response to the rising enthusiasm in the United States for the formation of a universal collective security organization, the United Nations. Secretary of State Cordell Hull, for example, argued that postwar antagonism between Russia and the West was unthinkable and that a third world war was the only conceivable alternative to full cooperation. Great power cooperation must be embedded in a world organization, a resurrection of the Wilsonian League of Nations. From 1944 onward Roosevelt and his advisers were fully committed to the early establishment of the United Nations as the only way to lasting peace. They became increasingly suspicious of Churchill's ideas. Ironically, many Americans came to believe that British imperialism and continued adherence to the idea of the balance of power were greater threats to security than anything Soviet Russia might do.

This does not mean that American leaders were hostile to Great Britain; rather they looked upon Britain as a misguided friend unfortunately wedded to dangerous and outmoded patterns of behavior. It was the duty of the United States to set this friend right for her own good and the good of the world. Russia, in contrast, was seen as the unfairly maligned giant, a bear too long harassed by an unsympathetic world. Russia had been so badly treated in the past that it was now necessary for the United States and Great Britain to make an extra effort to be warm and understanding. Roosevelt and many of his advisers believed that inwardly the Soviets yearned to be friends with the West, but were too scarred with unhappy memories to take the initiative. Russia's enormous loss of life in the war, approximately ten times Anglo-American losses, strongly reinforced the sympathetic American attitude. How callous it seemed to think ill of a nation that was suffering so horribly in what Americans thought of as the common cause of humanity against the barbaric Axis. In the face of this suffering, to treat Russia as a potential adversary, as the British were inclined to do, would perpetuate the atmosphere of suspicion.

While Roosevelt, Churchill, and their advisers privately wrestled with different theories for the maintenance of peace, the official public declaration of Anglo-American war aims remained the Atlantic Charter, a generalized statement drafted by the two leaders in August 1941, and subsequently accepted by all countries joining the war against the Axis. The Atlantic Charter denied that its adherents sought self-aggrandizement; it condemned territorial changes against the will of the peoples concerned, and favored self-government, liberal international trading arrangements, freedom from fear and want, and permanent security against aggression. Soviet Russia adhered to the Charter with the capacious qualification that "the practical application of these principles will necessarily adapt itself to the circumstances, needs, and historic peculiarities of particular countries." In other words, Russia would not be deflected in the slightest by the Charter from the pursuit of her own aims in her own way.

Roosevelt thought that Russia wanted nothing but security from attack and that this could easily be granted. Personally uninterested in theory and President of a country where ideological passion was out of style, Roosevelt tended to assume that national security meant approximately the same thing in Moscow as it did in Washington. Unfortunately, even the Russians could not say where the line lay between the normal requirements of national security and the imperatives of Communist ideology. Russia's minimum territorial objectives in Europe were clearly stated. They included restoration of the June 1941 boundary, which meant that Russia would enjoy the full fruits of the 1939 Nazi-Soviet pact, specifically the annexation of the three Baltic states, nearly half of prewar Poland, and pieces of Finland and Rumania. Germany was to be dismembered into a cluster of weak separate states and hunks of territory were to be given to Poland and Russia. Politically, Russia insisted on "friendly" governments along her central European borders. In practice this came to mean Communist regimes imposed by totalitarian means. In Asia the Soviets sought the expulsion of Japan from the mainland and the restoration of Russia's position as it existed at the height of the Tsarist imperial power in 1904. This would entail serious limitations on Chinese sovereignty in Manchuria.

The United States shared these aims as far as they applied directly to Germany and Japan, but everything beyond that was in actual or potential conflict with the Atlantic Charter. By postponing decisions on these conflicts, Roosevelt convinced himself that he was preventing discord with Russia without making concessions that violated the Charter. But inwardly the President was quite prepared to concede these Russian aims on the assumption that once they were attained Russia would feel secure and would cooperate without reservations in the new world organization.

In retrospect it seems clear that Roosevelt's basic assumption was false. The evidence indicates that Soviet leaders believed that their state and ideology could never be secure as long as the world contained any large concentration of non-Communist power. Defensively they could assign no limits to the requirements of security; offensively they were under a compulsion rooted in Russian history as well as Communist ideology to expand the area of their domination wherever practical. Russian security and expansion were two sides of the same coin. A collective security organization was for the Russians an instrument to be joined or abandoned solely in terms of its usefulness in advancing Russian power in the world of irreconcilable conflict between capitalism and Communism; it was not the beneficent organization of universal cooperation envisioned by the more idealistic Americans.

Historically, most wars have been accompanied by considerable diplomatic contact between enemies; the two sides test each other's determination and bargain quietly over terms while the guns are still firing. In the Second World War, the war of unconditional surrender, the United States engaged in little diplomacy of this type. Germany and Japan, however, carried on negotiations within their spheres which significantly influenced the outcome of the war. To generalize, the Axis lost through blundering many of the advantages gained by force of arms. Had Germany and Japan been as skilled at dealing with each other, with neutrals, and with conquered peoples as they were in launching military offensives, the plight of the Allies would have been far more drastic than it was. Instead, Axis diplomacy was one of the greatest assets enjoyed by the Allies.

Hitler and the militarists of Japan came to power because the German and Japanese people were dissatisfied with the conditions that prevailed after the First World War and found a totalitarian new order appealing. In like manner, Germany and Japan scored great initial military success because many of their adversaries lacked the will to take risks in defense of an international status quo which had not brought security, prosperity, or happiness. In order to exploit this advantage it was necessary for Germany and Japan to coordinate their activities and to convince the neutrals and the conquered that, as their propaganda claimed, the new orders for Europe and Asia offered genuine benefits for those willing to cooperate. They failed utterly on both counts.

In every war between coalitions one group seeks to drive wedges into the other. It was not necessary for the Allies to seek to separate Germany and Japan because they were never together, notwithstanding the alliance signed in September 1940. The two countries were profoundly suspicious of each other and withheld information with a fervor of secrecy more appropriate among enemies. The major, fateful decisions of each—Germany's invasion of Russia and Japan's attack on the United States—were made without informing the other in advance. Ultimately, these decisions meant defeat; perhaps it could not have been otherwise given the inferiority of the Axis in population and economic resources. But true coordination diplomatically arranged might have placed the outcome in doubt.

Geographical separation was, of course, a huge obstacle to coordination, but military action might have brought the two countries into contact. Far more divisive was ideological antipathy. Japanese propaganda stressed opposition to European imperialism and appealed to the idea of Asia for the Asians. It was thus most difficult to sympathize with the boundless growth of German power. Would Germany insist on acquiring new imperial status in the Far East? The Japanese could not be sure. Hitler's ideological dislike for the Japanese was even stronger. He was a believer in "the Yellow Peril" and found the spectacle of Japanese victories over white people most disturbing even when the whites were his enemies. In short, there was "a fundamental inconsistency in the alliance between Nazi Germany, the champion of the concept of Nordic racial superiority, and Japan, the self-appointed defender of Asia against Western imperialism." In March 1942, to illustrate this point, Hitler is reported to have indulged in the thought that it would be satisfying to send England twenty divisions to help throw back the yellow horde.

Few countries have ever been as brutally and selfishly nationalistic as Germany and Japan during the Second World War. They went to war to satisfy that nationalism and lost partly because their nationalism prevented their cooperation. Still less could they cooperate with smaller countries and colonial peoples who had no love for the Allies and who might have been made into effective collaborators if the Axis had tried seduction instead of rape. In Europe Hitler had an opportunity of winning support from anti-Communists in the Balkans, Poland, and the Ukraine. But he imposed slavery where he might have made friends. He could have had far greater support from Vichy France and Franco's Spain if he had decided to offer them advantages in the new Europe. Different diplomacy and military strategy could have brought Hitler control of the Mediterranean and all of North Africa. He then might have exploited anti-British sentiment in the Middle East and brought that sparsely defended and crucial area into his orbit. India was also susceptible to anti-British appeals and if India fell, Germany and Japan would be united in control of the southern rim of Eurasia. This would have brought incalculable adversity to the Allies.

Similarly, in Asia Japan had great opportunities as she conquered colonies whose populations longed to be rid of European rule. By acting genuinely in tune with their propaganda and granting some scope to the national aspirations of these peoples, the Japanese might have forged a chain of allies across Southeast Asia. In many places they did receive a tentative welcome at first, but soon the arrogance and brutality of conquerors produced bitter hatred. The colonial peoples knew that European imperialism was bad, but Japanese imperialism was worse.

GERMANY THREATENS AMERICAN SECURITY

When war broke out in Europe in September, 1939, the United States immediately proclaimed its neutrality. President Roosevelt did succeed in getting Congress to repeal the arms embargo section of the Neutrality Act and replace it with a cash-and-carry plan that permitted England and France to purchase war supplies in the United States, provided they paid cash and used their own ships to bring the goods back across the Atlantic. The chain of German victories stimulated increasing sympathy for England, and when the Nazi effort to bomb the British into submission failed in the fall of 1940, Americans were greatly relieved. They respected the courage the English had displayed, and they realized that Britain was the only power that stood between the United States and Hitler's plans for world conquest.

In early December of 1940, Winston Churchill sent a long message describing the state of the war to President Roosevelt, who was relaxing on a Caribbean cruise after his reelection to a third term. Near the end of this dispatch, the British leader warned that his country was running out of dollars to pay for purchases in the United States; unless Roosevelt could alter the cash-and-carry policy, Britain would have to stop buying war supplies. When he returned to Washington, Roosevelt announced a bold new policy to answer Churchill's need and yet avoid the granting of loans which would inevitably saddle the two nations with the troublesome issue of war debts. Announcing that his goal was to eliminate the dollar-sign, Roosevelt asked Congress to enact a Lend-Lease program whereby the United States would simply give Britain and her allies the arms and supplies they needed to wage war against Nazi Germany. Isolationists, still a powerful and articulate minority in Congress, protested vehemently, and the House Foreign Affairs Committee decided to hold public hearings before acting on the administration's request. The first witness to testify before the committee was Cordell Hull, a lean Tennessean who had been Roosevelt's Secretary of State since 1933 and who was a cautious but sincere internationalist.

CORDELL HULL, *The Lend-Lease Bill*

Secretary Hull: Mr. Chairman, members of the Committee on Foreign Affairs, we are here to consider a bill designed to promote the defense of the United States. I shall not discuss the technical details of the proposed measure, since that will be done by other departments of the Government more directly concerned with these matters. I shall place before you briefly the controlling facts relating to the manner in which the dangers that now confront this hemisphere and, therefore, this Nation, have arisen, and the circumstances which render imperative all possible speed in our preparation for meeting these dangers.

During the past 8 years, our Government has striven, by every peaceful means at its disposal, to secure the establishment in the world of conditions under which there would be a reasonable hope for enduring peace. We have proceeded in the firm belief that only if such conditions come to exist will there be a certainty that our country will be fully secure and safely at peace. The establishment of such conditions calls for acceptance and application by all nations of certain basic principles of peaceful and orderly international conduct and relations.

Accordingly, in the conduct of our foreign relations, this Government has directed its efforts to the following objectives: (1) Peace and security for the United States with advocacy of peace and limitation and reduction of armament as universal international objectives; (2) support for law, order, justice, and morality and the principle of nonintervention; (3) restoration and cultivation of sound economic methods and relations, based on equality of treatment; (4) development, in the promotion of these objectives, of the fullest practicable measure of international cooperation; (5) promotion of the security, solidarity, and general welfare of the Western Hemisphere.

Observance and advocacy of the basic principles underlying these policies and efforts toward their acceptance and application became increasingly important as three nations, one after another, made abundantly clear, by word and by deed, their determination to repudiate and destroy the very foundations of a civilized world order under law and to enter upon the road of armed conquest, of subjugation of other nations, and of tyrannical rule over their victims.

The first step in this fatal direction occurred in the Far East in 1931 with forceful occupation of Manchuria in contravention of the provisions of the Nine Power Treaty and of the Kellogg-Briand Pact. The equilibrium

"Lend-Lease Bill," *Hearings before the House Foreign Affairs Committee,* 77th Congress, 1st Session (Washington, Government Printing Office, 1941), pp. 2-7.

in the Far East which had been established by the Washington Conference treaties of 1921–22 became seriously disturbed by the setting up by forceful means in a part of China of a regime under Japanese control under the name of "Manchukuo." This control over Manchuria has been marked by the carrying out of a policy of discrimination which has resulted in forcing out American and other foreign interests.

During the years that followed, Japan went steadily forward in her preparations for expansion by force of arms. In December 1934 she gave notice of her intention to terminate the naval treaty of February 6, 1922. She then proceeded with intensified construction of military and naval armaments, at the same time undertaking, from time to time, limited actions directed toward an extension of her domination over China and involving disregard and destruction of the lawful rights and interests of other countries, including the United States.

In July 1937 the armed forces of Japan embarked upon large-scale military operations against China. Invading forces of more than a million men occupied large areas along the seaboard and in the central provinces. In these large areas there were set up puppet regimes which instituted systems of controls and monopolies discriminatory in favor of the interests of the invading country.

It has been clear throughout that Japan has been actuated from the start by broad and ambitious plans for establishing herself in a dominant position in the entire region of the western Pacific. Her leaders have openly declared their determination to achieve and maintain that position by force of arms and thus to make themselves masters of an area containing almost one-half of the entire population of the world. As a consequence, they would have arbitrary control of the sea and trade routes in that region.

Previous experience and current developments indicate that the proposed "new order" in the Pacific area means, politically, domination by one country. It means, economically, employment of the resources of the area concerned for the benefit of that country and to the ultimate impoverishment of other parts of the area and exclusion of the interests of other countries. It means, socially, the destruction of personal liberties and the reduction of the conquered peoples to the role of inferiors.

It should be manifest to every person that such a program for the subjugation and ruthless exploitation by one country of nearly one-half of the population of the world is a matter of immense significance, importance and concern to every other nation wherever located.

Notwithstanding the course which Japan has followed during recent years, this Government has made repeated efforts to persuade the Japanese Government that her best interests lie in the development of friendly relations with the United States and with other countries which believe in orderly and peaceful processes among nations. We have at no time made any threats.

In Europe, the first overt breach of world order was made by Italy, when, in 1935, that country invaded and conquered Ethiopia, in direct contravention of solemnly accepted obligations under the Covenant of the League of Nations and of the Kellogg-Briand Pact. In 1939 Italy seized Albania in violation of unequivocal treaty obligations. In the summer of 1940 she entered the European war on the side of Germany with the openly avowed purpose of participating with that country in a remodeling of the world on the basis of a "new order" founded upon unlimited and unrestricted use of armed force. Finally, without provocation, she has attacked Greece.

Throughout this period, the Government of the United States made known to the Government of Italy its anxious concern over the growing deterioration of peaceful international relationships. Both on the occasion of the Italo-Ethiopian controversy and during the period preceding Italy's entry into the European war, this Government addressed numerous communications to the Government of Italy in an effort to prevent new breaches of world order.

Germany, from the time that Hitler and his associates came to power in 1933, began feverishly to construct vast armaments, while following a program of repeatedly made and repeatedly broken promises as a part of a skillful diplomatic game designed to lull the suspicions of other countries. After employing for several months at the Disarmament Conference in Geneva tactics which have since become a distinct pattern of German policy—further demands as previous demands are met—Germany, in October 1933, rendered impossible any effective international agreement for limitation of armaments by withdrawing from the Disarmament Conference. There then followed nearly 6 years during which Germany, having determined upon a policy of unlimited conquest, moved inevitably toward the catastrophe of war.

Germany's work of preparation followed two main lines. The first consisted in the creation of armed force. To this end, her entire national economy was transformed into a highly regimented and highly disciplined war economy. Every phase of national activity became harnessed to the requirements of preparation for war. More than half of the national income was expended for military purposes. Foreign trade and foreign payments became rigidly controlled for the same purpose. The production of planes and tanks and guns and all the other countless accessories of a modern war machine became the immediate objective of the whole national effort.

The second line consisted of a series of steps directed toward improving the strategic position of Germany. The first of these was the occupation and fortification of the Rhineland in 1936, in direct violation of the Locarno Treaty, voluntarily entered into by Germany 10 years earlier. Then followed, in rapid succession, the absorption of Austria, in direct violation of pledges given by Hitler to respect the sovereignty and independence of that country; the dismemberment and final seizure of Czechoslovakia, in spite of Hitler's assurances after the seizure of Austria that Germany desired no additional territory in Europe and in violation of a solemn pledge to respect the independence of that country, officially given in October 1938; the annexation of Memel; and finally, on September 1, 1939, a brutal attack upon, and the devastation and partitioning of Poland.

The period of the war has witnessed the invasion and occupation of Denmark, Norway, Holland, Belgium, and Luxemburg, in violation of the scrupulously observed neutrality of these countries and in contravention, in the cases of some of these countries, of assurances expressly given by Germany of her intention to respect their independence and sovereignty; the invasion and partial occupation of France; the splitting up of Rumania and the German occupation of the remaining portion of that country.

These seizures have been accomplished through a combined use of armed force applied from without and of an almost unbelievable amount of subversive activity from within. Each of the invaded and occupied countries has been subjected to a reign of terror and despotism. By word and by deed, the invaders have made unmistakably clear their determination to impose permanently upon these unfortunate countries a rule of tyranny frequently reminiscent of the worst pages of ancient history.

So long as there seemed to remain even a faint hope of inducing the leaders of Germany to desist from the course which they were following, the Government of the United States neglected no opportunity to make its voice heard in restraint. It went further, and repeatedly offered its assistance in economic readjustments which might promote solution of the existing difficulties by peaceful means. All hope disappeared when the Nazi legions struck at Poland and plunged Europe into a new war.

Since then, it has become increasingly apparent that mankind is today face to face, not with regional wars or isolated conflicts, but with an organized, ruthless, and implacable movement of steadily expanding conquest. We are in the presence of forces which are not restrained by considerations of law or principles of morality; which have fixed no limits for their program of conquest; which have spread over large areas on land and are desperately struggling now to seize control of the oceans as an essential means of achieving and maintaining their conquest of the other continents.

Control of the high seas by law-abiding nations is the key to the security of the Western Hemisphere in the present-day world situation. Should that control be gained by the partners of the Tripartite Pact, the danger to our country, great as it is today, would be multiplied manyfold.

It is frequently said that there can be no danger of an invasion of the New World. It is said: As Germany has not been able to cross the British Channel, how can she cross the Atlantic?

German forces could cross the channel in an hour's time were it not for the fact that Britain, now thoroughly prepared and well armed, is fighting every hour of the day to prevent that crossing, and is fortified with every known device to repel a landing. The 20 miles of water between continental Europe and Britain are under British, not German, control. Were Britain defeated, and were she to lose command of the seas, Germany could easily cross the Atlantic—especially the South Atlantic—unless we were ready and able to do what Britain is doing now. Were the Atlantic to fall into German control, the Atlantic would offer little or no assurance of security.

Under these conditions our national security would require the continuous devotion of a very great part of all our work and wealth for defense production, prolonged universal military service, extremely burdensome taxation, unending vigilance against enemies within our borders, and complete involvement in power diplomacy. These would be the necessities of a condition as exposed as ours would be.

Great Britain is today a veritable fortress. So will this country be when our preparations for armed defense are completed. Most likely, however, it will not be by direct and frontal attack that the would-be invaders will undertake the conquest of this country, if they ever have a chance to embark upon such an enterprise. It is rather to be anticipated that their efforts would first be directed against other portions of this hemisphere, more vulnerable than this country, and then against us.

Subversive forces are hard at work in many American countries, seeking to create internal dissension and disunion as a now familiar prelude to armed invasion. Today these forces are held in check and are being steadily eradicated. But the entire situation would change if control of the high seas were to pass into the hands of the would-be attackers. Under such conditions, the difficulties of continental defense would demand from us vastly greater efforts than we are now called upon to envisage.

The most serious question today for this country is whether the control of the high seas shall pass into the hands of powers bent on a program of unlimited conquest. It is in this light, above all, that we should order our present-day thinking and action with respect to the amount of material assistance which our country is prepared to furnish Great Britain.

On no other question of public policy are the people of this country so nearly unanimous and so emphatic today as they are on that of the imperative need, in our own most vital interest, to give Great Britain and other victims of attack the maximum of material aid in the shortest possible space of time. This is so because it is now altogether clear that such assistance to those who resist attack is a vital part of our national self-defense. In the face of the forces of conquest now on the march across the earth, self-defense is and must be the compelling consideration in the determination of wise and prudent national policy.

For us to withhold aid to victims of attack would not result in a restoration of peace. It would merely tend to perpetuate the enslavement of nations already invaded and subjugated and provide an opportunity for the would-be conquerors to gather strength for an attack against us.

The protagonists of the forces against which we are today forging the instrumentalities of self-defense have repudiated in every essential respect the long-accepted principles of peaceful and orderly international relations. They have disregarded every right of neutral nations, even of those to which they themselves had given solemn pledges of inviolability. Their constantly employed weapons for the Government of their unfortunate victims are unrestricted terrorization; firing squads; deceit; forced labor; confiscation of property; concentration camps; and deprivations of every sort.

The most scrupulous observance by peaceful countries of legal concepts provides today no security whatever. Many nations which trusted to the integrity of their intentions and the care with which they observed their legal obligations have been destroyed.

I am certain that the day will come again when no nation will have the effrontery and the cynicism to demand that, while it itself scoffs at and disregards every principle of law and order, its intended victims must adhere rigidly to all such principles—until the very moment when its armed forces have crossed their frontiers. But so long as such nations exist, we cannot and must not be diverted—either by their threats or by their hypocritical protests—from our firm determination to create means and conditions of self-defense wherever and in whatever form we find essential to our own security.

The present bill sets up machinery which will enable us to make the most effective use of our resources for our own needs and for the needs of those whom, in our own self-defense, we are determined thus to aid. The great problem of democracy is to organize and to use its strength with sufficient speed and completeness. The proposed legislation is an essential measure for that purpose. This bill will make it possible for us to allocate our resources in ways best calculated to provide for the security of this Nation and of this continent in the complex and many-sided conditions of danger with which we are and are likely to be confronted. Above all, it will enable us to do all these things in the speediest possible manner. And, overwhelmingly, speed is our greatest need today.

AN ISOLATIONIST DISAGREES

The foremost isolationist spokesman to appear at the Lend-Lease hearings was Charles A. Lindbergh. The aviator-hero of the 1920's had avoided the public spotlight after the tragic kidnapping death of his son in 1934. He had taken a trip to Germany in the mid-1930's, and he came back impressed with the technological and industrial progress that nation was making under Hitler's leadership. After the European war began, he broke his public silence to speak out against American involvement in the hostilities. When the America First organization was formed in the fall of 1940, Lindbergh became its most effective orator, addressing mass rallies throughout the nation.

In his appearance before the House Foreign Affairs Committee, he spoke as an expert on air power to rebut the administration's contention that Germany was a threat to the security of the United States. He was frequently interrupted by Representative Charles Eaton of New Jersey, a Republican member of the Committee and a strong internationalist.

CHARLES A. LINDBERGH, *The Lend-Lease Bill*

Colonel Lindbergh: . . . I understand that I have been asked to appear before this committee to discuss the effect of aviation upon America's position in time of war. I believe that this effect can be summed up briefly by saying that our position is greatly strengthened for defense and greatly weakened for attack.

"Lend-Lease Bill," *Hearings before the House Foreign Affairs Committee,* 77th Congress, First Session (Washington, Government Printing Office, 1941), pp. 371, 380-381.

I base this statement upon two facts. First, that an invading army and its supplies must still be transported by sea. Second, that aviation makes it more difficult than ever before for a navy to approach a hostile shore.

In support of these facts, I cite, for the first, the minute carrying capacity of aircraft in relation to the weight of equipment and supplies required for a major expeditionary force; and for the second, the experience of the British Navy off the Norwegian coast and in the North Sea.

I do not believe there is any danger of an invasion of this continent, either by sea or by air, as long as we maintain an Army, Navy, and Air Force of reasonable size and in modern condition, and provided we establish the bases essential for defense. . . .

Mr. Eaton: Colonel Lindbergh, you have given us a very illuminating discussion of the possibility of an invasion of this country. Our main problem here is a bill which has been presented to us ostensibly for the aid of England. What are your views, if you care to express them, on the provisions of this bill? Are you in favor of it or opposed to it, or what?

Colonel Lindbergh: No, sir; I am opposed to this bill for two reasons. One, I think it is one more step away from democracy and the democratic system. And the other one is that I think it is one step closer to war, and I do not know how many more steps we can take and still be short of war.

Mr. Eaton: Divorcing the question of our aid to England from the provisions of the bill, are you in favor of our continuing to aid England to any extent?

Colonel Lindbergh: That is a very difficult question to answer, sir. I think that our aid, aside from the Neutrality Act originally, has brought us closer to war. I believe it has added to bloodshed abroad. I do not believe it will prove to have much effect on the outcome of the war. So that I was, and am still, opposed to our having left the provisions of the Neutrality Act. I am still inclined to believe that our encouragement of the waging of this war in Europe will not have very much effect on the outcome; that it will increase the hatred against us in Europe, in every country, bar none, when the war is over; and that it will have added to the bloodshed in Europe without much constructive result aside.

Mr. Eaton: So that, logically, you would be willing now to drop all aid to England and let the devil take the hindmost?

Colonel Lindbergh: This country having taken a stand that aid would be given to England, I do not believe we can justify simply dropping the position we have taken. I do believe that we should endeavor to bring peace to Europe and not encourage war in Europe. I believe that is possible for us to do, if we desire that.

Mr. Eaton: Will you indicate the steps that we could take toward peace under present conditions in Europe?

Colonel Lindbergh: I am not prepared to indicate what steps we should take. I should say that the first step is to create among our people a desire for peace in Europe. And I believe that when people fully understand conditions in Europe and what this war is leading to, peace will be desired.

Mr. Eaton: Colonel Lindbergh, of course, our people are nearly unanimous in their hatred of war, and that rests upon the soundest of reasons. The democratic system is impossible of continuance except on a basis of peace. It is the incarnation of the peace principle—the democratic system of life —in my judgment. But we have the announcement of Mr. Hitler and his echoes in Japan and Italy that they propose now to create a new world order—not a European order, but a world order—and they propose to do that by force. And they propose, when they have crushed the world by force, to place one race—their race—in control of the rest of us who will then be the producing slaves in the interests of our owners and superiors. Under those circumstances how can we possibly begin negotiations for a peace, unless Mr. Hitler has a change of mind, if he ever does have any change of mind?

How can we?

Colonel Lindbergh: I believe, sir, that no matter what is desired in Europe and in Asia—and that I do not know—we are strong enough in this Nation and in this hemisphere to maintain our own way of life regardless of what the attitude is on the other side. I do not believe we are strong enough to impose our way of life on Europe and on Asia. Therefore my belief is that the only success for our way of life and our system of government is to defend it here at home and not attempt to enter a war abroad, which is already in a position where I think it is of great doubt that we could have much effect upon it.

THE FOUR POLICEMEN

Two weeks after Pearl Harbor, Winston Churchill arrived in Washington to confer with Franklin Roosevelt on the conduct of the war. The two men quickly agreed that Germany was the more deadly opponent and therefore that the European theater of operations should receive priority. On January 1, 1942, the two leaders signed the Declaration of the United Nations, a statement affirming their determination to wage war against the Axis powers and agreeing not to sign a separate peace. Twenty-four other nations, including the Soviet Union and China, also subscribed to this statement and thus became charter members in the United Nations coalition.

In the spring of 1942, the Soviets were in a desperate situation. German armies had penetrated deep within Russia in 1941, overrunning the rich agricultural and industrial areas of the Ukraine and the Don Basin and reaching to within thirty miles of Moscow before the terrible winter cold halted the offensive. When the snow began to melt in April, Hitler began a new offensive in southern Russia, planning to drive to the Caucasus and gain control of the Baku oil fields. Though the United States was extending Lend-Lease aid, Roosevelt felt that it was essential to relieve the German pressure on the Soviet Union. On April 1, he approved a plan to launch a second front invasion of Europe in 1943, with provision for a small-scale emergency landing in France in September, 1942, if Russia was on the verge of surrender to Germany. With great reluctance, the British endorsed this plan. Roosevelt then asked Stalin to send a representative to Washington to discuss the course of the war. Vyacheslav Molotov, the Soviet Foreign Minister, received the assignment. After spending several days in Britain, he arrived in Washington on May 29. That evening he met with Roosevelt at the White House. Samuel Cross, the President's interpreter, made the following notes on this meeting.

Conversation between Roosevelt and Molotov

After the customary introductions and greetings, Mr. Molotov presented Mr. Stalin's good wishes, which the President heartily reciprocated. To

Foreign Relations of the United States, 1942 (Washington, Government Printing Office, 1961), III, pp. 566-567, 568-569.

the President's inquiry as to Mr. Stalin's health, Mr. Molotov replied that, though his Chief had an exceptionally strong constitution, the events of the winter and spring had put him under heavy strain.

Mr. Molotov described his flight from Moscow to London and thence to Iceland, Labrador, and Washington as not especially unpleasant or wearing. His plane had flown from Moscow to London direct, over the front and Denmark, in about 10 hours, but this was not particularly good time, as the same trip has been made before in $7^1/_2$ hrs. He explained that his military adviser had broken his kneecap in an automobile accident in London, and was, thus, detained in England. Mr. Molotov consequently regretted that he would have to act as both diplomat and soldier. The President remarked that none present were military specialists, but that Mr. Molotov would have an opportunity next day to talk with General Marshall and Admiral King.

Mr. Molotov expressed his intention to discuss the military situation fully. He had covered it in detail with Mr. Churchill, who had not felt able to give any definite answer to the questions Mr. Molotov raised, but had suggested that Mr. Molotov should return through London after his conversations with the President, at which time a more concrete reply could be rendered in the light of the Washington discussions.

The President noted that we had information as to heavy Japanese naval concentration in the Fuchia and Mariana Islands, but that we could not tell as yet whether they were directed against Australia, Hawaii, Alaska, or perhaps Kamchatka. Mr. Molotov said he was not informed about this, but he had no doubt the Japanese would do anything in their power to intimidate the Soviets.

To Mr. Molotov's remark that Hitler was the chief enemy, the President noted his agreement and mentioned his repeated statements to the Pacific Conference that we should remain on the defensive in the Pacific until the European front was cleared up. It had been difficult, he added, to put this view across, but, in his opinion it was now accepted. . . .

While serving cocktails, the President discussed at length certain basic considerations on post-war organization. Mr. Churchill (he said) had expressed some idea of reestablishing a post-war international organization which was in effect a revived League of Nations. The President had given Mr. Churchill his own opinion that such an organization would be impractical, because too many nations would be involved. The President conceived it the duty of the four major United Nations (Britain, U.S., U.S.S.R., and China, provided the last achieves a unified central government, opposite which there was still a question-mark) to act as the policemen of the world. The first step was general disarmament. But the four major nations would maintain sufficient armed forces to impose peace, together with inspection privileges which would guard against the sort of clandestine rearmament in which Germany had notoriously engaged during the prewar years. If any nation menaced the peace, it could be blockaded and then if still recalcitrant, bombed. The President added that which concerned him was the establishment of a peace which would last 25 years, at least the lifetime of the present generation. He and Mr. Stalin were over 60, Mr. Molotov 53; his aim was thus peace in our time. He thought that all other nations save the Big Four should be disarmed (Germany, Japan, France, Spain, Belgium, Netherlands, Scandinavia, Turkey, Rumania, Hungary, Poland, Czechoslovakia, etc.).

Mr. Molotov remarked that this might be a bitter blow to the prestige of Poland and Turkey. "The Turks," he added, "are an extremely pretentious people." He also inquired about the reestablishment of France as a great power. The President replied that might perhaps be possible within 10 or 20 years. He added that other nations might eventually be accepted progressively at various times among the guarantors of peace whenever the original guarantors were satisfied of their reliability. This might be peace by dictation, but his hope was that it might be so administered that the peoples of the previous aggressor nations might eventually come to see that they have infinitely more to gain from permanent peace than from periodically recurrent wars.

Mr. Molotov observed warmly that the President's ideas for the preservation of mutual peace would be sympathetically viewed by the Soviet government and people.

THE PROMISE OF A SECOND FRONT

The next day, May 30, Molotov and Roosevelt conferred again, with the American military leaders, General George C. Marshall and Admiral Ernest J. King, on hand to discuss ways in which the United States could help the beleaguered Russians. Again Samuel Cross kept minutes of the conversations.

Conversation between Roosevelt and Molotov

After a brief private conference between the President and Mr. Molotov, conversations were resumed at 11 A.M. The President asked Admiral King whether there was any special news from the Pacific. The Admiral replied that there was nothing of importance save some momentary disagreement between General MacArthur and Admiral Nimitz as to an operation against the Solomon Islands. Admiral King thought this difference was due to a misunderstanding, since Admiral Nimitz had in mind a specific project for destruction of installations rather than anything like a permanent occupation.

Opening the general discussion, the President remarked to Admiral King and General Marshall that he first wished to place them *au courant* with the questions Mr. Molotov had raised, and he hoped that Mr. Molotov himself would then put the situation before them in detail. Mr. Molotov, the President continued, had just come from London, where he had been discussing with the British authorities the problem of a second (invasion) front in Western Europe. He had, the President added, been politely received, but had as yet obtained no positive commitment from the British. There was no doubt that on the Russian front the Germans had enough superiority in aircraft and mechanized equipment to make the situation precarious. The Soviets wished the Anglo-American combination to land sufficient combat troops on the continent to draw off 40 German divisions from the Soviet front. We appreciated, he continued, the difficulties of the situation and viewed the outlook as serious. We regarded it as our obligation to help the Soviets to the best of our ability, even if the extent of this aid was for the moment doubtful. That brought up the question, what we can do even if the prospects for permanent success might not be especially rosy. Most of our difficulties lay in the realm of ocean transport, and he would in this connection merely remark that getting any one convoy through to Murmansk was already a major naval operation. The President then suggested that Mr. Molotov should treat the subject in such detail as suited his convenience.

Mr. Molotov thereupon remarked that, though the problem of the second front was both military and political, it was predominantly political. There was an essential difference between the situation in 1942 and what it might be in 1943. In 1942 Hitler was the master of all Europe save a few minor countries. He was the chief enemy of everyone. To be sure, as was devoutly to be hoped, the Russians might hold and fight on all through 1942. But it was only right to look at the darker side of the picture. On the basis of his continental dominance, Hitler might throw in such reinforcements in manpower and material that the Red Army might *not* be able to hold out against the Nazis. Such a development would produce a serious situation which we must face. The Soviet front would become secondary, the Red Army would be weakened, and Hitler's strength would be correspondingly greater, since he would have at his disposal not only more troops, but also the foodstuffs and raw materials of the Ukraine and the oil-wells of the Caucasus. In such circumstances the outlook would be much less favorable for all hands, and he would not pretend that such developments were all outside the range of possibility. The war would thus become tougher and longer. The merit of a new front in 1942 depended on the prospects of Hitler's further advantage, hence the establishment of such a front should not be postponed. The decisive element in the whole problem lay in the question, when are the prospects better for the United Nations: in 1942 or in 1943?

Amplifying his remarks, Mr. Molotov observed that the forces on the Soviet front were large, and, objectively speaking, the balance in quantity of men, aviation, and mechanized equipment was slightly in Hitler's favor. Nevertheless, the Russians were reasonably certain they could hold out. This was the most optimistic prospect, and the Soviet morale was as yet unimpaired. But the main danger lay in the probability that Hitler would try to deal the Soviet Union a mighty crushing blow. If, then, Great Britain and the United States, as allies, were to create a new front and to draw off 40 German divisions from the Soviet front, the ratio of strength would be so altered that the Soviets could either beat Hitler this year or insure beyond question his ultimate defeat.

Mr. Molotov therefore put this question frankly: could we undertake such offensive action as would draw off 40 German divisions which would be, to tell the truth, distinctly second-rate outfits? If the answer should be in the affirmative, the war would be decided in 1942. If negative, the Soviets would fight on alone, doing their best, and no man would expect more from them than that. He had not, Mr. Molotov added, received any positive answer in London. Mr. Churchill had proposed that he should return through London on his homeward journey from Washington, and had promised Mr. Molotov a more concrete answer on his second visit. Mr. Molotov admitted he realized that the British would have to bear the brunt of the action if a second front were created, but he also was cognizant of the role the United States plays and what influence this country exerts in questions of major strategy. Without in any way minimizing the risks entailed by a second front action this summer, Mr. Molotov declared his government wanted to know in frank terms what position we take on the question of a second front, and whether we were prepared to establish one. He requested a straight answer.

The difficulties, Mr. Molotov urged, would not be any less in 1943. The chances of success were actually better at present while the Russians still have a solid front. "If you postpone your decision," he said, "you will have eventually to bear the brunt of the war, and if Hitler becomes the undisputed master of the continent, next year will unquestionably be tougher than this one."

The President then put to General Marshall the query whether developments were clear enough so that we could say to Mr. Stalin that we are preparing a second front. "Yes," replied the General. The President then authorized Mr. Molotov to inform Mr. Stalin that we expect the formation of a second front this year.

FIRST MEETING OF THE BIG TWO

The Second Front did not materialize in 1942. During the summer, the British suggested that instead of an emergency landing in France the United States and Britain land in French North Africa in order to drive General Erwin Rommel's Afrika Korps out of Libya and win control of the Mediterranean. Roosevelt reluctantly agreed, since this seemed to be the only way American troops could be put into action against Germany in 1942. Ignoring General Charles de Gaulle who had formed a Free French Committee in London, the United States relied on General Henri Giraud to help win over the French garrison in Algeria and Morocco. Giraud proved to be a poor choice, but a last minute deal with Admiral Darlan, the vice-premier of Vichy France who happened to be in North Africa, halted the French resistance and insured the success of the invasion. The campaign against Rommel was slow in developing, but finally in May the combined Anglo-American armies defeated the Germans in Tunisia. Then, following a policy decision reached by Roosevelt and Churchill at the Casablanca conference in January, the Allied forces invaded Sicily and finally the mainland of Italy in the Summer of 1943. These operations

Courtesy of the State Historical Society of Wisconsin and the Office of War Information.

War posters, combat casualties: World War II.

toppled Mussolini's government, but German troops quickly overran much of Italy, and a long and exhausting campaign ensued. Meanwhile, the Second Front in France was deferred until 1944, to the intense disappointment and growing suspicion of the Soviet Union.

In the east, the decisive battle was fought at Stalingrad. In the fall of 1942, the German army was stopped at this strategic point on the Volga. The battle raged for several months, but finally the Soviets encircled Field Marshall Paulus' entire army and effectively halted the German invasion of Russia. From this time on, Russia had the strategic initiative as Stalin launched a massive counterattack that gradually drove the Germans off Russian soil.

The Allied victories made the need for diplomatic coordination more essential than ever. In October, 1943, Cordell Hull flew to Moscow to attend a Foreign Ministers Conference. The diplomats agreed on a declaration calling for a new world organization for peace at the war's end, and they made the arrangements for the first Big Three conference, to take place at Tehran in late November.

On the way to this summit conference, Roosevelt stopped off in Cairo to confer with Churchill and Chiang Kai-shek about the war against Japan in the Far East. Then Roosevelt and Churchill continued on to Tehran, arriving on November 27. The next morning, the President had a private meeting with Joseph Stalin prior to the opening of the conference. Charles Bohlen, an experienced State Department officer and expert on Russia, served as interpreter and made the following notes on the conversation.

Conversation between Roosevelt and Stalin at Tehran

The President greeted Marshal Stalin when he entered with "I am glad to see you. I have tried for a long time to bring this about."

Marshal Stalin, after suitable expression of pleasure at meeting the President, said that he was to blame for the delay in this meeting; that he had been very occupied because of military matters.

The President inquired as to the situation on the Soviet battlefront.

Marshal Stalin answered that on part of the front, the situation was not too good; that the Soviets had lost Zhitomir and were about to lose

Foreign Relations of the United States: The Conferences at Cairo and Tehran, 1943 (Washington, Government Printing Office, 1961), pp. 483-486.

Koresten [Korosten]—the latter an important railroad center for which the capture of Gomel could not compensate. He added that the Germans have brought a new group of divisions to this area and were exercising strong pressure on the Soviet front.

The President then inquired whether or not the initiative remained with the Soviet forces.

Marshal Stalin replied that, with the exception of the sector which he had just referred to, the initiative still remains with the Soviet Armies, but that the situation was so bad that only in the Ukraine was it possible to take offensive operations.

The President said that he wished that it were within his power to bring about the removal of 30 or 40 German divisions from the Eastern front and that that question, of course, was one of the things he desired to discuss here in Tehran.

Marshal Stalin said it would be of great value if such a transfer of German divisions could be brought about.

The President then said that another subject that he would like to talk over with Marshal Stalin was the possibility that after the war a part of the American-British merchant fleet which, at the end of the war, would be more than either nation could possibly utilize, be made available to the Soviet Union.

Marshal Stalin replied that an adequate merchant fleet would be of great value, not only to the Soviet Union, but for the development of relations between the Soviet Union and the United States after the war, which he hoped would be greatly expanded. He said, in reply to the President's question, that if equipment were sent to the Soviet Union from the United States, a plentiful supply of the raw materials from that country could be made available to the United States.

The Conference then turned to the Far East.

The President said that he had had an interesting conversation with Chiang Kai-shek in Cairo, on the general subject of China.

Marshal Stalin remarked that the Chinese have fought very badly but, in his opinion, it was the fault of the Chinese leaders.

The President informed Marshal Stalin that we were now supplying and training 30 Chinese divisions for operations in Southern China and were proposing to continue the same process for 30 additional divisions. He added that there was a new prospect of an offensive operation through North Burma to link up with China in Southern Yun[n]an and that these operations would be under the command of Lord Louis Mountbatten.

Marshal Stalin then inquired as to the situation in the Lebanon.

The President gave a brief description of the background and events leading up to the recent clashes, and in reply to Marshal Stalin's question said that it had been entirely due to the attitude of the French Committee and General De Gaulle.

Marshal Stalin said he did not know General De Gaulle personally, but frankly, in his opinion, he was very unreal in his political activities. He explained that General De Gaulle represented the soul of sympathetic France, whereas, the real physical France engaged under Petain in helping our common enemy Germany, by making available French ports, materials, machines, etc., for the German war effort. He said the trouble with De Gaulle was that this [his?] movement had no communication with the physical France, which, in his opinion, should be punished for its attitude during this war. De Gaulle acts as though he were the head of a great state, whereas, in fact, it actually commands little power.

The President agreed and said that in the future, no Frenchman over 40, and particularly no Frenchman who had ever taken part in the present French Government, should be allowed to return to position in the future. He said that General Giraud was a good old military type, but with no administrative or political sense, whatsoever. He added that there were approximately 11 French divisions, partly composed of Algerians and other North Africans, in training in North Africa.

Marshal Stalin expatiated at length on the French ruling classes and he said, in his opinion, they should not be entitled to share in any of the benefits of the peace, in view of their past record of collaboration with Germany.

The President said that Mr. Churchill was of the opinion that France would be very quickly reconstructed as a strong nation, but he did not personally share this view since he felt that many years of honest labor would be necessary before France would be reestablished. He said the first necessity for the French, not only for the Government but the people as well, was to become honest citizens.

Marshal Stalin agreed and went on to say that he did not propose to have the Allies shed blood to restore Indochina, for example, to the old French colonial rule. He said that the recent events in the Lebanon made public service the first step toward the independence of people who had formerly been colonial subjects. He said that in the war against Japan, in his opinion, that in addition to military missions, it was necessary to fight the Japanese in the political sphere as well, particularly in view of the fact that the Japanese had granted at least nominal independence to certain colonial areas. He repeated that France should not get back Indochina and that the French must pay for their criminal collaboration with Germany.

The President said he was 100% in agreement with Marshal Stalin and remarked that after 100 years of French rule in Indochina, the inhabitants were worse off than they had been before. He said that Chiang Kai-shek had told him China had no designs on Indochina but the people of Indochina were not yet ready for independence, to which he had replied that when the United States acquired the Philippines, the inhabitants were not ready for independence which would be granted without qualification upon the end of the war against Japan. He added that he had discussed with Chiang Kai-shek the possibility of a system of trusteeship for Indochina which would have the task of preparing the people for independence within a definite period of time, perhaps 20 to 30 years.

Marshal Stalin completely agreed with this view.

The President went on to say that Mr. Hull had taken to the Moscow Conference a document which he (the President) had drawn up for the purpose of a National [International?] Committee to visit, every year, the colonies of all nations and through use of instrumentalities of public opinion to correct any abuse that they find.

Marshal Stalin said he saw merit in this idea.

The President continued on the subject of colonial possessions, but he felt it would be better not to discuss the question of India with Mr. Churchill, since the latter had no solution of that question, and merely proposed to defer the entire question to the end of the war.

Marshal Stalin agreed that this was a sore spot with the British.

The President said that at some future date, he would like to talk with Marshal Stalin on the question of India; that he felt that the best solution would be reform from the bottom, somewhat on the Soviet line.

Marshal Stalin replied that the India question was a complicated one, with different levels of culture and the absence of relationship in the castes. He added that reform from the bottom would mean revolution.

It was then 4 o'clock and time for the General Meeting.

The President, in conclusion, stated that an additional reason why he was glad to be in this house was that of affording the opportunity of meeting Marshal Stalin more frequently in completely informal and different [sic] circumstances.

THE BIG THREE AND THE POSTWAR WORLD

For the next four days, Roosevelt, Churchill, and Stalin conferred in formal conference sessions with their advisers, in more informal dinners marked by frequent vodka toasts, and in private conversations. The Big Three agreed on final plans for the Second Front in the spring of 1944, with Stalin assuring the Americans and the British that he would launch a great offensive from the East to keep the Germans from massing in France. There was less harmony on political topics. The leaders discussed the future of Germany at length without reaching any consensus. The most serious problem, however, was the fate of Poland.

In the fall of 1939, Russian troops had entered eastern Poland while the Germans invaded from the west, and as a result, Russia had regained control over a large portion of Poland that once had been part of Czarist Russia. After the fall of Poland, a Polish government in exile had been established in London, and this group asked the British to help them convince the Russians that the postwar boundary of Poland should include the territory that Soviets had seized in 1939. Stalin was determined to retain the area he had taken, and in April 1943, after the Polish government charged Moscow with the murder of 8000 Polish officers at Katyn, the Soviet Union broke off relations and began forming a Communist-dominated Polish committee in Russia.

At a dinner meeting on the second day of the Tehran conference, Churchill, Roosevelt, and Stalin ranged broadly over the postwar problems that now began to loom as potentially divisive issues for the wartime coalition. Bohlen once again kept minutes of the discussion.

Conversation between Roosevelt, Churchill, and Stalin at Tehran

During the first part of the dinner the conversation between the President and Marshal Stalin was general in character and dealt for the most part with a suitable place for the next meeting. Fairbanks seemed to be considered by both the most suitable spot.

Foreign Relations of the United States, Tehran, pp. 509-512.

Reprinted by permission of Brown Brothers.

Stalin, Roosevelt, and Churchill during the Tehran conference, 1943

Marshal Stalin then raised the question of the future of France. He described in considerable length the reasons why, in his opinion, France deserved no considerate treatment from the Allies and, above all, had no right to retain her former empire. He said that the entire French ruling class was rotten to the core and had delivered over France to the Germans and that, in fact, France was now actively helping our enemies. He therefore felt that it would be not only unjust but dangerous to leave in French hands any important strategic points after the war.

The President replied that he in part agreed with Marshal Stalin. That was why this afternoon he had said to Marshal Stalin that it was necessary to eliminate in the future government of France anybody over forty years old and particularly anybody who had formed part of the French Government. He mentioned specifically the question of New Caledonia and Dakar, the first of which he said represented a threat to Australia and New Zealand and, therefore, should be placed under the trusteeship of the United Nations. In regard to Dakar, the President said he was speaking for twenty-one American nations when he said that Dakar in unsure hands was a direct threat to the Americas.

Mr. Churchill at this point intervened to say that Great Britain did not desire and did not expect to acquire any additional territory out of this war, but since the 4 great victorious nations—the United States, the Soviet Union, Great Britain and China—will be responsible for the future peace of the world, it was obviously necessary that certain strategic points throughout the world should be under the [their?] control.

Marshal Stalin again repeated and emphasized his view that France could not be trusted with any strategic possessions outside her own border in the postwar period. He described the ideology of the Vichy Ambassador to Moscow, Bergery, which he felt was characteristic of the majority of French politicians. This ideology definitely preferred an agreement with France's former enemy, Germany, than with her former allies, Great Britain and the United States.

The conversation then turned to the question of the treatment to be accorded Nazi Germany.

The President said that, in his opinion, it was very important not to leave in the German mind the concept of the Reich and that the very word should be stricken from the language.

Marshal Stalin replied that it was not enough to eliminate the word, but the very Reich itself must be rendered impotent ever again to plunge the world into war. He said that unless the victorious Allies retained in their hands the strategic positions necessary to prevent any recrudescence of German militarism, they would have failed in their duty.

In the detailed discussion between the President, Marshal Stalin and Churchill that followed Marshal Stalin took the lead, constantly emphasizing that the measures for the control of Germany and her disarmament were insufficient to prevent the rebirth of German militarism and appeared to favor even stronger measures. He, however, did not specify what he actually had in mind except that he appeared to favor the dismemberment of Germany.

Marshal Stalin particularly mentioned that Poland should extend to the Oder and stated definitely that the Russians would help the Poles to obtain a frontier on the Oder.

The President then said he would be interested in the question of assuring the approaches to the Baltic Sea and had in mind some form of trusteeship with perhaps an international state in the vicinity of the Kiel Canal to insure free navigation in both directions through the approaches. Due to some error of the Soviet translator Marshal Stalin apparently thought that the President was referring to the question of the Baltic States. On the basis of this understanding, he replied categorically that the Baltic States had by an expression of the will of the people voted to join the Soviet Union and that this question was not therefore one for discussion. Following the clearing up of the misapprehension, he, however, expressed himself favorably in regard to the question of insuring free navigation to and from the Baltic Sea.

The President, returning to the question of certain outlying possessions, said he was interested in the possibility of a sovereignty fashioned in a collective body such as the United Nations; a concept which had never been developed in past history.

After dinner when the President had retired, the conversation continued between Marshal Stalin and Mr. Churchill. The subject was still the treatment to be accorded to Germany, and even more than during dinner Marshal Stalin appeared to favor the strongest possible measures against Germany.

Mr. Churchill said that he advocated that Germany be permitted no aviation of any character—neither military or civilian—and in addition that the German general staff system should be completely abolished. He proposed a number of other measures of control such as constant supervision over such industries as might be left to Germany and territorial dismemberment of the Reich.

Marshal Stalin to all of these considerations expressed doubt as to whether they would be effective. He said that any furniture factories could be transformed into airplane factories and any watch factories could make fuses for shells. He said, in his opinion, the Germans were very able and talented people and could easily revive within fifteen or twenty years and again become a threat to the world. He said that he had personally questioned German prisoners in the Soviet Union as to why they had burst into Russian homes, killed Russian women, etc., and that the only reply he had received was they had been ordered to do so.

Mr. Churchill said that he could not look more than fifty years ahead and that he felt that upon the three nations represented here at Tehran rested the grave responsibility of future measures of assuring in some manner or other that Germany would not again rise to plague the world during the [that?] period. He said that he felt it was largely the fault of the German leaders and that, while during war time no distinction could be made between the leaders and the people particularly in regard to Germany, nevertheless, with a generation of self-sacrificing, toil and education, something might be done with the German people.

Marshal Stalin expressed dissent with this and did not appear satisfied as to the efficacy of any of the measures proposed by Mr. Churchill.

Mr. Churchill then inquired whether it would be possible this evening to discuss the question of Poland. He said that Great Britain had gone to war with Germany because of the latter's invasion of Poland in 1939 and that the British Government was committed to the reestablishment of a strong and independent Poland but not to any specific Polish frontiers. He added that if Marshal Stalin felt any desire to discuss the question of Poland, that he was prepared to do so and he was sure that the President was similarly disposed.

Marshal Stalin said that he had not yet felt the necessity nor the desirability of discussing the Polish question (After an exchange of remarks on this subject from which it developed that the Marshal had in mind that nothing that the Prime Minister had said on the subject of Poland up to the present stimulated him to discuss the question, the conversation returned to the substance of the Polish question).

Mr. Churchill said that he personally had no attachment to any specific frontier between Poland and the Soviet Union; that he felt that the consideration of Soviet security on their western frontiers was a governing factor. He repeated, however, that the British Government considered themselves committed to the reestablishment of an independent and strong Poland which he felt a necessary instrument in the European orchestra.

Mr. Eden then inquired if he had understood the Marshal correctly at dinner when the latter said that the Soviet Union favored the Polish western frontier on the Oder.

Marshal Stalin replied emphatically that he did favor such a frontier for Poland and repeated that the Russians were prepared to help the Poles achieve it.

Mr. Churchill then remarked that it would be very valuable if here in Tehran the representatives of the three governments could work out some agreed understanding on the question of the Polish frontiers which could then be taken up with the Polish Government in London. He said that, as far as he was concerned, he would like to see Poland moved westward in the same manner as soldiers at drill execute the drill "left close" and illustrated his point with three matches representing the Soviet Union, Poland and Germany.

Marshal Stalin agreed that it would be a good idea to reach an understanding on this question but said it was necessary to look into the matter further.

The conversation broke up on this note.

DOMESTIC POLITICS AND FOREIGN POLICY

Roosevelt kept silent during the conference discussions on Poland, pre-ferring to let Churchill carry on the debate alone against Stalin. In addition to Poland, the fate of the Baltic states of Latvia, Estonia, and Lithuania was also at stake. These countries, once part of Czarist Russia, had won their independence during the Russian Revolution but had been reincor-porated into the Soviet Union in 1940. Many Americans felt that the principle of self-determination championed by Woodrow Wilson after World War I still was valid and they saw the Russian treatment of the Baltic states and Poland as a vital test of Soviet behavior. In a brief private meeting with Stalin on December 1, Roosevelt tried to explain, as the Bohlen minutes reveal, American attitudes on these territorial issues.

Conversation between Roosevelt and Stalin at Tehran

The President said he had asked Marshal Stalin to come to see him as he wished to discuss a matter briefly and frankly. He said it referred to internal American politics.

He said that we had an election in 1944 and that while personally he did not wish to run again, if the war was still in progress, he might have to.

He added that there were in the United States from six to seven million Americans of Polish extraction, and as a practical man, he did not wish to lose their vote. He said personally he agreed with the views of Marshal Stalin as to the necessity of the restoration of a Polish state but would like to see the Eastern border moved further to the west and the Western border moved even to the River Oder. He hoped, however, that the Marshal would understand that for political reasons outlined above, he could not participate in any decision here in Tehran or even next winter on this subject and that he could not publicly take part in any such arrange-ment at the present time.

Marshal Stalin replied that now the President explained, he had under-stood.

The President went on to say that there were a number of persons of Lithuanian, Latvian, and Estonian origin, in that order, in the United States.

Foreign Relations of the United States, Tehran, pp. 594-595.

He said that he fully realized the three Baltic Republics had in history and again more recently been a part of Russia and added jokingly that when the Soviet armies reoccupied these areas, he did not intend to go to war with the Soviet Union on this point.

He went on to say that the big issue in the United States, insofar as public opinion went, would be the question of referendum and the right of self-determination. He said he thought that world opinion would want some expression of the will of the people, perhaps not immediately after their reoccupation by Soviet forces, but some day, and that he personally was confident that the people would vote to join the Soviet Union.

Marshal Stalin replied that the three Baltic Republics had no autonomy under the last Czar who had been an ally of Great Britain and the United States, but that no one had raised the question of public opinion, and he did not quite see why it was being raised now.

The President replied that the truth of the matter was that the public neither knew nor understood.

Marshal Stalin answered that they should be informed and some propaganda work should be done.

He added that as to the expression of the will of the people, there would be lots of opportunities for that to be done in accordance with the Soviet constitution but that he could not agree to any form of international control.

The President replied it would be helpful for him personally if some public declaration in regard to the future elections to which the Marshal had referred, could be made.

Marshal Stalin repeated there would be plenty of opportunities for such an expression of the will of the people.

THE EAGLES AND THE SONG BIRDS

A year passed before the three leaders met again at Yalta in early February, 1945. During that year, the course of the war changed dramatically. June, 1944, saw the long awaited cross-channel invasion, and by the end of the summer Paris had been liberated and the Germans driven from French soil. But in December, Hitler had launched a desperate counterattack, sending his remaining reserve forces on a drive that opened a great bulge on the western front. The American forces finally closed the gap in January, but Hitler's last offensive had slowed the momentum of Eisenhower's push into Germany. On the eastern front the Russian armies swept over Poland despite fierce German resistance, and by early 1945 Marshal Zhukov's forces were poised for the final drive on Berlin. As the Big Three prepared to meet to discuss the future of Europe, Stalin clearly held the strongest position, with his armies in command of all Eastern Europe. The United States, hoping to secure a Russian pledge to enter the war against Japan once Germany was defeated, was in a weak bargaining position with its wartime ally.

The conference was held at Yalta, a summer resort in the Crimea by the shores of the Black Sea. The agenda facing the Big Three was staggering, including such complex topics as the treatment of a defeated Germany, the fate of Russian-controlled Poland and the Balkans, the nature of a post-war world organization, and the question of Soviet entry into the Pacific war. Yet the meeting lasted only eight days and many of the vital issues were either ignored or dealt with in haste.

President Roosevelt and the American delegation placed the greatest emphasis on completing plans for a postwar international organization— the future United Nations. Cordell Hull had carefully supervised the drafting of a charter in the State Department, and at a conference at Dumbarton Oaks, in the Georgetown section of Washington in the fall of 1944, British, Soviet, and Nationalist Chinese representatives had approved its main features. A dispute arose, however, about how much power the great nations would have on the all-important Security Council. There was agreement that they should have a veto on all decisions involving the use of force to maintain peace, but the United States and Britain wanted to restrict the veto as far as possible, to permit the smaller nations

181

to have a greater voice, while the Soviet Union insisted on the right to veto any action by the Security Council, including even the question of whether to discuss an issue raised by a smaller power.

At the first dinner meeting of the Big Three at Yalta, Stalin stated his views on the role of the great powers to Roosevelt and Churchill. Charles Bohlen, still serving as FDR's interpreter, made the following minutes.

Conversation between Roosevelt, Churchill, and Stalin at Yalta

Before dinner and during the greater part of the dinner the conversation was general and personal in character. Marshal Stalin, the President and the Prime Minister appeared to be in very good humor throughout the dinner. No political or military subjects of any importance were discussed until the last half hour of the dinner when indirectly the subject of the responsibility and rights of the big powers as against those of the small powers came up.

Marshal Stalin made it quite plain on a number of occasions that he felt that the three Great Powers which had borne the brunt of the war and had liberated from German domination the small powers should have the unanimous right to preserve the peace of the world. He said that he could serve no other interest than that of the Soviet state and people but that in the international arena the Soviet Union was prepared to pay its share in the preservation of peace. He said that it was ridiculous to believe that Albania would have an equal voice with the three Great Powers for failure to take into consideration the rights of these small powers.

Marshal Stalin said that he was prepared in concert with the United States and Great Britain to protect the rights of the small powers but that he would never agree to having any action of any of the Great Powers submitted to the judgment of the small powers.

The President said he agreed that the Great Powers bore the greater responsibility and that the peace should be written by the Three Powers represented at this table.

The Prime Minister said that there was no question of the small powers dictating to the big powers but that the great nations of the world should discharge their moral responsibility and leadership and should exercise their power with moderation and great respect for the rights of the smaller nations. (Mr. Vyshinski said to Mr. Bohlen that they would never agree to

---

Foreign Relations of the United States: The Conferences at Malta and Yalta, 1945 (Washington, Government Printing Office, 1955), pp. 589-590.

Courtesy of the Office of War Information.

U.S. tank in France, World War II.

the right of the small powers to judge the acts of the Great Powers, and in reply to an observation by Mr. Bohlen concerning the opinion of American people he replied that the American people should learn to obey their leaders. Mr. Bohlen said that if Mr. Vyshinski would visit the United States he would like to see him undertake to tell that to the American people. Mr. Vyshinski replied that he would be glad to do so.)

Following a toast by the Prime Minister to the proletariat masses of the world, there was considerable discussion about the rights of people to govern themselves in relation to their leaders.

The Prime Minister said that although he was constantly being "beaten up" as a reactionary, he was the only representative present who could be thrown out at any time by the universal suffrage of his own people and that personally he gloried in that danger.

Marshal Stalin ironically remarked that the Prime Minister seemed to fear these elections, to which the Prime Minister replied that he not only did not fear them but that he was proud of the right of the British people to change their government at any time they saw fit. He added that he felt that the three nations represented here were moving toward the same goal by different methods.

The Prime Minister, referring to the rights of the small nations, gave a quotation which said: "The eagle should permit the small birds to sing and care not wherefor they sang."

THE POLISH DILEMMA

Despite his firm views, Stalin finally yielded on the veto issue; he agreed to a compromise which would permit a great power to block action by the Security Council but which guaranteed freedom of discussion and debate even if one of the Big Three objected. At the end of the conference, Churchill, Stalin, and Roosevelt called on all the members of the wartime coalition to meet at San Francisco to draft a final charter for the United Nations.

The other issues proved more troublesome, and none more than the problem of Poland, which was destined to become the starting point of the Cold War. The question of boundaries, discussed at Tehran, still was unsettled when the Big Three met at Yalta. The London Poles insisted on the prewar eastern frontier, while the Soviets countered with a demand for recognition of the boundary they had established in 1939, and which closely approximated a line suggested by Lord Curzon at the Paris Peace Conference in 1919. To sweeten their proposal, the Russians suggested that Poland be compensated with a slice of German territory in the west.

The question of who was to rule postwar Poland was even more crucial. In the summer of 1944 the Soviets had created a Polish Committee of

National Liberation at Lublin, and at the end of the year Stalin recognized this Communist group as the provisional government of Poland. The London Polish government pleaded with Britain and the United States to back its claims, but with the Red Army in control of the country, the future of Poland was clearly in Soviet hands. The British and Americans urged the London Premier, Stanislaw Mikolajczyk, to compromise with the Russians on the boundary issue, but he refused, thus making it all the more difficult for Churchill and Roosevelt to stand up for the government in exile.

Roosevelt appeared to be indifferent to the fate of Poland; it was Churchill who battled Stalin tooth-and-nail on this issue throughout the Yalta conference. The Russians insisted on recognition of the Lublin government, conceding only that this group would be expanded by admitting a few of the London Polish leaders into its ranks. Churchill wanted an entirely new government, consisting of representatives from London, from Lublin, and from the underground army which had been waging guerilla war against the Germans and had suffered terribly in the abortive Warsaw uprising in the fall of 1944.

On the afternoon of February 6, the Big Three began their long discussion on Poland. Once again, Bohlen kept a record of the conversation.

Conversation between Roosevelt, Churchill, and Stalin at Yalta

The President inquired whether the Polish question should be taken up now or postponed until the next meeting.

The Prime Minister said that he hoped that at least a start could be made today.

The President said that the United States was farther away from Poland than anyone else here, and that there were times when a long distance point of view was useful. He said that at Tehran he had stated that he believed the American people were in general favorably inclined to the Curzon Line as the eastern frontier of Poland, but he felt that if the Soviet Government would consider a concession in regard to Lwow and the oil deposits in the Province of Lwow that would have a very salutary effect. He said that he was merely putting forth this suggestion for consideration and would not insist on it. He said that in regard to the govern-

---

Foreign Relations of the United States, Yalta, pp. 667-671.

ment he wished to see the creation of a representative government which could have the support of all the great powers and which could be composed of representatives of the principal parties of Poland. He said one possibility which had been suggested was the creation of a Presidential Council composed of Polish leaders which could then create a government composed of the chiefs of the five political parties—Workers Party, Peasant Party, Socialist Party, etc. He said that one thing must be made certain and that was that Poland should maintain the most friendly and cooperative relations with the Soviet Union.

Marshal Stalin replied that Poland should maintain friendly relations not only with the Soviet Union but with the other Allies.

The President said he had merely put forth a suggestion but he thought if we could solve the Polish question it would be a great help to all of us. He added he didn't know personally any members of the London government or Lublin government, but he had met Mr. Mikolajczyk who had made a deep impression on him as a sincere and an honest man.

The Prime Minister said that he had consistently declared in Parliament and elsewhere that the British Government would support the Curzon Line, even leaving Lwow to the Soviet Union. He had been criticized for this and so had Mr. Eden, but he felt that after the burdens which Russia had borne in this war the Curzon Line was not a decision of force but one of right. He said he remained in that position. Of course, he added, if the mighty Soviet Union could make some gesture to the much weaker country, such as the relinquishment of Lwow, this act of magnanimity would be acclaimed and admired. He said he was much more interested in sovereignty and independence of Poland than in the frontier line— he wanted to see the Poles have a home where they could organize their lives as they wished. That was an objective that he had often heard Marshal Stalin proclaim most firmly, and he put his trust in those declarations. He said that he therefore had not considered the question of the frontier as a question of vital importance. It must not be forgotten, however, that Great Britain had gone to war to protect Poland against German aggression at a time when that decision was most risky, and it had almost cost them their life in the world. He said Great Britain had no material interest in Poland, but the question was one of honor and that his government would therefore never be content with a solution which did not leave Poland a free and independent state. The freedom of Poland, however, did not cover any hostile designs or intrigue against the U.S.S.R., and none of us should permit this. It is the earnest desire of the British Government that Poland be mistress in her own house and captain of her soul. He said that the British Government recognized the present Polish government in London but did not have intimate contact with it. He said he had known Mr.

Mikolajczyk, Mr. Grabski, and Mr. Romer and had found them good and honest men. He inquired whether there might be some possibility of forming a government here for Poland which would utilize these men. If this could be done all the great powers could then recognize it as an interim government until such time as the Poland government [Polish people?] by free vote could select and form their own government. He concluded by saying he was interested in the President's suggestion.

At the suggestion of Marshal Stalin, there was a ten-minute intermission.

Marshal Stalin then gave the following summary of his views on the Polish question: Mr. Churchill had said that for Great Britain the Polish question was one of honor and that he understood, but for the Russians it was a question both of honor and security. It was one of honor because Russia had many past grievances against Poland and desired to see them eliminated. It was a question of strategic security not only because Poland was a bordering country but because throughout history Poland had been the corridor for attack on Russia. We have to mention that during the last thirty years Poland twice was weak. Russia wants a strong, independent and democratic Poland. Since it was impossible by the force of Russian armies alone to close from the outside this corridor, it could be done only by Poland's own forces. It was very important, therefore, to have Poland independent, strong and democratic. It is not only a question of honor for Russia, but one of life and death. It was for this reason that there had been a great change from the policies of the Czars who had wished to suppress and assimilate Poland. In regard to the questions raised here on which we have different opinions, the following might be said:

In regard to the Curzon Line, concessions in regard to Lwow and the Lwow Province, and Mr. Churchill's reference to a magnanimous act on our part, it is necessary to remind you that not Russians but Curzon and Clemenceau fixed this line. The Russians had not been invited and the line was established against their will. Lenin had opposed giving Bialystok Province to the Poles but the Curzon Line gives it to Poland. We have already retreated from Lenin's position in regard to this province. Should we then be less Russian than Curzon and Clemenceau? We could not then return to Moscow and face the people who would say that Stalin and Molotov have been less sure defenders of Russian interest than Curzon and Clemenceau. It is, therefore, impossible to agree with the proposed modification of the line. I would prefer to have the war go on although it will cost us blood in order to compensate for Poland from Germany. When he was in Moscow Mr. Mikolajczyk was delighted to hear that Poland's frontier would extend to the West Neisse River and I favor the Polish frontier on the West Neisse and ask the conference to support this proposal.

As to the question of the Polish government, Mr. Churchill has said it would be good to create a Polish government here. I am afraid that was a slip of the tongue, for without participation of the Poles it is impossible to create a Polish government. I am called a dictator and not a democrat, but I have enough democratic feeling to refuse to create a Polish government without the Poles being consulted—the question can only be settled with the consent of the Poles. Last autumn in Moscow there was a good chance for a fusion of the various Polish elements and in the meeting between Mikolajczyk, Grabski and Lublin Poles various points of agreement were reached as Mr. Churchill will remember. Mikolajczyk left for London but did not return since he was expelled from office precisely because he wanted agreement. . . . I am prepared to support any attempt to reach a solution that would offer some [chance] of success. Should we ask the Warsaw Poles to come here or perhaps come to Moscow? I must say that the Warsaw government has a democratic base equal at least to that of de Gaulle.

As a military man I demand from a country liberated by the Red Army that there be no civil war in the rear. The men in the Red Army are indifferent to the type of government as long as it will maintain order and they will not be shot in the back. The Warsaw, or Lublin, government has not badly fulfilled this task. There are, however, agents of the London government who claim to be agents of the underground forces of resistance. I must say that no good and much evil comes from these forces. Up to the present time they have killed 212 of our military men. They attack our supply bases to obtain arms. Although it has been proclaimed that all radio stations must be registered and obtain permission to operate, agents of the London government are violating these regulations. We have arrested some of them and if they continue to disturb our rear we will shoot them as military law requires. When I compare what the agents of the Lublin government have done and what the agents of the London government have done I see the first are good and the second bad. We want tranquility in our rear. We will support the government which gives us peace in the rear, and as a military man I could not do otherwise. Without a secure rear there can be no more victories for the Red Army. Any military man and even the nonmilitary man will understand this situation.

The Prime Minister said that he must put on record the fact that the British and Soviet Governments have different sources of information in Poland and therefore they obtain different views of the situation there. He said it is possible that their reports are mistaken as it is not always possible to believe everything that anyone tells you. He believed, he added, that with the best of all their information he could not feel that the Lublin government represents more than one third of the people and would be maintained in power if the people were free to express their opinion. One of the reasons why the British have so earnestly sought a solution had been the fear that the Polish underground army would come into collision with the Lublin government, which would lead to great bloodshed, arrests and deportations which could not fail to have a bad effect on the whole Polish question. The Prime Minister said he agreed that anyone who attacks the Red Army should be punished, but he repeated that the British Government could not agree to recognizing the Lublin government of Poland.

The Conference then adjourned until four o'clock tomorrow.

BRAVE NEW WORLD

The Yalta conference ended on February 11. The Big Three issued an official communiqué which announced that the leaders had agreed on zones of occupation for Germany, called for a United Nations Conference to draft the charter of the new world organization at San Francisco in April, and promised free elections for the countries of Eastern Europe liberated from German rule. Churchill, Roosevelt, and Stalin also disclosed the agreement they had finally reached on Poland, which was heavily weighted toward the original Soviet proposal. The Lublin government was to be expanded by the addition of "democratic leaders from Poland itself and from Poles abroad," the eastern frontier was to follow the Curzon Line, and Poland was to receive "substantial accessions of territory in the north and west" from Germany. In the months that followed, the Russian army drove millions of Germans from a broad strip of land between the old Polish border and the Oder and western Neisse rivers and turned this area over to Poland. The United States has never recognized the legality of the Oder-Neisse boundary, and it remains one of the major items on the Cold War agenda down to the present.

After the conference, Roosevelt flew to the Mediterranean, where he boarded the cruiser Quincy. After a brief conference with King Farouk of Egypt, Haile Selassie of Ethiopia, and Ibn Saud of Arabia, the President stopped off at Algiers to confer with Charles de Gaulle, who had not been invited to the Yalta Conference. De Gaulle indicated his displeasure by failing to appear.

As the Quincy sailed back across the Atlantic, Sam Rosenman, the President's speech-writer, tried to get Roosevelt to work with him on an address to Congress on the Yalta conference. But the President, exhausted by the journey and the hectic negotiations, refused, staying in his cabin and emerging only for his meals. Toward the end of the trip, Roosevelt did go over a draft with Rosenman, but he remained depressed and listless.

On March 1, three days after he arrived back in the United States, the President went to the Capitol to address a joint session of Congress. For the first time since he had become President, he spoke to the lawmakers from a seated position, too weak to stand in his braces at the House rostrum. Though he was tanned from his days at sea, his gaunt visage and grey pallor were unmistakable signs of the illness that would take his life six weeks later. Departing frequently from his prepared text, he tried to adopt an informal style which gave his speech an uncertain quality. Yet despite his weariness, Roosevelt's bright hopes for the future shone radiantly through the halting words of his last major address.

FRANKLIN D. ROOSEVELT, *Address to Congress on the Yalta Conference*

I come from the Crimea Conference with a firm belief that we have made a good start on the road to a world of peace.

There were two main purposes in this Crimea Conference. The first was to bring defeat to Germany with the greatest possible speed, and the smallest possible loss of Allied men. That purpose is now being carried out in great force. The German Army, and the German people, are feeling the ever-increasing might of our fighting men and of the Allied armies. Every hour gives us added pride in the heroic advance of our troops in Germany—on German soil—toward a meeting with the gallant Red Army.

The second purpose was to continue to build the foundation for an international accord that would bring order and security after the chaos

Samuel Rosenman, ed., *The Public Papers and Addresses of Franklin D. Roosevelt: Victory and the Threshold of Peace* (New York, Harper and Brothers, 1950), pp. 571, 572-573, 577-578, 581-583, 585-586. Reprinted by permission of the publisher.

of the war, that would give some assurance of lasting peace among the Nations of the world.

Toward that goal also, a tremendous stride was made. . . .

When we met at Yalta, in addition to laying our strategic and tactical plans for the complete and final military victory over Germany, there were other problems of vital political consequence.

For instance, first, there were the problems of the occupation and control of Germany—after victory—the complete destruction of her military power, and the assurance that neither the Nazis nor Prussian militarism could again be revived to threaten the peace and the civilization of the world.

Second—again for example—there was the settlement of the few differences that remained among us with respect to the International Security Organization after the Dumbarton Oaks Conference. As you remember, at that time, I said that we had agreed ninety percent. Well, that's a pretty good percentage. I think the other ten percent was ironed out at Yalta.

Third, there were the general political and economic problems common to all of the areas which had been or would be liberated from the Nazi yoke. This is a very special problem. We over here find it difficult to understand the ramifications of many of these problems in foreign lands, but we are trying to.

Fourth, there were the special problems created by a few instances such as Poland and Yugoslavia.

Days were spent in discussing these momentous matters and we argued freely and frankly across the table. But at the end, on every point, unanimous agreement was reached. And more important even than the agreement of words, I may say we achieved a unity of thought and a way of getting along together.

Of course, we know that it was Hitler's hope—and the German war lords'—that we would not agree—that some slight crack might appear in the solid wall of Allied unity, a crack that would give him and his fellow gangsters one last hope of escaping their just doom. That is the objective for which his propaganda machine has been working for many months.

But Hitler has failed.

Never before have the major Allies been more closely united—not only in their war aims but also in their peace aims. And they are determined to continue to be united with each other—and with all peace-loving Nations—so that the ideal of lasting peace will become a reality.

The Soviet, British, and United States Chiefs of Staff held daily meetings with each other. They conferred frequently with Marshal Stalin, and with Prime Minister Churchill and with me, on the problem of coordinating the strategic and tactical efforts of the Allied powers. They completed their plans for the final knock-out blows to Germany. . . .

Of equal importance with the military arrangements at the Crimea Conference were the agreements reached with respect to a general international organization for lasting world peace. The foundations were laid at Dumbarton Oaks. There was one point, however, on which agreement was not reached at Dumbarton Oaks. It involved the procedure of voting in the Security Council. I want to try to make it clear by making it simple. It took me hours and hours to get the thing straight in my own mind—and many conferences.

At the Crimea Conference, the Americans made a proposal on this subject which, after full discussion was, I am glad to say, unanimously adopted by the other two Nations.

It is not yet possible to announce the terms of that agreement publicly, but it will be in a very short time.

When the conclusions reached with respect to voting in the Security Council are made known, I think and I hope that you will find them a fair solution of this complicated and difficult problem. They are founded in justice, and will go far to assure international cooperation in the maintenance of peace.

A conference of all the United Nations of the world will meet in San Francisco on April 25, 1945. There, we all hope, and confidently expect, to execute a definite charter of organization under which the peace of the world will be preserved and the forces of aggression permanently outlawed.

This time we are not making the mistake of waiting until the end of the war to set up the machinery of peace. This time, as we fight together to win the war finally, we work together to keep it from happening again. . . .

One outstanding example of joint action by the three major Allied powers in the liberated areas was the solution reached on Poland. The whole Polish question was a potential source of trouble in postwar Europe —as it has been sometimes before—and we came to the Conference determined to find a common ground for its solution. And we did—even though everybody does not agree with us, obviously.

Our objective was to help to create a strong, independent, and prosperous Nation. That is the thing we must always remember, those words, agreed to by Russia, by Britain, and by the United States: the objective of making Poland a strong, independent, and prosperous Nation, with a government ultimately to be selected by the Polish people themselves.

To achieve that objective, it was necessary to provide for the formation of a new government much more representative than had been possible while Poland was enslaved. There were, as you know, two governments —one in London, one in Lublin—practically in Russia. Accordingly, steps were taken at Yalta to reorganize the existing Provisional Government in Poland on a broader democratic basis, so as to include democratic leaders now in Poland and those abroad. This new, reorganized government will be recognized by all of us as the temporary government of Poland. Poland needs a temporary government in the worst way—an ad interim government, I think is another way of putting it.

However, the new Polish Provisional Government of National Unity will be pledged to holding a free election as soon as possible on the basis of universal suffrage and a secret ballot.

Throughout history, Poland has been the corridor through which attacks on Russia have been made. Twice in this generation, Germany has struck at Russia through this corridor. To insure European security and world peace, a strong and independent Poland is necessary to prevent that from happening again.

The decision with respect to the boundaries of Poland was, frankly, a compromise. I did not agree with all of it, by any means, but we did not go as far as Britain wanted, in certain areas; we did not go so far as Russia wanted, in certain areas; and we did not go so far as I wanted, in certain areas. It *was* a compromise. The decision is one, however, under which the Poles will receive compensation in territory in the North and West in exchange for what they lose by the Curzon Line in the East. The limits of the western border will be permanently fixed in the final Peace Conference. We know, roughly, that it will include—in the new, strong Poland— quite a large slice of what now is called Germany. And it was agreed, also, that the new Poland will have a large and long coast line, and many new harbors. Also, that most of East Prussia will go to Poland. A corner of it will go to Russia. Also, that the anomaly of the Free State of Danzig will come to an end; I think Danzig would be a lot better if it were Polish.

It is well known that the people east of the Curzon Line—just for example, here is why I compromised—are predominantly white Russian and Ukrainian—they are not Polish; and a very great majority of the people west of the line are predominantly Polish, except in that part of East Prussia and eastern Germany, which will go to the new Poland. As far back as 1919, representatives of the Allies agreed that the Curzon Line represented a fair boundary between the two peoples. And you must remember, also, that there had not been any Polish government before 1919 for a great many generations.

I am convinced that the agreement on Poland, under the circumstances, is the most hopeful agreement possible for a free, independent, and prosperous Polish state. . . .

The Conference in the Crimea was a turning point—I hope in our history and therefore in the history of the world. There will soon be presented to the Senate of the United States and to the American people a great decision that will determine the fate of the United States—and of the world —for generations to come.

There can be no middle ground here. We shall have to take the responsibility for world collaboration, or we shall have to bear the responsibility for another world conflict.

I know that the word "planning" is not looked upon with favor in some circles. In domestic affairs, tragic mistakes have been made by reason of lack of planning; and, on the other hand, many great improvements in living, and many benefits to the human race, have been accomplished as a result of adequate, intelligent planning—reclamation of desert areas, developments of whole river valleys, and provision for adequate housing.

The same will be true in relations between Nations. For the second time in the lives of most of us this generation is face to face with the objective of preventing wars. To meet that objective, the Nations of the world will either have a plan or they will not. The groundwork of a plan has now been furnished, and has been submitted to humanity for discussion and decision.

No plan is perfect. Whatever is adopted at San Francisco will doubtless have to be amended time and again over the years, just as our own Constitution has been.

No one can say exactly how long any plan will last. Peace can endure only so long as humanity really insists upon it, and is willing to work for it—and sacrifice for it.

Twenty-five years ago, American fighting men looked to the statesmen of the world to finish the work of peace for which they fought and suffered. We failed them then. We cannot fail them again, and expect the world again to survive.

The Crimea Conference was a successful effort by the three leading Nations to find a common ground for peace. It ought to spell the end of the system of unilateral action, the exclusive alliances, the spheres of influence, the balances of power, and all the other expedients that have been tried for centuries—and have always failed.

We propose to substitute for all these, a universal organization in which all peace-loving Nations will finally have a chance to join.

I am confident that the Congress and the American people will accept the results of this Conference as the beginnings of a permanent structure of peace upon which we can begin to build, under God, that better world in which our children and grandchildren—yours and mine, the children and grandchildren of the whole world—must live, and can live.

And that, my friends, is the principal message I can give you. But I feel it very deeply, as I know that all of you are feeling it today, and are going to feel it in the future.

The Right Frame